PERHAPS TODAY

Living every day in the light of Christ's return

Tyndale House books by
Tim LaHaye and Jerry B. Jenkins

The Left Behind® series
Left Behind
Tribulation Force
Nicolae
Soul Harvest
Apollyon
Assassins
The Indwelling
The Mark
Desecration
Book 10—available summer 2002

Left Behind®: The Kids

#1: *The Vanishings*	#10: *On the Run*
#2: *Second Chance*	#11: *Into the Storm*
#3: *Through the Flames*	#12: *Earthquake!*
#4: *Facing the Future*	#13: *The Showdown*
#5: *Nicolae High*	#14: *Judgment Day*
#6: *The Underground*	#15: *Battling the Commander*
#7: *Busted!*	#16: *Fire from Heaven*
#8: *Death Strike*	#17: *Terror in the Stadium*
#9: *The Search*	#18: *Darkening Skies*

Tyndale House books by Tim LaHaye
Are We Living in the End Times?
How to Be Happy Though Married
Perhaps Today
Spirit-Controlled Temperament
Transformed Temperaments
Why You Act the Way You Do

Tyndale House books by Jerry B. Jenkins
And Then Came You
As You Leave Home
Still the One

PERHAPS

LIVING EVERY DAY IN THE LIGHT OF CHRIST'S RETURN

TODAY

TIM LaHaye
JERRY B. JENKINS

TYNDALE HOUSE PUBLISHERS, INC.
WHEATON, ILLINOIS

Visit Tyndale's exciting Web site at www.tyndale.com

Discover the latest Left Behind news at www.leftbehind.com

Designed by Julie Chen

Chart on page 88 adapted from *Rapture Under Attack*, © 1992, 1998 by Tim LaHaye. Used by permission of Multnomah Publishers, Inc.

Published in association with the literary agency of Alive Communications, Inc., 7680 Goddard Street, Suite 200, Colorado Springs, CO 80920.

Library of Congress Cataloging-in-Publication Data

LaHaye, Tim F.
   Perhaps today : living every day in the light of Christ's return / Tim LaHaye, Jerry B. Jenkins.
     p. cm.
   ISBN 0-8423-3601-X
   1. Eschatology—Biblical teaching.   I. Jenkins, Jerry B.   II. Title.
   BS680.E8 L34 2001
   236'.9—dc21   2001003096

Printed in the United States of America

09   08   07   06   05   04   03   02   01
10   9   8   7   6   5   4   3   2   1

To all those who want spiritual inspiration and prophetic instruction at the same time we dedicate this book. It is our prayer that you will not only not be left behind but will be ready when He comes again.

CONTENTS

INTRODUCTION

THE SECOND coming of Jesus Christ is the most vital of subjects for Christians. History will one day end, and that which we call "time" will be swallowed up in God's glorious tomorrow. The New Testament's focus is salvation, which is the point of Christ's original coming. But His second coming is the next most prominent subject in Scripture. It is mentioned 318 times in the New Testament alone.

The return of Christ is mentioned by every New Testament writer. It was the consuming interest of the church during its first three hundred years of existence—the most evangelistic period of Christian history. Following these first three centuries of vitality, the Bible slipped from esteem and the promise of Christ's return was nearly lost. For centuries thereafter, the church and the world experienced moral and spiritual decay. The church's teaching on holy living and evangelism all but died. This period of time is fittingly called the "Dark Ages" and lasted eleven hundred years!

But God's plan for the ages was not forgotten. With the Reformation and the widespread publishing of the Bible during the sixteenth and seventeenth centuries, the doctrine of the Second Coming emerged. Once again the church was inspired to holy living in an unholy age. Evangelism and missionary passion were born anew with great zeal. Our Lord's great commission became global.

The last two centuries of church history, like the first three, have witnessed worldwide evangelism. In these five centuries, more Christians have lived consecrated lives and more missionaries have shared their faith than in all other centuries combined.

The reason? The Bible!

Wherever God's people have used their Bibles, they have learned that the glory of the Scriptures is prophecy. "For the testimony of Jesus is the spirit of prophecy" (Revelation 19:10, NKJV). The future God has for us will be wonderful, and many Bible scholars believe that future is now at hand.

M. R. DeHaan of Grand Rapids, Michigan, was a medical doctor who had a profound effect on American believers. When my mother was young she began attending his Friday night Bible classes. Those studies eventually grew into the *Radio Bible Class*—the "Scripture school" for millions of listeners.

From where did Dr. DeHaan gain such insight and power?

Early in his life he was an alcoholic who had all but ruined his health through excessive drinking, nearly dying in his thirty-sixth year. Then grace arrived, and he became a Christian! In time he became an avid teacher of Bible prophecy.

In time, my mother's prayers were answered and I was called to preach. I became pastor of my first church at age twenty-three. It was a little country congregation not rich enough to afford a more seasoned minister. I can't say how well or poorly I did. Sermons were difficult for me, and my study was long. I was always desperate to find good sermon material.

It was during those days I came across Dr. DeHaan's book, *The Second Coming of Christ*. But it turned out to be more than a source of sermons for a fledgling preacher. I preached it, and it had a profound influence on me. It molded my thinking on prophecy, evangelism, and sanctification for over five decades and gave me a worldwide missionary vision.

Years later I visited the *Radio Bible Class* headquarters in Grand Rapids and was permitted to see Dr. DeHaan's study. What impressed me most was not his great library but a single plaque that seemed to radiate truth from his bookshelf. In large black letters it read *PERHAPS TODAY*.

May that theme characterize the hope for every reader of this book. Even so, come quickly, Lord Jesus. It is our prayer that all who read this book will be challenged to live every day as if it were the day of Christ's coming. May the words of this book call to mind this promise: "I am going to prepare a place for you. . . . When everything is ready, I will come and get you, so that you will always be with me where I am" (John 14:2-3).

Jesus' words could be fulfilled any day now. He could come any time: Every prophecy concerning His return has been fulfilled. Nothing remains to prevent this final joy! This glorious immediacy should influence the way every Christian lives. The daily reading of this devotional book should thrill and inspire you. Can any be glum? Any morose? The Lord is at hand.

1 JESUS PROMISED TO TAKE US TO HIS FATHER'S HOUSE

"Don't be troubled. You trust God, now trust in me. There are many rooms in my Father's home, and I am going to prepare a place for you. If this were not so, I would tell you plainly. When everything is ready, I will come and get you, so that you will always be with me where I am. And you know where I am going and how to get there."

"No, we don't know, Lord," Thomas said. "We haven't any idea where you are going, so how can we know the way?"

Jesus told him, "I am the way, the truth, and the life. No one can come to the Father except through me." JOHN 14:1-6

CHRIST is the way! Many Christians have memorized this promise. Those attending the funerals of saints gather hope from its truth. Sunday schools teach it to children. It is Christ's personal remedy for the troubled heart.

Trouble in this life is certain. "People are born for trouble as predictably as sparks fly upward from a fire" (Job 5:7). It bypasses none! Even becoming a Christian doesn't exempt us from adversity. But Jesus owns a remedy: "You trust God, now trust in me." And He has given us one of the most important promises in the Bible: "I will come and get you, so that you will always be with me where I am." We have His word for it: Even now, He is preparing a "place" for us. He will come again and personally conduct us to His Father's house.

Therefore, see trouble as it is. In the midst of life's greatest trials, take comfort in the promise our Lord delivered to His disciples in the upper room just hours before His crucifixion. That promise still serves. No matter what our trials may be, Jesus is coming, and we will all someday take up residence in His Father's house.

This house is grand indeed! It has enough rooms to house the saints of both the Old Testament and New Testament eras. Do you question the size of such a house? Don't. It is our Savior's word. Let us dwell in the promise of this grand house! I cannot think of its glory without remembering my godly mother. Life was hard for her. When she was only twenty-eight years old, she was left a widow with three children. She worked tirelessly in a factory to raise us, attending Bible college at night for nine years and finally receiving her degree so she could become a child evangelism director. She served Christ in this capacity for twenty-three years. She often lived in one-bedroom apartments or mobile homes. Still, she served in surrender with little emphasis on the material things. She never owned a home of her own. But in heaven things will be different! There's a grand house on the way! Her real home! She will enjoy this house forever. It is a house prepared by her Savior. It is built from her unceasing service and her life of single focus: her love for the Builder.

In this passage, Jesus first mentions the rapture of His church. This was the first time Jesus spoke of taking His believers up to His Father's house. In His previous references to the Second Coming, He spoke of coming down to the earth to set up His kingdom. But here is set out the first phase of His coming, often referred to as the Rapture. It will be glorious. It will be sudden. Best of all, it may be soon!

Today's Prayer

Dear heavenly Father, thank You for Your encouraging promise. Give us joy in Your pledge that You are literally coming again to take us to Your house, which Your Son even now prepares. May we be found faithful in serving You as long as we have life. And for today, lead us to make all our decisions in the light of Jesus' coming.

Further, make us so sensitive to Your leading that we, in joy, reach out to share the promise with others. In Jesus' name, Amen.

2 OUR DUAL CITIZENSHIP

> But we are citizens of heaven, where the Lord Jesus Christ lives. And we are eagerly waiting for him to return as our Savior. He will take these weak mortal bodies of ours and change them into glorious bodies like his own, using the same mighty power that he will use to conquer everything, everywhere.
> PHILIPPIANS 3:20-21

IN 1998 the Mexican government joined several other countries in allowing its citizens to retain their native citizenship and also become citizens of another country. Millions of Mexican citizens are now applying for dual citizenship. America, on the other hand, requires that you surrender your U.S. citizenship if you choose to become a citizen of another country. There is, of course, one exception. No law prohibits us from being both citizens of the U.S. and citizens of heaven. This citizenship occurs when we are "born again" by faith in Jesus Christ.

Our natural citizenship is free to the native born, but it is not one we choose. Our citizenship in heaven is the free gift of God to those of us who invite God's Son to rule over our hearts in faith. Natural citizenship is physical and earthly; heavenly citizenship is spiritual and forever.

Citizens are expected to obey the laws of their homeland. They must also pay taxes to support their government and vote in elections to choose those who govern them. In a similar way, Christian citizens are also expected to obey their Lord and all He requires them to believe. God's laws focus on living the consecrated life. Jesus calls us to deny ourselves, take up our crosses daily, and follow Him (Luke 9:23). Kingdom citizens are called to keep eternal perspectives always in view.

What is this eternal perspective?

It is the great possibility of history!

The apostle Paul described it as "eagerly waiting for him to return as our Savior." This not-so-secret key to success in the Christian life is never to lose sight of this perspective. As citizens of heaven, we must never forget that our Lord could come at any time. Then He will take us to be with Him forever. This current age will not endure. This present moment could be our last day on Earth.

When *People* magazine did a special story on our Left Behind series of novels, they insisted that my coauthor, Jerry B. Jenkins, and I pose for special photographs looking heavenward. We thought it a little weird that at three different locations they had us pose for five hours looking skyward to get the one picture they actually used with the article. Their photograph seemed to imply that we were so heavenly minded we were no earthly good.

Quite the contrary!

We are citizens of heaven. We expect our Lord to return at any time. This day could be our last on Earth. We therefore seek to make life's major decisions in the light of eternity. Like Moses (Hebrews 11:24-25), we want to deny ourselves some of the pleasures of our momentary life to enjoy His approval forever.

Citizens of only one country are often "earthly minded." But dual citizens make the major decisions of life as they wait for the Savior who will "take these weak mortal bodies of ours and change them into glorious bodies like his own" (Philippians 3:21). Heaven is forever! Therefore, "set your affection on things above," not on the things of this world (Colossians 3:2, KJV).

Today's Prayer

Dear Lord, thank You for making me a citizen of heaven freely by Your grace. I do not deserve this privilege, but I thank You for it. I sincerely desire to live each day in conformity to Your will. Help me to avoid earthly minded decisions and "set [my] affection on things above." May I commit all my ways to You. Use my life as You see fit. In Jesus' name, Amen.

3 THE MOST DEFINING RAPTURE TEXT IN SCRIPTURE

And now, brothers and sisters, I want you to know what will happen to the Christians who have died so you will not be full of sorrow like people who have no hope. For since we believe that Jesus died and was raised to life again, we also believe that when Jesus comes, God will bring back with Jesus all the Christians who have died. I can tell you this directly from the Lord: We who are still living when the Lord returns will not rise to meet him ahead of those who are in their graves. For the Lord himself will come down from heaven with a commanding shout, with the call of the archangel, and with the trumpet call of God. First, all the Christians who have died will rise from their graves. Then, together with them, we who are still alive and remain on the earth will be caught up in the clouds to meet the Lord in the air and remain with him forever. So comfort and encourage each other with these words.   1 THESSALONIANS 4:13-18

CHRISTIANS often disagree about when the rapture of the church will occur. Some say it will come before the Tribulation, others think it will be in the middle of the Tribulation, and still others believe the Rapture will occur when the Tribulation is over. But most agree that there will be a future moment when all Christians living or dead will hear a shout from heaven and be "caught up" (or "raptured," from a

Latin word root) "to meet the Lord in the air" and thereafter forever be with their Lord!

This Scripture not only defines the rapture of the church, it was sent for her comfort. It answers the age-old question, "What happens to Christians after death?" I have searched throughout all world religions and found nothing hopeful in their views of life after death. This text stands as a preface to Christ's establishment of His future kingdom. Here, Paul gives us a detailed description of the resurrection of all Christians. It is a statement of hope for all living believers who have ever lost a loved one.

First Thessalonians was very likely the first book of the New Testament ever to be written. It was penned only eighteen years after Jesus ascended into heaven, preceding the earliest of the Gospels by as much as ten years.

Paul, the intrepid evangelist, had founded the little church in Thessalonica, a city given over completely to idolatry and immorality. There were Jews there who rejected his resurrection message and quickly drove him out of the city. But in the brief weeks before they drove him out, he had taught them much prophecy.

Then within six months of that expulsion, he received word that some of their members had died and those who remained wanted to know where the deceased had gone. They were afraid these buried loved ones would be left behind when Jesus came again. In answering their doubts, Paul answers for the rest of us. You too may have loved ones who have died. If so, you cannot read this text too often. It is our blessed hope presented in just six verses.

Jesus is coming again for both the dead and the living. He will then "catch up" His entire church. We who are alive at His coming will not precede "those who are in their graves." In fact, the dead will respond before the living. Then all of us will be "caught up in the clouds to meet the Lord in the air."

Our departed loved ones will be given a new resurrected body.

All earthly bodies will be transformed instantly into heavenly bodies. Then comes that breathtaking moment! We shall see Jesus! But more than simply seeing Him, we will "remain with him forever"!

Can you imagine being with our Lord forever? Life eternal! No more death! Health forever from Him who is the great physician. Peace with Him who quells all war. No more want! Nothing that defiles or harms.

Sadly, this marvelous promise is not for all. Only those who have personally received Jesus Christ by faith can ever hope to be a part of those "who are still living when the Lord returns." Only "those who have fallen asleep in Christ" will be His when He comes to rapture His church (1 Corinthians 15:18, NKJV). The apostle Paul reminds us in verse 14, "Since we believe that Jesus died and was raised to life again, we also believe that when Jesus comes, God will bring back with Jesus all the Christians who have died." Thus the Rapture can only serve those who "believe." Believe what? The gospel!

In 1 Corinthians 15:1-4, Paul limits salvation to those who believe that Jesus died and rose again. Jesus gave himself once for all as a sacrifice for our sins. He rose again, proving God's acceptance of His sacrifice and showing His power over death. Each person must believe this to be a Christian. Church doctrine alone offers no hope. Nor does any denominational policy. Faith in Christ's death and resurrection is God's bottom line for salvation. If you have any doubt that you know the resurrected Christ as your Savior, you should bow your head and invite Him into your life by faith. Then the promise and the hope will be yours.

Today's Prayer
Dear heavenly Father, thank You for sending Jesus Your Son to die on the cross for my sins. Thank You for raising Him from the dead. I here and now confess the sin of my rebellion to You. I accept Your will for my life. I invite Your resurrected Son into my

life as Lord and Savior. I formally surrender my life and my future to You. In Jesus' name I pray, Amen.

4 LOOKING FOR THE BLESSED HOPE AND GLORIOUS APPEARING

For the grace of God that brings salvation has appeared to all men, teaching us that, denying ungodliness and worldly lusts, we should live soberly, righteously, and godly in the present age, looking for the blessed hope and glorious appearing of our great God and Savior Jesus Christ, who gave Himself for us, that He might redeem us from every lawless deed and purify for Himself His own special people, zealous for good works.

TITUS 2:11-14, NKJV

TWO DISTINCT phases of our Lord's appearing come as a pair in Scripture. "The blessed hope" always refers to the rapture of the church. The "Glorious Appearing" refers to our Lord's return "with power and great glory" (Matthew 24:30). In this final event He will conquer the Antichrist and establish His thousand-year reign of peace (Revelation 19:11-21).

These two events will be separated by seven years, during which He judges both His saints in heaven and those still on this earth. This time will be so turbulent that Jesus called it the "great Tribulation." He taught that not "since the beginning of the world until this time," have such trials fallen on humanity (Matthew 24:21, NKJV). The Glorious Appearing will come at the end of the Tribulation. The Rapture will precede it.

Paul challenges Christians to look forward to both of these

PERHAPS

events. In fact, our eager awaiting of these events will enable us to deny ungodly lusts and to "live soberly, righteously, and godly in the present age." But becoming a Christian can never cancel our fallen nature. Nor will it exempt us from seducing temptations. To help us be strong in these matters, God has given us "the blessed hope" of His Glorious Appearing. As we gain the upper hand over all temptation, we can devote ourselves to God's wonderful plan for our future.

What Christian would want the Lord to come while he or she is in the midst of some sin? Since we know neither the day nor the moment when He will come, we are to live our lives continually as if that moment is now—as though this day is our last. Anticipating this glory—"looking for the blessed hope"—will reduce our temptations to manageable size.

The pastor of a village parish was walking to church one Sunday morning to preach. He passed the home of one of his members who had not attended church in several weeks. As he got even with the house, he heard wood being chopped. Detouring a bit to the backyard, he saw the man dressed in work clothes and chopping wood near the back of his lot. Cupping his hands to his mouth, the pastor shouted, "Brother, the Lord is coming!" and walked on to church. About ten minutes into the service, the woodchopper slipped sheepishly into the back of the church, surprising his wife. We all need reminding that even in the midst of our petty agendas we must take stock of Christ's coming. The man's great sin was not in chopping wood, but in forgetting the great priority of the church on the Lord's Day.

"Looking for the blessed hope" means we should conduct our entire lives in anticipation of that event when He shall rapture us to be with Him. Are we then never to enjoy the blessings God has provided us? Of course we are. Life must go on even as we anticipate His coming. Some Christians, therefore, will be on vacation when He comes. Others will be busy at work earning a living for their families. Many Christian mothers will be home raising and nurturing their children. Some will even be engaged in sporting activities or the arts. But all who love Him must anticipate His coming.

Recently one of my grandsons interviewed for a well-paying but very secular job. At first he was tempted to take it. After all, he felt he deserved a great employment opportunity. He had scrimped and saved as he worked his way through a Christian college for years. After attending a full day of company orientation, he felt he could do the work well. He even felt that this job would help a lot of people. Still, as he drove across the city of Los Angeles at the conclusion of his first day he thought, *While it's a good job, it has no eternal value.* He then pulled off the freeway and recommitted his life to Christ. Suddenly he felt exhilarated by a new sense of calling as a youth pastor.

A short time later he saw a sign pointing to Talbot Seminary. He had previously thought about attending there for his master's degree. So he drove on to the campus. He found a registrar still there for the day, and he enrolled in seminary. He is now at peace with himself, his Lord, and his future. If Jesus comes while he is in seminary, the Lord will be served. If He doesn't come until after he has had a chance to minister to youth, the Lord will still be served. Either way, he now finds himself "looking for the blessed hope and glorious appearing of our great God and Savior Jesus Christ."

The "blessed hope" is not the kind of hope that says, "I *hope* someone will come see me" or "I *hope* to see you again." This word for hope has much more certainty to it. It is a Bible word that speaks of "a blessed confidence."

Hope here is used to indicate a future event that has long been guaranteed by God Himself. This hope is future, but it is as certain as the one hundred Old Testament prophecies that speak of our Lord's first coming. Now we can see His coming is a historical fact. The second coming of Jesus will itself one day be history. It will happen. Until it does, live your life in joyous anticipation. Look for the blessed hope! Make your expectation confident!

Dear Lord, thank You for the promise of Your return. Thank You for revealing in advance the certainty of my future. I want to be so faithful that even when tempted by the passions and lusts of this present world, I will keep on "looking" for Your coming on a daily basis. In Jesus' name I pray, Amen.

5

THE COMFORT OF HIS COMING

And now, brothers and sisters, I want you to know what will happen to the Christians who have died so you will not be full of sorrow like people who have no hope. For since we believe that Jesus died and was raised to life again, we also believe that when Jesus comes, God will bring back with Jesus all the Christians who have died. I can tell you this directly from the Lord: We who are still living when the Lord returns will not rise to meet him ahead of those who are in their graves. For the Lord himself will come down from heaven with a commanding shout, with the call of the archangel, and with the trumpet call of God. First, all the Christians who have died will rise from their graves. Then, together with them, we who are still alive and remain on the earth will be caught up in the clouds to meet the Lord in the air and remain with him forever. So comfort and encourage each other with these words.   1 Thessalonians 4:13-18

SEVENTEEN DAYS before my tenth birthday, my father suddenly died of a heart attack. I was devastated! My five-year-old sister was also overwhelmed by his sudden disappearance from our lives. Our seven-week-old brother would never know a father's love. For the first and only time in my life, I no longer wanted to live. I was so horrified I could hardly stand to view his remains at the funeral home. The absence of his hearty laughter, his warm hugs, his lifting touch—all were gone. Life had lost all hope.

Fortunately for us, the minister who had led my parents to Christ six years earlier believed the Scriptures. While conducting my father's graveside service, this pastor spoke of hope. Like a bolt of lightning in a dark place, he offered me a confident hope that has never died.

Pointing his finger heavenward toward the low overhanging skies of Michigan, he said, "This world has not heard the last of Frank LaHaye! One of these days Jesus will descend from heaven with a shout . . . and the dead in Christ shall rise first. Then we who are alive and remain shall be caught up together with them in the clouds to meet the Lord in the air. And thus we shall always be with the Lord." Then he added, "Therefore comfort one another with these words."

That teaching has provided a lifetime of comfort for me, and not for me only, but for millions of Christians everywhere. This passage of Scripture and its parallel in 1 Corinthians 15:50-58 are read or quoted at more funeral services than any other words of hope. Poems and eulogies are nice, but they cannot offer the comfort of such passages. The counsel of these verses offers us hope for a wonderful life after death.

Have you ever noticed that many people who ignore Jesus and His claim on their lives will frequently use these Scriptures at the loss of a loved one? At such times, even exalted minds like those of Tennyson, Wordsworth, and Russell have little hope to offer. Only Jesus has "the words that give eternal life" (John 6:68).

In verse 13 of the above text, Paul said he was giving this teaching so they would "not be full of sorrow like people who have no hope." It is no shame to feel sorrow when we lose our loved ones to death. Grief is natural. Why? Because we miss our loved ones' presence and company. But we should never sorrow for them as though their souls or spirits are homeless after death. They are with the Lord in our Father's house. So our sorrow

PERHAPS

should never be as hopeless as the sorrow of those who have no faith.

The unsaved, however, have no such hope. The hardest thing that I ever had to do during my forty years as a pastor was to conduct funerals for the unsaved. It was all so hopeless. Among such remembrances I can still see the three Texans who wept uncontrollably at the funeral of their unsaved father. They had paid handsomely for the glass-covered, airtight casket they had purchased to be sure their father's dead body could be preserved as long as possible. Glass coffins are a vain attempt at hope! Better their father had surrendered to Jesus while still alive.

There is nothing in Scripture that offers hope to those who die without faith in Christ. As Christians, our hope comes not from us or from anything we have done. It comes only from Christ's finished work on Calvary and the power of His resurrection.

I saw this graphically illustrated one day while conducting the funeral for a Christian friend. His wife, Olivia, shared his faith in Jesus at his memorial service. His wife's unsaved sister was at the service, and as they were leaving the grave site this sister began weeping profusely. The loving widow put her arm around her and said, "Don't take on so, dear. I will see my husband again when Jesus comes."

That only made her grieving sister weep even more, for she knew she had no such hope. But need is the beginning of all things wonderful. The sister's need caused her to trust in Christ before she returned home. Comforted by her newfound salvation and our Lord's promise to come again, she has since become a faithful witness.

Today's Prayer

Dear Lord, thank You so much for the comforting truth that I again shall one day meet all my loved ones who have died in the faith. What other religion can offer such life? Please help me to share my faith with others who have no such hope because they have not yet received You. I want to be used of Your Spirit today. In Jesus' name I pray, Amen.

6 WAITING FOR JESUS

> So you received the message with joy from the Holy Spirit in spite of the severe suffering it brought you. In this way, you imitated both us and the Lord. As a result, you yourselves became an example to all the Christians in Greece. And now the word of the Lord is ringing out from you to people everywhere, even beyond Greece, for wherever we go we find people telling us about your faith in God. We don't need to tell them about it, for they themselves keep talking about the wonderful welcome you gave us and how you turned away from idols to serve the true and living God. And they speak of how you are looking forward to the coming of God's Son from heaven—Jesus, whom God raised from the dead. He is the one who has rescued us from the terrors of the coming judgment.   1 THESSALONIANS 1:6-10

THE INFANT church of Thessalonica was filled with former pagan idolaters who worshiped with the immoral rituals common to the Greco-Roman culture. After their conversion, these onetime pagans had begun to "serve the true and living God," and were "looking forward to the coming of God's Son from heaven."

This is one of the many New Testament evidences that when any sinner comes to Christ, he or she begins a different way of life. So often contemporary Christians get it backwards. They try to change their way of life first to demonstrate their ability to become a Christian. Such attempts are futile. Without Christ, human beings can never stop sinning; they lack the moral force to accomplish it. Then they become frustrated and disillusioned and sometimes completely reject Christianity and return to their former way of life.

The Bible is clear on this: First we must accept Christ by faith, and then, as He gives us the spiritual resources to change our way of life, we are enabled to do it. One of the best motivations to implement moral change is a strong belief in Jesus' second coming. The apostle Paul was led by the Holy Spirit to teach these former pagans to anticipate Jesus' coming. He taught them that Christ came into this world to seek and save the lost. He reminded them often that Christ had died sacrificially for their sins and was resurrected on the third day just as the Old Testament prophets had predicted. He taught them that they were to live waiting for Jesus to come again. This anticipation, said the apostle, would help them to turn from idols to serve the living God.

What was the manner of their waiting? This was no easy-chair passivity. Waiting is a discipline that demands a life of prayer and intentional study. Paul has already commended them for becoming "followers of us and of the Lord" (verse 6, NKJV). Further, he goes on to say, "You yourselves became an example to all the Christians in Greece. And now the word of the Lord is ringing out from you to people everywhere, even beyond Greece, for wherever we go we find people telling us about your faith in God. We don't need to tell them about it." Evidently these new converts were energized with a second-coming zeal. This motivated them to preach the gospel to everyone in their area.

I once saw this graphically illustrated in the lives of a young dentist and his wife. They accepted Christ in our church many years ago. I don't recall any couple ever leading more unsaved people to Christ than these two. When I questioned this vibrant young man as to how he won so many, he replied, "Everyone I know is a pagan in need of Christ."

Later this evangelistic couple joined the Campus Crusade for Christ staff and served in the Churches Alive program. They spent the next thirty years teaching thousands of people how to share their faith in Christ. Recently they began to read our Left Behind series and wrote to tell us how much they enjoyed the books. In the same letter, they reminded me that shortly after their conversion I had been teaching the book of Revelation on Sunday nights. The man freely admitted, "In those days, I must confess, I didn't always understand what you were teaching even when my wife tried to explain it to me as we drove home from church. But one thing I did learn was that Jesus was coming and I had better get my house in order!"

Like the Thessalonians, this young couple had to totally change their lifestyle to "serve the true and living God." Do they have any regrets? Certainly not. In the dentist's letter he said, "It's been a great life." All through the years of my ministry I have never heard anyone complain that they had made a wrong decision in surrendering their lives to Christ. The reason is simple: The committed Christian life is the only meaningful way to live. And at the center of that meaning is the glorious hope of His coming.

TODAY'S PRAYER

Dear heavenly Father, I want to thank You for saving me and giving me direction in life. Without You I tend to scramble those decisions so important to my daily life. Thank You for all the promises of Jesus' second coming. May they always motivate me to turn from the idols of my past and serve You, the living Lord of glory. In Jesus' name, Amen.

7 SAVED FROM THE WRATH TO COME

Wait for His Son from heaven, whom He raised from the dead, even Jesus who delivers us from the wrath to come.   1 THESSALONIANS 1:10, NKJV

THE DOMINANT force in turning the young Christians of Thessalonica from serving idols to serving the living God was the

PERHAPS

promise of the Second Coming. Still, it was not the only motivation. In addition to the Second Coming we have the promise that Jesus "delivers us from the wrath to come." To understand we have been delivered from the wrath is to be compelled to live in holiness.

During his brief ministry in Thessalonica, Paul had taught the people much about Bible prophecy. His term "the wrath to come" was not new to them. He had evidently taught them what the Old Testament prophets had to say about wrath and suffering, trouble and travail. Although Paul had not heard Jesus' Olivet discourse, he knew that Christ had referred to the great Tribulation as "a time of greater horror than anything the world has ever seen or will ever see again" (Matthew 24:21). Paul also knew and probably pointed out to the Thessalonians that Daniel long before had said this tribulation would last seven years (Daniel 9:27).

And as bad as this time would be, Paul convinced these young believers that they would never have to live through it. This is not the only place that Paul mentioned this unique deliverance. The teaching is found also in Romans 5:9 and in 1 Thessalonians 5:9, where he states that "God did not appoint us to wrath" (NKJV).

Along with Paul, Jesus also mentions this deliverance. In His revelation to John (Revelation 3:10), He said that believers will be protected "from the great time of testing that will come upon the whole world." That "time of testing" can only mean the Tribulation period that will follow the Lord's rapture of His church.

Obviously, then, Paul used both the promise of our Lord's second coming and His promise of deliverance from the Tribulation to serve as a motivator for these former practitioners of paganism. And seeing the true course of final things, they turned from their sinful lifestyles "to serve the true and living God" (1 Thessalonians 1:9).

It is interesting to note that the first three centuries of church history in addition to the last two have seen more Christians turn from idols than all other centuries combined. These five centuries also have contained the brightest and strongest teachings about the Second Coming.

I never cease to be amazed at all that motivates people to accept Christ. Some are moved by our Lord's sacrificial death on the cross. Others are compelled by His great salvation. In my case I was so terrified of perishing in the flames of hell I turned instantly to Christ. One young man came forward weeping after a service in which I had preached, saying, "God wants to deliver me from the coming time of wrath." He, too, had gotten the message! He knew that if he did not accept Christ he would have to go through the Tribulation. I was challenged by his prayer: "Thank You, Lord, for saving me from the wrath to come."

TODAY'S PRAYER

Dear Lord, I cannot thank You enough for Your assurance that Jesus is coming to take us to Your heavenly house. Further, I thank You that I will not have to go through the Tribulation that may soon fall upon the whole world. Please help me to live each day so that I can share my faith in the power of Your Holy Spirit. In the name of Your Son I pray, Amen.

8 OUR HOPE, JOY, AND CROWN OF REJOICING

For what is our hope, or joy, or crown of rejoicing? Is it not even you in the presence of our Lord Jesus Christ at His coming? For you are our glory and joy.   1 THESSALONIANS 2:19-20, NKJV

THE APOSTLE Paul's greatest joys on this earth were those souls in Thessalonica who had turned from their pagan idols "to serve the true and living God" (1 Thessalonians 1:9). We have already seen that their conversion was accompanied by an incredible transformation in their lifestyles. In this text Paul is telling them how much they mean to him. They gave him pride in knowing his life and sacrifices were worthwhile. They were for him a hope, a joy, and an eternal crown.

Some Bible teachers believe this "crown of rejoicing" is one of the five crowns that any Christian may earn in this life. When understood in the light of eternity, this crown causes everything else in life to pale in significance. It is often called "the soul-winner's crown." It is a crown to be bestowed by Jesus at the judgment seat of Christ. It is a laurel of gold for those who made the conscious effort to win their friends and associates to faith.

This suggestion parallels Daniel's prophecy that after the coming of Christ, "Those who are wise will shine as bright as the sky, and those who turn many to righteousness will shine like stars forever" (Daniel 12:3).

We should keep in mind that this crown, like every crown, is a symbol of authority. It provides its wearer a position in which to rule and reign with Christ during the Millennium. While we will examine the other four crowns later in this book, this particular crown is the soul-winner's glory. It is an evidence of the special leadership status that all soul-winners will have during that thousand-year reign of Christ.

Often times Christians rationalize away their obligations to win souls by bragging about their service as deacons, Sunday school teachers, choir members, and so forth. And while these positions play an important part in the church, only the soul-winner's crown will provide a special reward of blessing due the evangelist. And this crown will last for at least a thousand years!

But that isn't all. Paul mentions that the conversions and life transformations of the Thessalonians were for him a source of "glory and joy." Their response and commitment to the living Christ increased his own confidence that the Lord is alive and well and will return someday to take us to Himself. Christ is our present joy. Ask any soul-winner and he or she will tell you there is no joy like leading another person to faith in Christ.

Many people have shared with me how they sent one or more of our novels to a lost or errant loved one. As a result that person came to faith in Christ.

Recently a young man stopped me in the hall at a Religious Broadcasters Convention to tell me how the novels were used of God to transform his sister, who had rebelled against her parents, left home, and wouldn't talk to the rest of the family. Since he was the only one she would talk to, he sent her our first book. She read it, recommitted her life to Jesus, and wrote him in a letter, "Ask Mom and Dad if I can come home!" Tears of joy ran down his face as he told us her triumphant story.

Years ago, I asked a young ophthalmologist in our church, "What is the greatest experience you have ever had?" I expected him to tell me of his first successful corneal transplant, which he had performed only ten days earlier. My question seemed to plunge him into silence. Suddenly, yet reflectively, he sat back on his stool, turned, stared ahead briefly, and began telling me about a woman he had recently led to Christ.

After the woman's surgery, the ophthalmologist had begun the slow process of removing the bandages from her eyes. Day by day as he removed successive layers of those bandages, he took the opportunity to show her the way to Christ. When he finished he asked, "Wouldn't you like to receive Christ?" She at first said no but then said yes.

Suddenly the doctor interrupted his narrative with a broad smile before he continued, "As we prayed, I sensed a presence in the room. When our prayer was over I looked up and saw that her husband was now standing at the side of her bed. I must confess I had always been afraid of her husband. He was a blunt and profane soul, intimidating in conversation. But when I looked up, tears were running down his face. I took courage and began to show him the way to Christ. He came to faith."

When the doctor finished his story, a wonderful quiet filled the room. I could only ask myself, "Why was leading a couple to faith the greatest experience that young doctor had ever had?" Because it's the most euphoric experience anyone can have on this earth. Nothing has more eternal significance than this.

Truly evangelism is a "crown of rejoicing."

TODAY'S PRAYER

Dear heavenly Father, thank You for saving my soul and thank You for those who had a part in leading me to Christ. Accepting Him has been the greatest experience of my life. Help me to share that experience with others and to start them on this wonderful road to heaven. Lead me to someone who needs You and use my lips to communicate Your grace in the power of Your Spirit. In Jesus' name I pray!

9 ABOUNDING IN LOVE

For what thanks can we render to God for you, for all the joy with which we rejoice for your sake before our God, night and day praying exceedingly that we may see your face and perfect what is lacking in your faith? Now may our God and Father Himself, and our Lord Jesus Christ, direct our way to you. And may the Lord make you increase and abound in love to one another and to all, just as we do to you, so that He may establish your hearts blameless in holiness before our God and Father at the coming of our Lord Jesus Christ with all His saints.   1 THESSALONIANS 3:9-13, NKJV

A YOUNG man whom we know wrote to us telling us of the one thing that had kept him from receiving Christ: He was harboring a deep-rooted, lifetime hatred for a person he believed was a hypocrite. Each time he saw the person, anger would well up in his heart. This anger had finally become a roadblock to faith.

Fortunately, he began reading *Left Behind.* Gradually he became convinced that in spite of what the other person had done, he himself needed Christ! He knew the dire truth: When Jesus raptured His church, this man's girlfriend would be taken and he would be left behind. So the next Sunday when the invitation was given he decided to go forward and say an eternal "yes" to Jesus Christ.

Then an amazing thing happened. As he walked down the aisle, an overpowering sense of love came over him. His long-term anger for the person he believed to be a hypocrite was washed away. The Spirit had cleansed his sin and replaced his animosity with love. He still felt the other person was wrong in his business dealings, but it no longer mattered. His transformation was complete!

Paul desired this kind of "abounding love" for the Thessalonians. This kind of love surpasses natural affection. Paul knew the dark captivity of the Greco-Roman religion. These gods were base deities indeed. They were gods who thrived on hate, jealousy, and pride. Revenge was common to the gods in their dealing with each other. But now Christ had come. Christianity had offered the incomparable love of God who gave His only Son for the sins of a rebellious world (John 3:16). And it was that kind of love that Paul wanted these former idolaters to emulate.

Paul's yearning was at last realized in their lives. Even secular history reveals that the first-century Christians were famous for loving one another. Yet he admonished them to "increase more and more" in love toward one another (1 Thessalonians 4:10, NKJV). All of us know problem people who can cause a root of bitterness to grow up within us and stifle our love for God even as it ruins our relationships with others.

We should take a "love inventory" of all our relationships. Is there someone I truly dislike? Is there anyone who causes me to grieve the Spirit by forcing me to live in bitterness? God wants me to forgive and love that person. I should never let my victory in Christ be defeated by a grudge. I must seize the high ground. I will, in Christ, forgive everyone their pettiness and meanness of spirit. I will love them in spite of themselves. Jesus is coming. I will make love my way of life.

TODAY'S PRAYER
Dear heavenly Father, thank You for Your unconditional love! Forgive me when I am unloving. Particularly help me forgive those whose selfish ways offend me. May I never allow any lack of forgiveness to be brought against me at the judgment seat of Christ. I am powerless to be Christlike on my own. Help me to love like You, beginning today. In Jesus' name I pray.

10 REWARDS FOR MARTYRS

Don't be afraid of what you are about to suffer. The Devil will throw some of you into prison and put you to the test. You will be persecuted for "ten days." Remain faithful even when facing death, and I will give you the crown of life.   REVELATION 2:10

God blesses the people who patiently endure testing. Afterward they will receive the crown of life that God has promised to those who love him.   JAMES 1:12

CASSIE BERNALL was described by her fellow students as "vivacious, filled with faith, hope, and love." Although it had been only three years since she received Jesus Christ at a youth camp, He literally transformed her life. Coming home on the weekend she told her mother, "You have a different girl, Mom; I have committed my life to

Christ." She instantly turned from rebellion and drugs and became the child her parents had always dreamed she might be.

One unforgettable day, Cassie went into her school library in Littleton, Colorado, to study for an exam. Suddenly two gunmen began firing weapons at their fellow classmates. Then one of them approached Cassie and asked her if she believed in God. She hesitated only a moment before saying, "Yes, I believe." Point-blank, her assassin shot her in the face.

Her memorial service rocked the entire nation. Her personal testimony via video was presented at this service. It had been filmed at her church youth group just two days before her death. In her own words, she spoke her message of life clearly: "I just try to not contradict myself. [I want] to get rid of all the hypocrisy and just live for Christ." Cassie was one of twelve students gunned down by these teenage killers who worshiped Satan and admired Adolf Hitler.

The memorial service for all the students drew an overflow of seventy thousand mourners to be consoled by evangelist Franklin Graham and other evangelical pastors who had lost young people in the shooting. The whole service was carried live on CNN, MSNBC, and C-SPAN. While Christian clergy are always brought in to minister at such times, they are usually not made welcome on school campuses. Prayer, Bible reading, and the acknowledgment of God and creation are usually forbidden in the halls of education. Yet in seasons of crisis, ministers suddenly are made welcome.

Have you ever wondered why?

It's really quite simple: The Bible is the only real source that offers hope for life in the next world! When loved ones are taken from us, the best poems, philosophy, and human wisdom won't cut it. Real hope is found only in the resurrection life of Jesus. He has prepared for us a home indestructible in the heavens. No other religion, no secular vision could ever come close to the wonderful plan God has for all who put their faith in Christ.

What about Cassie? Wasn't she cut off even before the prime of her youth? Don't mourn for her. Weep for her parents, perhaps. Yes, pray for them. Pray for her school, for all there will miss the ever personable Cassie. But as for herself, she has come to know that to be "absent from the body" is "to be present with the Lord" (2 Corinthians 5:7, NKJV). Henceforth there is laid up for her "the crown of life" that will never fade!

Twice in the Scripture, Revelation 2:10 and James 1:12, we find the mention of "the crown of life" as the premier reward to faithful believers who have no fear of standing before the judgment seat of Christ. All who stand before Christ at that judgment will be born-again believers like Cassie.

How shall we understand these crowns? How are they to be defined? No one knows for sure. Still we can say that these crowns will be given to reward Christian leadership during the Millennium.

Kings wear crowns on special ceremonial occasions. But these are poor diadems indeed. These merely earthly crowns represent authority and sovereignty. We know from the Scriptures that we will "reign with [Christ] a thousand years" (Revelation 20:6). We can only conclude therefore, that Cassie and all other Christian martyrs will wear crowns that represent their service to the Lord they loved and died for.

Christians throughout history have suffered agony, and many have been martyred for their faith. But all martyrs will be handsomely rewarded. They will receive the martyr's crown. Their rewards will last forever.

TODAY'S PRAYER

Dear heavenly Father, thank You for the example of courage and faith that Cassie showed in her last moments of life. And thank You for welcoming her into heaven that very instant. Then, please, I beg You, help me to live every moment in the light of

Christ's coming, that I may be prepared at every moment to be with You. In Jesus' name I pray, Amen.

11 LACKING NOTHING AT THE RAPTURE

God has called us to be holy, not to live impure lives. Anyone who refuses to live by these rules is not disobeying human rules but is rejecting God, who gives his Holy Spirit to you. But I don't need to write to you about the Christian love that should be shown among God's people. For God himself has taught you to love one another. Indeed, your love is already strong toward all the Christians in all of Macedonia. Even so, dear brothers and sisters, we beg you to love them more and more. This should be your ambition: to live a quiet life, minding your own business and working with your hands, just as we commanded you before. As a result, people who are not Christians will respect the way you live, and you will not need to depend on others to meet your financial needs.   1 THESSALONIANS 4:7-12

THERE are standards in the Christian life. And those offered in the passage above immediately precede what we recently examined and called the most important Rapture passage in the Bible (1 Thessalonians 4:13-18). This text offers us one of the Bible's most significant challenges on how to live in the light of His any-moment coming.

In this passage, Paul offers us a fivefold approach to holiness in prayer.

First, "God has called us to be holy" (verse 7).

Earlier in the chapter, Paul challenged the young converts of Thessalonica to sanctify their bodies by keeping "clear of all sexual sin" (1 Thessalonians 4:3), because it is a constant threat to holiness. God is holy, and if we are going to enjoy intimate fellowship with Him, we must seek holiness. Elsewhere in the New Testament Peter admonished believers, saying, "But now you must be holy in everything you do, just as God—who chose you to be his children—is holy" (1 Peter 1:15).

But how are we to arrive at holiness? One of the first obligations of prayer is to ask God for forgiveness. Why? Unconfessed sin keeps our prayers from being heard. Because as David said in the Old Testament, "If I had not confessed the sin in my heart, the Lord would not have listened" (Psalm 66:18). Have you ever felt that your prayers never went any higher than the ceiling? This powerlessness can usually be traced to a lack of holiness.

In the Old Testament the *shekinah* glory of God resided in the Holy of Holies. The Holy of Holies was that inner sanctuary of the temple where only the high priest could go once a year. It was forbidden to all others ever to enter it. So when the priest was assigned to minister there, he had an elaborate method of cleansing his entire body before he did so. Then before he entered, a special rope was tied around his ankle. If he had not confessed all his sins and God struck him dead while he was alone in the Holy of Holies, his body could be pulled out under the curtains by the other priests not permitted to enter. God demands that we be holy in preparation for His coming. So when approaching God in prayer, we should acknowledge and confess all sin. Once we have done this, we must freely accept His forgiveness and not beat ourselves with guilt and self-condemnation. A single sincere confession is enough. Asking once for forgiveness is all that is required to own instant holiness.

Second, we must increase our love for other Christians (verse 10).

Love is the first fruit of the Spirit working in our lives. If there is anyone in your church toward whom you feel bitterness, ask God to forgive you and replace that bitterness with His love.

Third, aspire to "live a quiet life" (verse 11).

Riotous living is a characteristic of those who do not have a personal relationship with God. These have no internal peace of heart. The more peace a person has on the inside, the less noise he craves on the outside. The closer we get to the end of the age the more we can expect this world to be dominated by secular people. These individuals are prone to violence and noise, and often rebel against Christlikeness. Paul said Christians should seek an opposite lifestyle: the quiet, obedient life.

Fourth, "[mind] your own business" (verse 11).

Minding our own business is a call to avoid being busybodies. We are to allow each individual to live his or her life in Christ. We are never to try to answer to God for anyone else's behavior.

Fifth, "[work] with your hands" (verse 11).

The Bible has never encouraged laziness. In fact, it teaches—especially in regard to the Second Coming—that he who will not work should not be provided for by those who do (2 Thessalonians 3:10).

When I was pastoring my first church, we lived in the parsonage right next to the church. A truckload of sod had been delivered the very day I began to pastor. I intended to lay all this sod myself. A bricklayer also arrived that day to build a new church sign. The bricklayer had a negative view of preachers, thinking them all lazy and unproductive. Little did I realize that as he was building the new church sign, he was watching me very carefully. We both started the day at 7:30 A.M., but before I started laying sod I introduced myself to him. I told him I had an early meeting to attend. I am sure he doubted that I would ever return to actually lay the sod. But as soon as my early meeting was over, I rushed back, changed clothes, and laid sod. However, it was not long before the telephone rang. I had to change out of my "grubbies," get into dress clothes, and go make a call. Then once again I returned, changed clothes, and put down some more sod. My interruptions continued throughout the day. When we both quit at about 5 P.M., the bricklayer observed that I had changed my clothes six times that day.

The next Sunday he brought his family to church. A month later, he accepted Christ as his Savior. I think he was won by the simple example of honest labor. He not only changed his mind about preachers, he changed his mind about the Savior who inspires believers to do honest work.

The purpose of these five challenges is to call us to remember that people are watching us. When we take a stand for Jesus Christ and let it be known in our office, shop, or school, the people of the world expect us to live and work well. Paul challenged these early believers to "walk properly toward those who are outside, . . . that you may lack nothing" (verse 12, NKJV). In other words, a Christian is not to enjoy the luxury of living as an island unto himself or herself.

We Christian sports fans take delight in those star players who give a ready witness to Christ. There are many such Christians in the National Football League. A few years ago, one of the best quarterbacks in the NFL attributed his incredible success to his conversion experience. At his open testimony, even secular sports writers had to acknowledge his spiritual integrity. In contrast, another Christian athlete on the night before the Super Bowl was arrested for a crime that brought disgrace to him, his family, and the Christ he claimed to love. His "walk" did not match his "talk" and left room for sportscasters to mock his testimony and life.

A young woman I read about was determined to seduce a Christian man in her office. He had witnessed to the woman, hoping to bring her to Christ. For weeks she tried to seduce him. He was gracious, never humiliating her, but just as determined to stay true to his Lord and his wife. In fact, he was careful never to be found in the slightest compromising situation. Finally the young woman admitted in frustration, "You must be the real thing." He was. He knew he was not perfect, but he was determined to live every day so that if his Lord suddenly returned for him, he would be ready.

TODAY'S PRAYER

Dear heavenly Father, forgive me for those times when I have not lived up to Your standards. I want to be a faithful follower of Your Son Jesus and be ready for His coming. Make me strong in temptation. Enable me to provide all those on "the outside" with a consistent and faithful witness to my Lord, in whose name I pray, Amen.

12 GOD'S WILL FOR YOU AT HIS COMING

How we thank God for you! Because of you we have great joy in the presence of God. Night and day we pray earnestly for you, asking God to let us see you again to fill up anything that may still be missing in your faith. May God himself, our Father, and our Lord Jesus make it possible for us to come to you very soon. And may the Lord make your love grow and overflow to each other and to everyone else, just as our love overflows toward you. As a result, Christ will make your hearts strong, blameless, and holy when you stand before God our Father on that day when our Lord Jesus comes with all those who belong to him. Finally, dear brothers and sisters, we urge you in the name of the Lord Jesus to live in a way that pleases God, as we have taught you. You are doing this already,

and we encourage you to do so more and more.
For you remember what we taught you in the
name of the Lord Jesus. God wants you to be holy,
so you should keep clear of all sexual sin. Then
each of you will control your body and live in holiness and honor—not in lustful passion as the
pagans do, in their ignorance of God and his ways.
Never cheat a Christian brother in this matter by
taking his wife, for the Lord avenges all such sins,
as we have solemnly warned you before. God has
called us to be holy, not to live impure lives.

1 THESSALONIANS 3:9–4:7

EVERY true pastor, like the apostle Paul, yearns that the members of
his congregation will always be found doing the will of God. Paul,
the intrepid evangelist, got his greatest joy in seeing these young converts turn from their idols to serve the living God. But he had one further desire for them. He also wanted them to walk in holiness and
love.

He called this walk of holiness "sanctification" (2 Thessalonians
2:13, NKJV). We hear so little these days of this biblical virtue. Yet the
Scripture is clear. We will be held accountable for sanctified living
when Jesus calls us to Himself.

In 1 Thessalonians 3:13, Paul describes sanctification as a heart
that is "blameless, and holy when you stand before God our Father
on that day when our Lord Jesus comes." In 1 Thessalonians 4:3, Paul
says that it is sanctification that causes us to "keep clear of all sexual
sin." Sexual sins are ever central to our human experience. God has
given human beings the gift of sex, and yet it is a gift that can become
Satan's tool to destroy inconsistent believers. Sometimes we wonder
why God has given us the sex drive. That answer is simple. If we
didn't have it, the human race might long ago have become extinct.
But like all other appetites—hunger, self-preservation, ambition—it

is often misused. To fail to control this drive is to be destroyed by it.

God has given us marriage as the context in which to express this great gift. Until we come to marriage, He has asked us to exercise self-control. In a practical sense, self-control begins in the mind, which the Bible instructs us to keep pure. I have seen many Christians lose the joy of living godly lives because their minds became indulgent in sexual license. Mental adulterers and fornicators of the heart are now rampant. Today's television programs and movies have universally corrupted hearts.

Long ago Jesus said, "You will know them by their fruits" (Matthew 7:16, NKJV). It doesn't take a theologian to realize that the entertainment industry is destroying any vestige of Judeo-Christian moral values. What movies, for instance, exalt virtue, fidelity, lasting love, or purity? What they do champion is perversion, sexual immorality, profanity, and blasphemy. The fruit of Hollywood's indulgence is seen on the screen every day. Today's "entertainers" continually turn the hearts of the nation toward Sodom. They have publicized a widely accepted lie: The personal life is no one else's business; it has no effect on our professional life.

The tragedy is not just that the unbelievers in our country accept this. Many Christians now buy into this kind of thinking. Too many Christians have the idea they can feed their minds on immorality and not be affected in their walk of faith. What folly! The Bible tells us that "as [a man] thinks in his heart, so is he" (Proverbs 23:7, NKJV). What we put into our minds fuels our emotions, which in turn determines our behavior in the world.

A twenty-one-year-old college student once told me, "Pastor, I think I am oversexed!" I felt his statement could have only been prompted by what he permitted to live in his mind. When I asked how he spent his free time, he admitted to reading *Playboy* and *Hustler* magazines. Then he protested, "I don't buy them; they are always available in our frat house." When I asked what TV and movies he had experienced, he finally admitted to watching the HBO channel and a steady diet of R-rated films.

I told him that he was probably not oversexed. It is just that at twenty-one, he was at the highest point of his sex drive and he was overstimulating that drive with pornography and sexually explicit entertainment. I also warned him that because he had been living on such a steady junk diet of the mind, that it would probably take him a couple of months to overcome his mental feeding habit. I told him that with spiritual discipline he could gradually replace those lustful thoughts with wholesome images. Then I designed a regular Bible reading and study program for him, including three weeks of Scripture memorization. After faithfully practicing this new discipline, his mental perversions were replaced and his mind was purified.

Your mind is the most important organ you possess. If you want to maintain pure emotions, you will have to "set your affection on things above, not on things on the earth" (Colossians 3:2, KJV). Your affections are you. But more than that, your affections are your destiny. What you love determines where you will spend eternity. Love material things and live in fear. Love God and all is well.

TODAY'S PRAYER

Dear heavenly Father, please forgive me for allowing my mind to be polluted by what I allow my eyes to see. I want to be sensitive to eternal things, not the temptations of this world. Help me to be discerning in what I read, view, or listen to. I want to maintain the vessel of my mind in honor and purity. Help me to live every day as though this is the day the Savior might call me up to be with Him forever. In Jesus' name, Amen.

13 SOBER LIVING IN THE "DAY OF THE LORD"

I really don't need to write to you about how and when all this will happen, dear brothers and sisters. For you know quite well that the day of the Lord will come unexpectedly, like a thief in the night. When people are saying, "All is well; everything is peaceful and secure," then disaster will fall upon them as suddenly as a woman's birth pains begin when her child is about to be born. And there will be no escape. But you aren't in the dark about these things, dear brothers and sisters, and you won't be surprised when the day of the Lord comes like a thief. For you are all children of the light and of the day; we don't belong to darkness and night. So be on your guard, not asleep like the others. Stay alert and be sober. Night is the time for sleep and the time when people get drunk. But let us who live in the light think clearly, protected by the body armor of faith and love, and wearing as our helmet the confidence of our salvation. 1 THESSALONIANS 5:1-8

HAVE YOU ever been robbed? We have—twice! Once, when we were out of town, a thief worked around our security system and threw a rock through the kitchen window. It was our only unsecured window. Then he took everything of value he could get through that window. One other time while my wife Beverly was speaking in a church, a thief broke into her hotel room and took all her jewelry.

Thieves count on our trust. They work on the element of surprise. The Second Coming has often been compared to the coming of a thief. When our Lord comes, most people will not expect Him. Even some of His followers will be caught unaware. In my preaching I have repeatedly urged my hearers to be ready every day of their lives for the inevitable and imminent second coming of Christ.

"The Day of the Lord" is referred to throughout Scripture. The term designates a time of judgment when God will move to take direct control of history. When the Hebrew prophets spoke of this day, they often had in mind a local judgment when God would rebuke Israel and Judah for their sins. Sometimes the Day of the Lord in the Old Testament referred to sieges or wars. Sometimes it was used to designate the Tribulation period and the Glorious Appearing of the Messiah's millennial kingdom.

In our text for today, "the day of the Lord" refers to those who will be transformed and snatched up instantly to be with the Savior. His coming, like that of a thief, will come when most people least expect Him.

Paul specifically challenges us as "children of the light" to live soberly and put on three things:

1. The body armor of faith. I only know one way to put on this body armor. It is accomplished through the regular reading of God's Word. I have never met a man or woman of faith who did not have a consistent devotional time of reading God's Word.
2. The body armor of love. Believers are to love all others, particularly the unlovely. Hate comes easy. But it takes the Spirit of God working through His Word to enable us to love those who do not love us.
3. The helmet (the confident expectation) of salvation. Our hope of salvation is not a hope-so affair. It is a confident expectation. It is a "know-so salvation." It is our assurance that He is able to save to the uttermost all who call upon Him.

Many times as a minister I have sat with dying people. Those without hope of eternal life die differently than Christians. I have never seen a Christian who did not die in peace. Not so with those who reject Christ. They often leave life kicking and screaming. For believers, Jesus removes all fear of death and replaces it with the confident expectation of eternal life. What could be better?

Today's Prayer
Dear Lord, thank You for sending Jesus to die for my sins and to save me. I freely admit I am unworthy, but I'm ever so grateful. Thank You for the confidence I have that "to be absent from the body [is] to be present with the Lord" (2 Corinthians 5:7, NKJV). Help me to take time each day to read Your Word and pray, to live a life pleasing to You, and always to love others. In Jesus' name I pray.

14 CHRISTIANS APPOINTED TO SALVATION, NOT WRATH

> For God did not appoint us to wrath, but to obtain salvation through our Lord Jesus Christ, who died for us, that whether we wake or sleep, we should live together with Him. Therefore comfort each other and edify one another, just as you also are doing. 1 Thessalonians 5:9-11, NKJV

SCRIPTURE can only be understood in the light of its context. In 1 Thessalonians 4:13-18, Paul delivered the most detailed description of the rapture of the church. He did it to help us rely on the truth that one day our Lord Himself will shout from heaven, raise the dead, transform the living, and gather all believers to His Father's house. We have seen the great comfort that Christ gives to grieving believers.

But here, Paul challenges us to avoid those who glibly preach, "Peace and safety!" Such naiveté is often followed by sudden destruction (1 Thessalonians 5:3). This destruction is the very image of that Tribulation period which will "come as a snare on all those who dwell on the face of the whole earth" (Luke 21:35, NKJV). This period is often called "The Day of the Lord," for it is the time that God's wrath will fall upon an entire generation. God will allow this to bring unbelievers to accept or reject the Savior. He will give those whom the Rapture leaves behind exactly seven years to make this important decision. But these seven years will also be a time when He pours out His wrath on all those who have persecuted His prophets and servants. Revelation 6:17 makes it very clear that this will be history's most horrible era.

After challenging believers not to be taken by surprise at the coming of Christ, Paul then makes an astounding statement: "God did not appoint us to wrath, but to obtain salvation through our Lord Jesus Christ." This is one of the most underappreciated promises in the Bible. Yet God will keep His pledge that Christians will be saved from the wrath to come (1 Thessalonians 1:10, NKJV). However, the most important part of this promise is that we who believe in Christ are appointed to "obtain salvation." That is not just for the generation living in the end time, but it pertains to believers in every era.

The Bible is clear that God has a plan to end this old world that has known more than its share of self-inflicted suffering. Sane people shudder when we think of the millions who have been killed or made to suffer due to the ultimate expression of man's inhumanity to man: war. In the twentieth century alone, it has been estimated that 180 million deaths have been caused by war and political oppression. Countless more millions have lost limbs and eyes, and made other bodily sacrifices to keep mad dictators from controlling the world. But freedom is never free. It always costs someone. Still there is a day when all suffering will come to a fiery end; when God will judge the thoughts and intentions of the heart. Millions will reject Him, but the great news is that "a vast crowd, too great to count," will receive Him

(Revelation 7:9). The Tribulation will be a period of momentous decisions—seven years of choice, of life, of destiny!

Christians, however, in whatever age they live, are appointed to salvation, to be delivered from wrath (verse 9). In other words, every unbeliever will have a final opportunity to "obtain salvation." This incredible hope should inspire joy in the hearts of believers. In that day all the injustices of life will be rectified. The wise of heart will be saved.

Most humble Christians respond, "But I don't deserve salvation." How right they are! Who could ever be worthy of the Cross? Yet we are guaranteed its blessings, not because of anything we have done, but because of His mercy. *Jesus paid it all,* says the hymn writer, *all to Him I owe; sin had left a crimson stain, He washed it white as snow.*

One of the most common responses to the offer of salvation that we have heard through the years is, "It sounds too easy." Can we really be made eternally free from the consequences of sin without some good works? Yes. Because Jesus paid it all. Whenever anyone says, "The Christian offer of salvation is too easy," I always answer, "No, it isn't! It cost God our Father the life of His only begotten Son." It cost the Son of God incomparable suffering, "even death on a cross" (Philippians 2:8, NASB). Our salvation cost so much more than the freedom it purchased us. It cost the dearest thing to the heart of God: the life of Christ.

"The joy of the Lord is [our] strength" (Nehemiah 8:10). There is no other joy like knowing Jesus and knowing that through His sacrifice we are appointed to obtain salvation through Him. No wonder Paul said in another place, "Thank God for his Son—a gift too wonderful for words!" (2 Corinthians 9:15).

Today's Prayer
Dear heavenly Father, I am humbled and awed at the gift of Your Son and His willing sacrifice for my soul's salvation! Just

saying thank You seems so little! Yet I must. Thank You for forgiving my sins. And thank You for saving my soul from wrath. I give You the only thing I can give: my life! Do with me as You see fit. And above all, please use me this day to share widely Your great salvation. In Jesus' blessed name I pray, Amen.

15 FURTHER ADMONITIONS IN LIGHT OF HIS COMING

So encourage each other and build each other up, just as you are already doing. Dear brothers and sisters, honor those who are your leaders in the Lord's work. They work hard among you and warn you against all that is wrong. Think highly of them and give them your wholehearted love because of their work. And remember to live peaceably with each other. Brothers and sisters, we urge you to warn those who are lazy. Encourage those who are timid. Take tender care of those who are weak. Be patient with everyone. See that no one pays back evil for evil, but always try to do good to each other and to everyone else. Always be joyful. Keep on praying. No matter what happens, always be thankful, for this is God's will for you who belong to Christ Jesus. Do not stifle the Holy Spirit. Do not scoff at prophecies, but test everything that is said. Hold on to what is good. Keep away from every kind of evil.   1 THESSALONIANS 5:11-22

IN OUR last study, we learned the news that in Christ we are not only saved from the wrath to come but we have also been appointed to God's salvation. It doesn't matter whether we are "awake or asleep," when Christ returns; the Rapture is for all of us who believe. Paul confirms it: we shall all "live with Him forever" (1 Thessalonians 9:10). And we know from our previous studies that the dead in Christ will be first in the Rapture and come with Christ in His Glorious Appearing. Then there will follow a millennium of life on the newly refurbished earth.

The apostle challenges us to be ready every moment for His coming. To live in this constant awareness we must do these thirteen things:

1. We must "encourage each other" with the promise of hope.
2. We must "build each other up." Christians should freely share what they know of this hope.
3. We must "think highly" of "those who are . . . leaders in the Lord's work." Simply stated, believers should honor those who are their true spiritual leaders and teachers. They should constantly encourage all those who edify others in the Lord.
4. We should "live peaceably with each other."
5. Christians are to be "patient with everyone," even the "lazy," the "timid," and the "weak." One of the hallmarks of the Christian life is that it should lead us to be more concerned about others than ourselves.
6. We should "always try to do good to each other."
7. We should "always be joyful."
8. We should "keep on praying." Among other things, we ought to pray that the lost will make themselves ready for the Lord's coming.
9. We should "always be thankful, for this is God's will for you who belong to Christ Jesus." Thankful people are happy people. Rejoicing and thanking go hand in hand. Taken together, they dissolve discouragement and destroy self-pity before it turns into depression.
10. We are not to "stifle the Holy Spirit." Usually this sin is the

result of unconfessed emotional or mental anger. Our minds, instead, should be fixed on things above—things like the coming of Jesus.

11. We should "not scoff at prophecies." Prophecy should be the believer's delight. (See Revelation 19:10.)

12. We should "test everything that is said. Hold on to what is good."

13. We should "keep away from every kind of evil."

Having been a pastor of three churches over forty years, I have observed that solid Bible teaching produces a harmonious church. Further, whenever I preached on the Second Coming, the church grew rapidly. Some who didn't like my expository preaching would get upset with me. From time to time, they tried to stir up trouble in an effort to derail my ministry. Still, my sermons on the Second Coming were always accompanied by an outpouring of the Holy Spirit on our services. Some came to Christ. Many answered the first-time call of God for missionary service. Still others rededicated their lives to Christ.

But those who were excited about the coming of Christ rarely became involved in the conflict. Even during times of tension, new Christians were particularly excited about Jesus' coming. Under the spell of their second-coming hope they witnessed to their friends, bringing them to the church, where many of them were saved. There is something about second-coming truth that reduces our little differences to their proper size.

After giving us twelve very positive things to do, the apostle reminds us that we should also "keep away from every kind of evil." We live in a sin-filled age that daily seems to become worse. We seem to get further and further from the Christian faith on which our nation was founded. Temptations to sin are all around us. When Christians begin doing the evil things of this world, they cease to honor these twelve positive things. The best way to abstain from evil in an increasingly evil age is to remind ourselves that Jesus is coming again.

TODAY'S PRAYER

Dear heavenly Father, thank You for reminding me to keep on looking for the coming of Christ. I get so entangled with the cares of everyday life that I sometimes lose sight of the fact that I am not living for You. Help me today to seek out those who are not ready for Your coming. Then give me the power of Your Spirit to share my faith with those not ready for His return. In Jesus' name I pray, Amen.

16 COMPLETE SANCTIFICATION AT HIS COMING

Now may the God of peace Himself sanctify you completely; and may your whole spirit, soul, and body be preserved blameless at the coming of our Lord Jesus Christ.   1 THESSALONIANS 5:23, NKJV

IN PAST generations, "sanctification" seemed to be a single experience of grace that was supposed to last for a lifetime. Unfortunately, in the crucible of human experience, it rarely worked out that way. All of us have been disillusioned by Christians we respected who committed sins that destroyed their testimonies for life. Some of these were sanctified at some time in their life but lost that sanctification because of some moral indiscretion that destroyed their usefulness to God.

Instead of criticizing such people (usually they have enough pain in their lives without our adding to it), we should learn from their tragic examples. None of us is exempt from any sin. Sanctification for all of us must be a day-by-day or hour-by-hour experience.

Nothing motivates us to this kind of sanctification like anticipating the coming of Christ.

I recently did a radio interview to talk about our Left Behind novels. The interviewer posed a question I am frequently asked: "Dr. LaHaye, how close do you think we are to the coming of the Lord?"

I started out by saying, "No one knows the day or the hour. It could be today, next month, or next year. In fact, it could be in the next century."

Then he asked, "Do you *really* believe He could come today?"

Unquestionably He could! It is important to realize that there are no signs set to precede the Rapture. Prophecy scholars call it "a sign-less event." So, understand this: There is nothing to be fulfilled before Jesus returns for His church. But this is not true for the Glorious Appearing that occurs at the end of the seven-year Tribulation period. There are lots of signs that pertain to this event: the revelation of the "man of sin," the signing of the covenant between the Antichrist and Israel for seven years, the twenty-one judgments of the book of Revelation, to name just a few examples. All these things must occur before our Lord comes in power to set up His kingdom. But absolutely nothing needs to happen before He comes to take His church out of the world.

Since there is to be no forewarning, every believer should live every day of his or her life as if it were the last. Such anticipation encourages us to live the sanctified life.

We saw in our last passage the twelve things Christians must do to live sanctified lives. But remember this: The sanctification of our body, soul, and spirit (our entire person) is a lifetime process. It begins at salvation and is completed only at the Second Coming when Christ will give us our resurrected "incorruptible" bodies (1 Corinthians 15:52, NKJV). When He gives us our new nature, we "are not the same anymore, for the old life is gone. A new life has begun!" (2 Corinthians 5:17). If we feed our mind, soul, and spirit by reading and studying the

Word of God regularly, the Spirit of God will reveal all the changes we need to make in our lives. As He does the work of sanctification in us through His Word, we gradually change and become conformed to His will. We will also be found "blameless" at His return.

TODAY'S PRAYER
Dear heavenly Father, thank You for the ultimate sanctification that is assured by Christ's coming. Thank You that He will transform my body, soul, and spirit and make me fit for heaven. In the meantime, give me a holy desire to live the godly life. If there is any sin in my life I am not aware of, please reveal it to me by Your indwelling Holy Spirit as I read Your Word. Help me to live in continual confession and yield the control of my life to You. In His dear name, Amen.

17 JUDGMENT AT HIS COMING

And in his justice he will punish those who persecute you. And God will provide rest for you who are being persecuted and also for us when the Lord Jesus appears from heaven. He will come with his mighty angels, in flaming fire, bringing judgment on those who don't know God and on those who refuse to obey the Good News of our Lord Jesus. They will be punished with everlasting destruction, forever separated from the Lord and from his glorious power when he comes to receive glory and praise from his holy people. And you will be among those praising him on that day, for you believed what we testified about him.   2 THESSALONIANS 1:6-10

WHEN JESUS comes, He will bring judgment on all those who have persecuted the prophets and saints in every age. Most martyrs died before their persecutors could see their own judgment approaching. Certainly these persecutors died before they could receive the just penalty for their evil acts. But reckoning is on the way. All their inhumanity will be justly dealt with when Jesus comes again.

The believers in Thessalonica were such turned-on Christians that Satan himself sent deceivers and persecutors into their midst in a vain attempt to nullify their effectiveness. Paul commended them for their "patience and faith in all [their] persecutions and tribulations" (2 Thessalonians 1:4, NKJV). He wanted their persecutors to know they would be repaid for the malicious evil they brought upon the church.

Some of these Christian abusers and persecutors appeared to get by with their evil deeds with no consequence. But when Jesus comes in glory and power, not even the best of lawyers will be able to get them acquitted. God's judicial system is just, righteous, and swift. "You will always reap what you sow" (Galatians 6:7).

Paul specifically says that when Jesus comes from heaven "with his mighty angels," no enemy, including Satan himself, will be able to stand against Him. We learn in Revelation 20 that even Satan will be bound and thrown into the bottomless pit. The Antichrist and false prophet will be cast alive into the lake of fire.

At that time, the Lord will avenge the martyrs, visiting on their persecutors "everlasting destruction, forever separated from the Lord." These people who have persecuted God's saints will pay for their persecutions.

History reveals that hundreds of martyrs have been burned at the stake by centuries of evil rulers. Many of these martyrs were killed for the single sin of translating the Bible into readable languages. The names of John Wycliffe, John Huss, Savonarola, William Tyndale, and many others come to mind. In most cases, their persecutors never paid for their evil deeds. John Wycliffe, called the "Morning Star of the Reformation," died unesteemed for his Bible translation. His bones were dug up long after his death and were burned in anger by those who resented his translating the Bible into the language of the people (the first English Bible).

There is, however, one incredible exception. Those who actually crucified or called for the crucifixion of Jesus were forgiven for the most notable of martyrdoms: Jesus of Nazareth. Our Lord forgave His persecutors, calling from His cross, "Father, forgive these people, because they don't know what they are doing" (Luke 23:34). Many Bible teachers believe that among the three thousand Jews who called on the name of the Lord on the Day of Pentecost were many who had participated in the Crucifixion.

It must be clear that if the sin of nailing Jesus to the cross has been forgiven, any other sin may be. This means that those rulers who killed the martyrs—even those who set the torch to their funeral biers—are welcome and encouraged to call upon Christ and be saved. This grace is even extended to today's blasphemers. Yet they must seek Him while they live.

In fact, because of the abundant mercy of God, we may see a grand reunion in heaven. Someday both the martyrs and killers may be reunited in His great mercy.

However, those who go into eternity unrepentant will one day be judged by the righteous Judge of all the universe. They will "be punished with everlasting destruction, forever separated from the Lord."

TODAY'S PRAYER
Dear heavenly Father, I stand in awe before the wonder of Your salvation. Thank You for saving me and forgiving my sins. Because of Your grace and faithfulness, I realize that all my sin is now under the blood. Please help me to leave the punishment of those who have persecuted me to You, praying that they will receive Your grace and forgiveness even as I have. Help me to forgive them for whatever they have done against me. I want to be

pure and free from all grudges at the coming of Jesus. In His
name I pray, Amen.

18 SAINTS GLORIFIED AT HIS COMING

These shall be punished with everlasting destruction from the presence of the Lord and from the
glory of His power, when He comes, in that Day,
to be glorified in his saints and to be admired
among all those who believe, because our testimony among you was believed.

2 THESSALONIANS 1:9-10, NKJV

ACCORDING to a national poll on religion in America, 64 percent
of the population believes that Jesus Christ is physically coming back
to this earth. The same poll indicates that an amazing 44 percent believe in some kind of a rapture of Christians. What makes that so incredible is that only 41 percent of the population claim to be "born
again." If my math is correct, 23 percent of Americans (about two out
of ten people) believe enough about Jesus that they could be converted if someone would just give them the gospel.

In our last study we saw that those who persecute believers will
be judged when He comes. But we did not mention the fact that those
who persecute believers will be left behind if they are not saved.
These then will be forced to go through the Tribulation and receive
the judgment of God for their deeds.

This is only one side of that story, however. The other side is that
Jesus will be glorified in His saints on that day. In the ongoing battle
between Satan and God, Jesus' greatest joy is believers who put their
trust in Him. Perhaps the saddest statement concerning the earthly

Jesus was, "Even in his own land and among his own people, he was not accepted" (John 1:11). But in joyous contrast John also wrote in verse 12, "But to all who believed him and accepted him, he gave the right to become children of God."

When Jesus raptures His church, He will be glorified in His saints because they will be the prize that Christ has snatched from Satan. The billions of individuals throughout the church age who received Christ are the saved. They are Christ's glorification. When they stand before Him at the judgment seat, He will be glorified. In their faithfulness, His victory is complete. Part of His glory will come in rewarding His saints for their good works.

In these verses, Paul uses the Second Coming as an encouragement to the young Thessalonian believers. There is a day coming when not only will their persecutors be judged for their works, but the inequities of those persecutions will also be punished. In the same way, the sacrifices of the saints will be rewarded.

At the risk of being too personal, let me use my own experience as a pastor for over forty years. While I admit some ministers have difficult churches (where even the saints seem to persecute them), my wife and I have been blessed with three loving congregations. Although we were willing to suffer and sacrifice our lives for whatever the Lord desired for us, we were never called on to offer any great sacrifice. Looking back over our lives, we have enjoyed blessing heaped upon blessing.

Our first full-time church in Minneapolis built us a brand-new parsonage the month after we arrived; we then spent six years living in that beautiful new home. Our California church allowed us to purchase our own home. There, once again, we had the experience of living in a brand-new house with a beautiful view. During these years of ministry, the Lord gave us four healthy, wonderful children. We have always worked to share our faith, and God has exceeded our fondest expectations in His blessings on our ministry.

However, not all who love Him have had it as easy. Some of the

PERHAPS

missionaries we saw God call have gone to very difficult places to serve their Lord. They were committed to serving Christ, just as we were, yet they had to struggle and sacrifice in ways we were not called to do. Some we know have lost children and loved ones ten thousand miles away from the land where they were born. Two of our friends still serve the Lord in the oppressive heat and poverty of Africa. One of these noble, unrecognized saints has arthritis. Yet, in spite of her pain, she goes daily into the jungles with her husband, jostling over ruts and unpaved roads to get the message out. They are faithful. They are reaching people who would never have heard about Jesus if they had not gone to Africa.

My question is this: Who will receive the greater reward? Probably not my wife or me. On that day when He is "glorified in His saints" (2 Thessalonians 1:10, NKJV), some of the most unknown saints of history will be the most glorified. We will all praise the name of the Lord as these—the virtually forgotten—will be given the glory they deserve. They never served Him to get the glory. They served Him because they loved Him. Still, when He comes, they will receive their reward, and the Savior they loved all their lives will be glorified!

"Ours is not to reason why; ours is but to do or die" goes the famous line of a wartime battle cry. We, too, are in a battle for the souls of men. We must decide to be either servants of the Savior or pawns of Satan. I am quite confident that you as a reader of this book desire to become a willing servant in the hands of Jesus your Lord.

Never ask why you have been blessed and never persecuted. Accept each day as one from Him and let Him do with your life whatever He chooses. Let Him be Lord. For some of you, He may ask you to quit your job and go to Bible school or seminary in order to be better equipped to serve Him. For some, He may ask you to serve Him by staying where you are and ministering in your office, shop, or classroom. The important thing is that each of us gives our total self to Him to do with us as He sees fit. Then when He comes He will glorify each of us accordingly, and that glorification will last forever!

TODAY'S PRAYER

Dear Lord, there is no question in my mind that Jesus is coming! I want to live every day of my life as though this is that day. You know my greatest desire is to be faithful each day, for I want You to be pleased with me when Jesus comes. Please help me to listen to Your Spirit's direction to do Your will both now and in the future. I am even now waiting on Your long-term instructions. Please help me be alert to the immediate opportunities I have to witness to my associates, neighbors, and loved ones. Thank You for the exciting future You have planned for me. In Jesus' name, Amen.

19 OUR GATHERING TOGETHER TO HIM

And now, brothers and sisters, let us tell you about the coming again of our Lord Jesus Christ and how we will be gathered together to meet him. Please don't be so easily shaken and troubled by those who say that the day of the Lord has already begun. Even if they claim to have had a vision, a revelation, or a letter supposedly from us, don't believe them. 2 THESSALONIANS 2:1-2

THIS SECOND chapter of 2 Thessalonians is one of the most important chapters in prophecy. In terms of its truth and insight, it rivals in importance our Lord's Olivet discourse in Matthew 24. This chapter includes many of the details of end-time events.

Both of Paul's Thessalonian letters were written ten or so years before the Gospels, and they contain those end-of-the-age doctrines that Paul characteristically taught to all his churches. In the first letter, Paul taught the details of the rapture of the church (1 Thessalonians 4:13-18) and challenged Christians to live as though Christ could come in their lifetime. In this second epistle (probably written within six months of the first), Paul was trying to clarify various cloudy details of the doctrine that the Thessalonians did not understand.

The general subject is "the coming again of our Lord Jesus Christ." The particular studies examine the Rapture, the man of sin being revealed, and the Glorious Appearing. In this verse, Paul specifically refers once again to Christ's gathering all people to Himself in the Rapture. He had written about this in his first epistle. The phrase "gathered together to meet him" was used widely in the early church to refer to the Rapture.

One example that has survived the passage of time came from Ephrem of Nisibis (A.D. 306-373), who wrote:

> Why therefore do we not reject every care of earthly actions
> and prepare ourselves for the meeting of the Lord Christ,
> so that he may draw us from the confusion, which over-
> whelms all the world? . . . *All the saints and elect of God are*
> *gathered together before the Tribulation, which is to come, and*
> *are taken to the Lord,* in order that they may not see at any
> time the confusion which overwhelms the world because
> of our sins.

It is interesting to note that as early as the fourth century this Bible scholar and prolific writer referred to the Rapture as "all the saints . . . gathered together before the Tribulation." This predates John Darby's first modern mention of the doctrine in 1828. In fact, our gathering together to Him was probably a commonly used term to describe the Rapture from the days Paul first mentioned it here in this text.

Frankly, I can't think of a more exciting truth owned by Christians in any age than the fact that His church will be "gathered together to meet him."

This challenge is exactly what that Syrian church father Ephrem of Nisibis gave to fourth-century Christians when he appealed to them to "reject every care of earthly actions and prepare [themselves] for the meeting of the Lord Christ." Now sixteen centuries later, we are still using this same promise of His coming to challenge His church to live in purity.

A pastor friend of mine told me of a ninety-one-year-old woman in his congregation to whom he supplies free office space. Every day she is found there from 8:00 A.M. until 5:00 P.M. She still teaches a Bible class, challenging people to come to Christ and live for Him. She has done this for over seventy years! That kind of consistent dedication is not uncommon for those who really believe Jesus could come at any time.

How does the fact that we "will be gathered together to meet him" affect the way you spend your life? Someone has said, "You can spend your life any way you like, but you can only spend it once!" I trust you are spending every moment of it in the light of His coming.

Today's Prayer

Dear heavenly Father, thank You for challenging us to live as though Jesus could come at any time. I don't want to lose sight of that fact in the press of all the day-to-day decisions I have to make. Help me to spend each moment as though this could be the day. I once again give myself to You. In Jesus' name I pray, Amen.

PERHAPS

20 DON'T GET SHAKEN UP ABOUT THE SECOND COMING

> And now, brothers and sisters, let us tell you about
> the coming again of our Lord Jesus Christ and
> how we will be gathered together to meet him.
> Please don't be so easily shaken and troubled by
> those who say that the day of the Lord has already
> begun. Even if they claim to have had a vision, a
> revelation, or a letter supposedly from us, don't
> believe them. Don't be fooled by what they say.
> For that day will not come until there is a great
> rebellion against God and the man of lawlessness
> is revealed—the one who brings destruction.
>
> 2 THESSALONIANS 2:1-3

YEARS AGO, a North Carolina fisherman found a fairly large rock in a stream where he was fishing and took it to his cabin home. Not having a mantel over his fireplace on which to place it, he used it as a doorstop. Years later, a geologist was hiking through that area and the man invited him in for coffee. This gesture turned out to be extremely profitable. As his guest began examining the rock, he found it was solid gold! In fact, it turned out to be the largest hunk of gold ever found east of Colorado.

To many Christians, the Second Coming is like that lump of gold. It is a valuable doctrine, mentioned in all the creeds of Christendom. It is in the doctrinal statements of most churches. But in too many of these churches it has become only a source of controversy among its members. Unfortunately, it has little place in most people's lives on a practical level. It is gold unrecognized and unclaimed.

The return of Christ is the second-most frequently mentioned doctrine in the Bible. Sadly, it does not hold a place of great importance in the lives of so many believers. Living each day with the thought of our Lord's soon return should have a profound effect on everyone's spiritual life. It should give each person a motivation to witness.

One of the things that causes many churches to ignore this cardinal doctrine is that it is a fearful subject. Yet Christ has encouraged us not to fear it but to anticipate it. Jesus Himself said of His coming, "Don't be troubled" (John 14:1). In His masterful Olivet discourse He warned His followers thirteen times to beware of false prophets, deceivers, false christs. Jesus knew that Satan would do everything he could to cause believers to disregard sound teaching. Jesus also knew that Satan's deceiving attacks would intensify at the end of the age.

The little church in Thessalonica had already felt the effect of Satan undermining the doctrine of the Rapture. These false teachers were troubling their confidence in the Rapture by "vision, a revelation, or a letter supposedly from us" (Paul was evidently referring to a false letter probably written in his name). How better can Satan confuse and discourage congregations than to rob them of the contagious nature of their faith?

It is the same today. No one who takes the Bible literally questions the fact of Jesus' second coming. It is the timing of the event that causes disagreements among Christians. What is the big question? When will Jesus come—before, in the middle of, or at the end of the Tribulation? Personally, my study of end-times passages convinces me that our Lord will rapture His church before the Tribulation in which He will try the whole earth.

I am deeply concerned that Christians today should not be lulled into thinking they have lots of time to prepare for our Lord's coming. I would rather them live every day as though this could be the day.

Some of my friends who believe the Rapture will occur in the middle of or after the Tribulation like to tell me I should be warning Christians to get ready to go through the worst time the world has ever seen or ever will see: the great Tribulation. My response is always, "Why should I? God didn't!" There is not one verse in the New Testament spoken by either Jesus, Paul, or Peter that tells us that Christians should prepare to endure the Tribulation. On the other hand, there are at least four passages that tell us we are to be "saved from the wrath to come."

Why is that? Simply put, we will not be here when the earth experiences that tribulation. So don't be troubled over the day of Christ. It has not come, nor will it come until Jesus shouts from heaven, calling His church home. When He does, we who believe will be instantly out of here. We will leave the unbelieving world to go through the Tribulation (Revelation 6–19). Instead of being "shaken" or "troubled" over this terrible time of trial, we should rejoice that our name is written in heaven.

A missionary home on furlough got a businessman in our church to manufacture thousands of pocket-sized crystal radio sets for him to take back into the jungles. The unique feature of these radios was that they could only receive one station signal—a Christian station. In fact, each radio had only one knob that both turned it on and controlled the volume. The station could not be changed.

That is similar to what happens when we are born again through the finished work of the Cross. The Holy Spirit comes into our lives and "tunes" us to the one wavelength of heaven. Regardless of whatever church we attend, when the Savior shouts from heaven, all of those on this one wavelength will respond to His call and be snatched up to be with Him in His Father's house.

TODAY'S PRAYER
Dear heavenly Father, thank You for sending Jesus Your Son into this world to die for my sins and the sins of the whole world. Thank You for His wonderful promise to take us up to Your house to be with Him. No one deserves such a treasure, but thank You for it. Help me this day to share Your wonderful message with those who are not yet prepared for His coming. In Jesus' name, Amen.

21 FIRST CHRIST—THEN ANTICHRIST

Now, brethren, concerning the coming of our Lord Jesus Christ and our gathering together to Him, we ask you, not to be soon shaken in mind or troubled, either by spirit or by word or by letter, as if from us, as though the day of Christ had come. Let no one deceive you by any means; for that Day will not come unless the falling away comes first, and the man of sin is revealed, the son of perdition, who opposes and exalts himself above all that is called God or that is worshiped, so that he sits as God in the temple of God, showing himself that he is God. Do you not remember that when I was still with you I told you these things? And now you know what is restraining, that he may be revealed in his own time. For the mystery of lawlessness is already at work; only He who now restrains will do so until He is taken out of the way. And then the lawless one will be revealed.

2 THESSALONIANS 2:1-8, NKJV

RECENTLY a California Christian college professor wrote a book suggesting that Christians should be looking more for the coming of the Antichrist than the coming of Christ. Such a view not only undermines a belief in the pre-Trib Rapture, it also encourages God's people to look for the wrong thing.

Paul makes it clear in this great text on the Second Coming that we are not to let anyone deceive us. The Glorious Appearing (or "the day of Christ," verse 2) will not come until two things have happened. First there must come the "falling away" or "the departing." Second, the man of sin must be revealed. The correct pecking order of last things is this. First, our gathering together unto Him (or "the departing," which we call the Rapture), second, the revelation of the man of sin (the Antichrist), and third, the Glorious Appearing.

Let us examine these three events in their proper order beginning with "the Day of the Lord." The King James Version of the Bible in some ways has done a great disservice to Bible students in the last two centuries. It translates the Greek term "Day of the Lord" as the "Day of Christ"! The "Day of the Lord" in Scripture designates that day when God intervenes in the affairs of men with judgment. In some cases, the term refers to the day when God begins the Tribulation, the prophetic time of wrath.

The Day of judgment will not come until the *apostesia* (in the Greek) has come. This apostasy is the second event in our triad of final things. All English translations of the Bible from Wycliffe to the Geneva Bible translate that word *apostesia* as "departing." The word occurs only twice in this verb form in the New Testament: here and in Acts 21:21, where the Pharisees accuse Paul of "departing" from the faith. The word here should be legitimately translated as the "departing" or the Rapture. So the "Day of the Lord" or the Tribulation period will not come until after the Rapture occurs. No one seems to know why the King James translators changed the meaning to "falling away" and why all subsequent translators have followed in kind. Admittedly, when the Tribulation begins there will be a "falling away" from faith by those left behind in the Rapture. After the Rapture, there will be an apostasy from the faith for there will be none on Earth who believe. Into this faithless, post-Rapture world will come the 144,000 witnesses of Revelation 7:1-15 to do their incredible work of evangelism.

No one knows how much time will elapse between the Rapture and the beginning of the Tribulation. It could be a day, a week, or several years. The first event of the Tribulation will be the signing of the covenant between Israel and the Antichrist that will last for seven years (Daniel 9:27). In our Left Behind series, Jerry and I chose to allow two weeks to elapse between the Rapture and the day that the Antichrist actually begins his takeover. Of course, our novel only offers an arbitrary length of time. The actual amount of time is known only to God.

The third step in our order of final things is the appearance of the Antichrist. This is the so-called "man of sin, the son of perdition." He is not some obscure character in prophecy. He is mentioned by Daniel, Paul, and John of the Apocalypse. He will be the most evil dictator who ever lived. In verse 4, it says he will exalt "himself above all that is called God or that is worshiped." He will even exalt himself as a god in the temple of God to be worshiped as God. He will be the most blasphemous person in the history of the world.

Why concern ourselves with this study of last things? Why have we written these books on Jesus' coming?

Recently we received a grateful letter from one of our readers telling us why we have devoted our lives to this issue. This reader confessed, after reading our novels, "My life has been transformed! I want to witness to everyone I meet so none will be left behind." Frankly, that is why we have given ourselves to study and preach the Rapture. That is why we have written these books! We don't want anyone to be left behind.

Today's Prayer

Dear Lord, thank You so much for so clearly describing the coming of Jesus prior to the Tribulation. I pray for all those who read the Left Behind series that Your Holy Spirit will speak to them so they will clearly understand and be ready for the Savior when He comes. And thank You, Lord, for those who gave me the good news of the gospel. In Jesus' name, Amen.

22 WHEN THE RESTRAINER IS GONE

And you know what is holding him back, for he can
be revealed only when his time comes. For this
lawlessness is already at work secretly, and it will
remain secret until the one who is holding it back
steps out of the way. Then the man of lawlessness
will be revealed.   2 Thessalonians 2:6-8

FORMER Vice President Dan Quayle is a bold, confessing Christian.
He incurred the wrath of the media during the 1992 elections by
pointing out that we are in a war for the soul of America. He boldly
spoke the truth. We are on the verge of losing that cultural battle.
They scathed him for criticizing Murphy Brown, a fictional TV character, for choosing to have a baby out of wedlock as a part of the popular sitcom. In real life, Candace Bergen, Murphy Brown's portrayer,
was a happily married mother. But on the show she was committing
immoral acts, implying that such immorality was good for the soul of
the nation.

The deterioration occurring in our culture is moving at high ve-
locity as such antimoral values have become our way of life. Can you
imagine what the culture will be like when the church is raptured and
its restraining influence is taken from an already corrupt culture?
Paul had this concept of moral force in mind when he taught that
"the one who is holding it back [the Holy Spirit in the church] steps
out of the way" (verse 7).

One of the tasks of the church today is to serve as a restraining influence against unrighteousness. Believe it or not, it's working.
Churches, schools, colleges, camps, and scores of other ministries
serve as restraining influences on immorality. Every evangelistic
Bible-teaching church—and there are multiplied thousands—in this
country is seeing people delivered from all kinds of addictions: drugs,

alcoholism, sex, violence. Further, we are seeing millions of lives transformed by the gospel. All of this is an evidence of the restraining influence of the Holy Spirit.

But after the Rapture, this restraining influence will be gone. To be sure, the Holy Spirit will still be in the world during the Tribulation. Joel 2:28-32 makes it clear He will not only be here but He will convict sinners of unrighteousness. His presence will empower the 144,000 Jewish witnesses to convert "a vast crowd, too great to count" (Revelation 7:9). But His all-pervasive force will not be the same as it is today. The huge body of believers will not be there to hold back the forces of evil. The church, the "sin restrainer," will simply have vanished.

The widespread crime that will follow the Tribulation is clearly defined in Revelation 9:20-21. After the seal and trumpet judgments, Scripture tells us "the people . . . still refused to turn from their evil deeds. They continued to worship demons and idols made of gold, silver, bronze, stone, and wood. . . . And they did not repent of their murders or their witchcraft or their immorality or their thefts." The abundance of such crimes in today's culture must already presage this time of future depravity when the church is gone.

In the meantime, we are told to "occupy" till Jesus comes (Luke 19:13, KJV). We are to let the Holy Spirit use our lives, our talents, our time, our families, and our resources to restrain the ever-increasing flow of evil.

Long ago, Dr. Francis Schaeffer, the philosopher prophet of the twentieth century, warned us that America had become a part of "the post-Christian culture." Today we have almost been silenced by anti-Christian forces claiming that *we* are trying to impose moral values on this rampant decadence. The truth is that *they* have tried to impose their immoral values on us. They are generally doing a better job of corrupting society than we are of cleansing it. May God help us to become the restraining influence we should be on a corrupt world.

Dear Lord, like Daniel of old, I come humbly to You to confess my sins and to deplore the sins of our whole nation. We have turned our back on You, Your moral standards, and the traditions of our fathers. Please awaken our leaders to the necessity of reestablishing God's righteous standard for our country. Help me to do all I can as a citizen to elect to leadership men and women deeply committed to Your moral values. In Your Son's name, Amen.

23 WHEN ANTICHRIST GETS HIS

Then the man of lawlessness will be revealed, whom the Lord Jesus will consume with the breath of his mouth and destroy by the splendor of his coming. This evil man will come to do the work of Satan with counterfeit power and signs and miracles.   2 THESSALONIANS 2:8-9

A FELLOW passenger on a recent flight startled me by asking, "Do you think the Antichrist is alive and in the world today?" No one could answer the young man's question for sure. If the time of our Lord's return is near, as many prophecy scholars think, he well could be. I do know when the Antichrist, or the "man of lawlessness," is coming. He is called by many names in Scripture: the Beast, the king of fierce countenance, the little horn, the Antichrist, and as in this text, the man of lawlessness. Whoever he is, he will eventually be seen as the embodiment of evil. But not at first!

When my sixteen-year-old grandson was halfway through *Left Behind,* he said, "I sure hope Nicolae Carpathia [the name we gave the Antichrist in our series] is not the Antichrist because I kind of like him." But by the time he got to *Tribulation Force*, he had changed his mind. Such is the way this evil man will enter history (Revelation 6:1-2). He is the rider on the first of the four horses of the Apocalypse. With a congenial diplomacy he will conquer the world. But when war breaks out and kills 25 percent of the population, people will begin to see him for what he is.

As a politician, this man will make many promises "with swelling words" (Jude 1:16, NKJV). He will, with great approval, convince a war-weary world to let him usher in world "peace." Preaching peace, he will become a global dictator. We have gotten used to politicians promising us anything to get elected and later forsaking all their promises. But as the Antichrist rules during the seven-year Tribulation period, he will not only forsake his political promises, he will become increasingly evil. Then in the middle of the seven years, he will be killed and miraculously resurrected as Satan takes over his body. He will then desecrate the temple of God, persecute the Jews, and kill the two witnesses of Revelation along with millions of believers.

Finally, he will be destroyed by Christ as He comes in His Glorious Appearing described in Revelation 19. But he will not be destroyed until he has done what Satan does best: brought about a great deception on the people of God. During the seven-year Tribulation period, everyone living on this earth will have to make a decision to either give himself to Christ or to the Antichrist. The consequences of that decision will, of course, be eternal. Finally, Revelation 19:20 reveals that when Jesus comes to set up His kingdom at the end of the Tribulation, He will cast the Antichrist and his false prophet into the "lake of fire that burns with sulfur."

The last days prior to and during the Tribulation period will be days of incredible deception. One of the many reasons so many think we are approaching the end times is that we have seen such an increase in false teachers and Christ impersonators. But the current mania will get even worse when the Antichrist arrives.

Consequently, God's people today should stay informed. Jerry and I have committed ourselves to this matter. We want to communicate through every possible means the thrilling plans God has for the future of mankind. We also want to warn people everywhere to avoid all deceptive teachings about God, salvation, and the future of the human race.

We hope this devotional study will whet your own appetite to read the book of Revelation and to test every future teaching you encounter against the truth of God's Word. Many say they cannot understand the book of Revelation. But you can. Maybe not all the intricate details, but by reading it carefully you will be amazed at how much can be learned.

Recently we received a letter from a reader of our fiction series who said, "Although I had read the rest of the Bible, I had never read the book of Revelation until I finished *Left Behind.* Since then, I have read it four times! And I am happy to say it now makes sense to me." It will to you also. In fact, it will bless you, for it is the only book in the Bible that promises a blessing to those who read it (Revelation 1:3). Frankly, although I have written a best-selling commentary called *Revelation Unveiled,* I do not claim to understand everything in the book. But I have been much enriched by what I do understand.

The story is told of a humble custodian who was reading the book of Revelation while waiting for some students to finish a basketball game. The custodian was employed by a liberal seminary that did not believe in the true teachings of Revelation. One of the seminarians saw him reading his Bible and asked what he was reading. The old man replied, "The book of Revelation." Thinking that no one could really understand it, the seminarian asked, "Do you understand what you are reading?"

The janitor replied with a smile, "I sure do."

"What does it say?" the seminarian asked.

"Jesus wins!" replied the janitor.

If you learn nothing else from reading Revelation other than the fact that Jesus wins, it is worth reading!

TODAY'S PRAYER

Dear heavenly Father, thank You for Your prophetic word that so predicts the future. This world can become a pretty dismal place sometimes, with its sin, chaos, and tragedy. Teach me to look forward to the day when Jesus will come and set all things right. Help me to anticipate that world where tears and sorrow will be replaced by peace and blessing. Use my life to share the good news of the final triumph of Christ. In Jesus' name, Amen.

24 WHEN GOD SENDS DECEPTION

The coming of the lawless one is according to the working of Satan, with all power, signs, and lying wonders, and with all unrighteous deception among those who perish, because they did not receive the love of the truth, that they might be saved. And for this reason God will send them strong delusion, that they should believe the lie, that they all may be condemned who did not believe the truth but had pleasure in unrighteousness. 2 THESSALONIANS 2:9-12, NKJV

OUR GOD is in the business of truth. Deception can never be any part of that business. Yet this passage tells of a time when God will send "strong delusion, that they should believe the lie. . . ." The time of that delusion will come during the Antichrist's reign, particularly during the latter half of the Tribulation.

All through the Bible God reveals His truth. In fact, Paul said,

"Long ago God spoke many times and in many ways to our ancestors through the prophets. But now in these final days, he has spoken to us through his Son" (Hebrews 1:1-2). Peter concurs when he said, "You must understand that no prophecy in Scripture ever came from the prophets themselves or because they wanted to prophesy. It was the Holy Spirit who moved the prophets to speak from God" (2 Peter 1:20-21).

And Jesus said of Himself, "I am the way, *the truth,* and the life. No one can come to the Father except through me" (John 14:6, italics mine).

Obviously, God was revealing truth all through the 1,600 years that He inspired more than forty authors to write the Bible. That revelation, consisting of sixty-six books, is without doubt the most authentic ancient book ever written. So why, when God characteristically reveals truth, would He give deception to mankind?

The time element of this deception is not hard to discern; it is after the man of sin has been revealed and just before the Lord Jesus returns to this earth to consume the Antichrist with His power. Whenever you consider this short seven-year period of the wrath of God on the earth, remember its purpose. It is designed by God with the precise purpose of forcing the world to make a decision to accept or reject Christ just prior to the Millennium.

God is "not willing that any should perish but that all should come to repentance" (2 Peter 3:9, NKJV). Still, He leaves it up to each individual to make that decision for himself or herself. Whichever he or she decides, of course, does not take God by surprise. He knew before the foundation of the world when each person would be born and then born again. During the turmoil of the Tribulation period, two kinds of decisions will be made. First, a "vast crowd, too great to count" (Revelation 7:9), will believe the truth of God as preached by the 144,000 witnesses and the two special witnesses who will have miraculous powers. Obviously, God will go to great lengths during that period to get the truth to all of those willing to receive it.

As it is in our day, the majority who live through the Tribulation will reject that truth because they find pleasure in unrighteousness (2 Thessalonians 2:12). It is for the same reason that many people reject the truth of the gospel today. Loving their indulgence in some particular sin, they are unwilling to give up that pleasure and receive Jesus. Thus, their indulgences damn their soul for eternity. These will accept the lies of Antichrist who will take the mark on the back of the right hand and place it on their forehead. Most of these will refuse to hear the preaching of the 144,000 servants of God and the two supernatural witnesses of the Tribulation (Revelation 7 and 11). They will choose Antichrist over Christ. They will not reverse that decision, once made. God will then send them a delusion to continue believing Satan's lies.

How wonderful that such is not the case today. I recently gave an invitation to a large audience at the end of a prophecy conference. Many received the Lord. But the best thing is that those who did not receive Him can still change their minds. This is why the Bible calls every day "the day of salvation" (2 Corinthians 6:2)—or, as we might phrase it, a "day of decision."

Today's Prayer

Dear heavenly Father, I marvel at Your patience with mankind. You have sent the prophets, the apostles, and even Your Son to warn us to "flee the wrath to come." I know that during the Tribulation You will raise up thousands of individuals to share the gospel with humanity. I pray for those of our own day who have not yet received Your Son as their Savior. Please send Your Holy Spirit to convict these of sin and use me to share Your good news that today is the day of salvation. In Jesus' name, Amen.

25 THE STONES THAT CRY OUT FOR BELIEF

> As Jesus was leaving the Temple grounds, his
> disciples pointed out to him the various Temple
> buildings. But he told them, "Do you see all these
> buildings? I assure you, they will be so completely
> demolished that not one stone will be left on top
> of another!"   MATTHEW 24:1-2

HAVING EXAMINED the apostle's view on the Rapture, let us consider what Jesus had to say about it. Shortly before His death, our Lord delivered His Olivet discourse just across the Brook Kidron from the city of Jerusalem.

This Olivet discourse (recorded in Matthew 24–25, Mark 13, and Luke 21) is considered the most important prophecy in the Bible for three reasons: First, it was given by our Lord who, having known the end from the beginning, must have been able to present an authoritative outline of God's plan for the future.

Second, this discourse is the most detailed description of end-time events, and the first to be given to His church. It wonderfully describes His return in power and glory at the end of the Tribulation period.

Third, it answers the question that most students of the Second Coming want answered: "What will be the sign of Your coming, and of the end of the age?" (Matthew 24:3, NKJV).

Personally, I believe the Olivet discourse should be used as a basic outline from which all other prophecies are studied. When other passages find their place in relation to this teaching of our Lord, a sense of rightness and wholeness is achieved. The books of Daniel and Revelation, for instance, fit nicely into the Savior's outline of future events.

First, however, we should examine the mini-prophecy with which Jesus begins this end-time prophecy. During the last week of Jesus' earthly life, He and His entourage came out of the temple. His disciples tried to impress Him with the grandeur of Herod's temple. Herod had spent several years and many tax dollars rebuilding that temple. It had been erected by the exiles after their return from Babylon 450 years earlier.

There is something humorous in this event. Imagine trying to impress the Creator of the universe with a building made by men! Still, to the disciples it was probably the most magnificent building they had ever seen. Jesus asked them, "Do you see all these buildings? I assure you, they will be so completely demolished that not one stone will be left on top of another!"

Just thirty-seven years later, it all happened as Jesus said. The armies of the Roman general Titus surrounded the city, laid siege to it, and destroyed it. History says he burned it to the ground. One account of the event says that General Titus gave the order not to destroy the temple building. He was not a Christian, but his beliefs made him respectful of religious buildings.

In those days Roman soldiers were not paid regular wages for serving their emperor. Instead, they pillaged and plundered their conquered enemies for whatever was of intrinsic worth or value. Obviously, one of the best things to plunder was gold, for it could be easily transported and could be readily exchanged for other goods.

As the fires raged out of control throughout Jerusalem, the intense heat rose to the temple dome and darkened its elaborate, gold-carved architecture. The molten gold ran down into the cracks and crevices of the stones that made up the temple. Once destroyed, the only remains of real value was the gold in the cracks. To get it, the Roman infantry had to take the temple apart stone by stone. When they had finished doing that, these pagan soldiers had unwittingly fulfilled the prophecy of Jesus.

All of us have seen the fulfillment of this prophecy on the evening news from time to time. Whenever the news cameras show us pictures of the Wailing Wall in Jerusalem, let us note particularly the large block stones near the foundation. Those are some of the remaining stones of the temple of Jesus' day. Because of their enormous weight, they had to be carried stone by stone from the site of the temple to their current place. This removal of these stones also fulfilled the prophecy of Jesus. Let this final account of Jesus' prophecy encourage our faith. Let the accuracy of this account assure us of the accuracy yet to be fulfilled in the events He has planned for our future.

TODAY'S PRAYER

Dear Lord, we are humbled at the way You reach out to us and encourage our faith. There are times in our lives when we become weak in the faith. Your second coming has already taken a long, long time. But Your Word and its fulfillment gives us the faith to keep on trusting and serving You. Help us to do this right up to the time when the Savior calls us to Himself. Today I yield my life and talents to You. Please lead me to share my faith with some lost soul. In Jesus' name, Amen.

26 WHAT SHALL BE THE SIGN OF YOUR COMING?

Later, Jesus sat on the slopes of the Mount of Olives. His disciples came to him privately and asked, "When will all this take place? And will there be any sign ahead of time to signal your return and the end of the world?" Jesus told them, "Don't let anyone mislead you. For many will come in my name, saying, 'I am the Messiah.' They will lead many astray."   MATTHEW 24:3-5

AFTER JESUS' opening remarks about the dissolution of the temple, the disciples asked the $64,000 question: "When will all this take place? And will there be any sign ahead of time to signal your return and the end of the world?"

At every prophecy conference I have spoken at in the last twenty years, the most popular question is always: "When will Christ return and what signs shall precede the Second Coming?" I always emphasize that "no one knows the day or the hour" (Matthew 24:36), and there are no signs that will precede the Rapture. The only sign that is certain for those who pretend to know the hour of our Lord's return is the clear sign that such a one is a false teacher!

Our Lord had His own focus on false teachers. Jesus, in answering the disciples' questions, did not rebuke them for asking about signs. Some Bible teachers act as if it is forbidden to examine the "signs of the times" to see how close we are to the return of Christ. In reality, it is a natural question to anyone who loves Him and longs for the day He returns.

However, it is important at the outset to warn all Christians, young and old, to be on the watch for the devilish deception of false teachers. Our Lord warns His disciples thirteen times in these two chapters not to "let anyone mislead you. For many will come in my name, saying, 'I am the Messiah.' They will lead many astray" (Matthew 24:4-5). "False messiahs and false prophets will rise up and perform great miraculous signs and wonders so as to deceive, if possible, even God's chosen ones" (Matthew 24:24).

We do not want to scare our readers, but we all need to be aware that in the last days there will be an increase of false teachers who will be incredibly believable. Some will even use supernatural signs and wonders to deceive the best of Christians. These deceivers will accompany their false doctrines with miracles and thus deceive millions. Remember this: Satan has the power to perform miracles. He can reverse those sicknesses he has brought on people. In the Tribulation, he will so intensify his deceptive practices that he will appear to duplicate the miracles of Jesus.

Satan has always been a liar and a deceiver. But in the last days his deceptions will increase. In our day there has been an incredible increase of false teachers both inside and outside the church. Although the tactics and antics of these false teachers are not new, their activities in occultism, demonism, Satan worship, and horoscopes are certainly becoming more popular.

In such a time, Christians need to continue to study God's Word in the fellowship of a good Bible-teaching church. This is the time for the saints of God to be active in a Bible-study group and faithful in their devotional lives. The apostle John was very careful to challenge Christians to "test the spirits" by the Word of God (1 John 4:1, NKJV). A teacher who presents any doctrine that cannot be supported by the Scriptures is a false teacher.

If you are a young Christian, we would urge you to pray for guidance whenever you hear of some new teaching or when your heart is troubled by some doubtful expositor. Remember, the Holy Spirit is within you and will give you a peaceful spirit concerning those who are properly teaching the Word of God. In a similar way, He will give you a troubled spirit when confronted by a false teacher.

Several years ago while pastoring in San Diego, I wrote a twenty-four-page tract entitled *Jesus—Who Is He?* It became the forerunner to my 1998 book of the same name. A young contractor and his wife who were being influenced by the Jehovah's Witnesses were troubled in spirit. They prayed one morning at the breakfast table for guidance. Later that day as this contractor was getting out of his pickup truck during a rainstorm, he looked down to see a little blue booklet floating in the gutter. He fished it out of the water, took it home, and his wife dried it out in the oven. Later they read it together and prayed to receive Christ as their Lord and Savior. Needless to say, they discontinued their weekly meetings with false teachers and became active in a Bible-teaching church.

Our heavenly Father loves to guide His children as they seek the truth. Therefore never hesitate to call on Him for advice. Remember the counsel of Scripture: "Seek his will in all you do, and he will direct your path" (Proverbs 3:5).

TODAY'S PRAYER

Thank You, heavenly Father, for giving us Your wonderful Word. Without it we would be easily led astray. Help me to be sensitive to Your Spirit and test those who present any "new truth or doctrine." And help me to care about the welfare of my friends lest they be swept into some false teaching. In Jesus' name I pray, Amen.

27

WHAT THE SIGNS ARE NOT!

Jesus told them, "Don't let anyone mislead you. For many will come in my name, saying, 'I am the Messiah.' They will lead many astray. And wars will break out near and far, but don't panic. Yes, these things must come, but the end won't follow immediately. The nations and kingdoms will proclaim war against each other, and there will be famines and earthquakes in many parts of the world."   MATTHEW 24:4-7

DECEIVERS and false prophets are now quite customary on the religious scene. They are often most persuasive in their attempt to mislead "even God's chosen ones" (Matthew 24:24). There is nothing new in this. The church has always had to contend with false teachers. But remember there are thirteen separate references to these teachers in Jesus' Olivet discourse.

Even though Jesus warned us that such would come, these false teachers are not a part of the sign the disciples requested. Nor was the next subject Jesus introduced: war. "And wars will break out near and far, but don't panic. Yes, these things must come, but the end won't follow immediately."

Obviously, false teachers and wars are not *the* sign that the end is near. False teachers most often fail to realize this. During the last half-century, many books have been written and even more pastors have preached their dire warnings that false teachers are here along with their unceasing falsehoods. These, they say, are a clear sign the end is approaching. But here Jesus makes it clear these things are *not* the sign! They may be a sign the end is approaching but they are not *the* final sign.

Jesus also said when you see these false teachers and hear of these wars, "don't panic." In John 14:1-2, He even offers the antidote to troubled hearts when He says, "Don't be troubled. You trust God, now trust in me. There are many rooms in my Father's home, and I am going to prepare a place for you. If this were not so, I would tell you plainly." Then, as we saw in an earlier study, He promises to come again and take us to His Father's house.

How are we to avoid having troubled hearts? We are to believe in God and anticipate the coming of Christ. No matter how many "wars and rumors of wars" we see on the world's scene (Matthew 24:6, NKJV), we must not let our hearts be troubled. We should instead look beyond the present crises to that wonderful day when Jesus raptures His church to be forevermore with Him.

When I was sixteen years old I had an early morning newspaper route. One Saturday an elderly customer with a strong British accent became irate toward me and said, "Young man, all you ever bring me in your paper is bad news—war, war, war. If you can't stop this gloomy news, I'm going to stop taking your paper!" Obviously she had a troubled heart; her native land, England, was even then being bombed by the Germans. She was naturally troubled at the devastation being heaped on her homeland.

Two years later I was a GI in the U.S. Air Force. After my basic training I was shipped to Europe. Naturally my widowed mother was troubled. But she was a dedicated Christian and a woman of the Word. So she committed me to God and allowed her firstborn to serve his country. She was willing for me to be in harm's way, and through faith she was able to overcome a troubled heart.

And so will faith serve you! God is never far from any of us. He wants to comfort us in times of trial and difficulty. You may not be faced with war or false teachers at the moment. But you may be facing your own dire circumstances in life. Trust in God, look to Him, read His Word, and anticipate Jesus. This is the perfect antidote for a troubled heart.

TODAY'S PRAYER

Dear heavenly Father, forgive me for the times that I have let the cares of my life "trouble" my heart. I know You have been there for me all the time, and I sin when I fail to trust You. Please increase my faith, then help me to allow my faith to quiet my troubled heart. In Jesus' name I pray, Amen.

28 WHAT THE SIGNS ARE

The nations and kingdoms will proclaim war against each other, and there will be famines and earthquakes in many parts of the world. But all this will be only the beginning of the horrors to come. MATTHEW 24:7-8

IN THE previous chapter covering Matthew 24:4-7, we saw that false teachers and wars are not the signs of the times. One scholar has counted 135 false christs during the first nineteen centuries of church history. If he were living today, he would have to raise that number to 150 or more.

I majored in history in college and became aware that the study of history is the study of wars. Occasionally we sped through a decade or two of history, enjoying a brief time of peace. But such respite is infrequent. One historian noted that there have been fifteen thousand wars in the history of mankind and that the most severe and barbaric of those were in the twentieth century. Yet all these wars tell us that the God of end-time prophecy is not directly involved in the decisions that nations make. Usually it is only the leaders of nations who make those decisions.

The Lord Jesus interjected God's view of "wars and rumors of wars" (Matthew 24:6, NKJV) into his answer to the disciples' question. Jesus pointed out that there would be a special world war that would be a clear sign of the end of the age. Jesus actually used this expression: "nation will rise against nation, and kingdom against kingdom" (Matthew 24:7, NKJV). This is an old Hebrew idiom that refers to a war between two nations in league with many surrounding nations.

The first worldwide conflict occurred between 1914 and 1918. Historians later called it World War I. It was the first such war in human history to ever be given this title. The war was sparked by a single atrocity: a Serbian zealot assassinated the Archduke of Austria. The Austrians then declared war on Serbia. Nation by nation, the world took sides on the issue. Eventually all but seven nations in the entire world officially sent troops to do battle on one side of the war or the other.

This world conflict stands out in history because more people died in that war than in any previous war. Estimates on this global slaughter say as many as fifteen million people died. Besides soldiers, millions of civilians were killed, crippled, and displaced.

But World War I alone does not constitute *the* sign Jesus gave. There are other parts of that sign that must be considered alongside the sign of war. Jesus indicated that following that war would be "famines and earthquakes in many parts of the world." Since there have always been famines and earthquakes, He must have meant unprecedented famines, etc. And there were! Following World War I came worldwide hunger. Between 1914 and 1918, untilled croplands from Crimea to Africa resulted in unprecedented famines. The flu epidemic that accompanied that famine took nineteen million lives in Europe and America. More perished in that epidemic than were lost on the battlefield. Not long after the war, the first multiple earthquakes in human history were recorded.

These unprecedented events (a world war, famines, pestilences, and simultaneous earthquakes) are four of the prophesied conditions indicating what *could* be the fulfillment of Jesus' sign of the end of the age.

Note carefully that Jesus did not say those conditions would usher in His second coming. What He did say is they would constitute the "beginning of the horrors to come" (literally, "travail"). The "beginning of horrors" is a common Hebrew idiom comparing the traumatic end-of-the-age events to the birth pains of a pregnant woman about to deliver her child.

Concerning birth pains, any mother will testify that in each case it has been the same. The first birth pain does not mean the baby is going to be born. But it does mean there will be other birth pains. As those pains get closer together they become more intense—just before the baby is born.

It is quite probable that Jesus intended that a special war would follow these famines, pestilences, and earthquakes and these would indicate other birth pains or signs were on the way. Most prophecy scholars see many other such signs. Israel's return to their homeland, Russia becoming a world player, people "[running] to and fro, and knowledge [being] increased" (Daniel 12:4, KJV)—all these signs are getting more intense and coming much closer together.

No man knows the day or the hour, but it is a wise Christian who studies these signs and in light of them considers how he or she will live. His coming could be a day or a week or a month away. It could be decades. But if ever a generation had reason to believe Christ might come in its lifetime, it must surely be ours. In light of all those things let us ready ourselves for the Rapture.

TODAY'S PRAYER

Dear heavenly Father, if scholars have "rightly divided" all prophecy, it is probable that Jesus' coming will be soon, perhaps even today. Help me to so live that when I see You face-to-face You will be pleased with my life. If there is some sin I have never fully surrendered to You, may Your Holy Spirit make me conscious of it. Help me to live every day with eternity's values in view. In Jesus' name I pray, Amen.

29 THE COMING TRIBULATION

Then you will be arrested, persecuted, and killed. You will be hated all over the world because of your allegiance to me. And many will turn away from me and betray and hate each other. And many false prophets will appear and will lead many people astray. Sin will be rampant everywhere, and the love of many will grow cold. But those who endure to the end will be saved.

MATTHEW 24:9-13

SCRIPTURE gives more space to the coming Tribulation period than any other seven-year period of time. It is a major theme of the Hebrew prophets, who mentioned it almost fifty times. Some call it "the time of Jacob's trouble" (Jeremiah 30:7, NKJV), others call it "a day of wrath"

(Zephaniah 1:15, NKJV). In the New Testament, it is mentioned by the apostle Paul and covered by Jesus in his Olivet discourse. It also occupies a major part of the book of Revelation (chapters 6–19).

The Lord Jesus called it the "great Tribulation" and described it as unlike anything that ever existed "since the beginning of the world until this time, no, nor ever shall be" (Matthew 24:21, NKJV). As we saw in an earlier study, this has not taken place yet. Nor have any of the events it describes ever taken place. It is all yet to come.

Without being technical, the seven years are divided into two periods of three and a half years each. Our Lord labels these the Tribulation and the great Tribulation. In the book of Revelation, it is separated into two periods of forty-two months and in Daniel, two periods of three and one-half years.

Those who believe that Christ will come in the middle of the Tribulation (mid-Tribulationists) or at its end (post-Tribulationists) seem not to take the Tribulation very seriously. In the case of the "mid-tribbers," they locate all the judgments in the last half of the period. This late suffering does not jibe with the fact that in Revelation the Tribulation period starts right off with the seven seal judgments that wipe out a quarter of Earth's population. Then, another third of the world's population is erased in the next seven trumpet judgments. Such natural and military devastation seems like full-term tribulation to us. The good news, of course, is that all Christians are to be saved "from the wrath to come" (1 Thessalonians 1:10, NKJV). Consequently, it can only be inferred that Christians will already have been raptured before that time of wrath begins.

What is the purpose of the Tribulation? The Hebrew prophet Daniel tells us it is to "bring in everlasting righteousness" (Daniel 9:24). That is, it will bring time, as we know it, to an end and usher in our Lord's thousand-year kingdom of peace. But in God's great redeeming heart, it will compress an entire generation's opportunity to accept Christ into the brief space of seven years. Doubtless everyone will make the same decision about God that they would make if they had a normal lifetime in which to make it.

This further confirms the abundant mercy and love of God toward humankind. As the Scripture says, the Lord "is not willing that any should perish but that all should come to repentance" (2 Peter 3:9, NKJV). God wants all to be saved and is willing to go to extreme measures to help those outside of grace come to Christ.

Just recently we had a young woman in our home to whom we had witnessed several times while she was doing some redecorating for us. The daughter of a liberal minister, she had never received Christ. Though we pressed the cause of Christ upon her, she would not make a decision at that time.

Two years later she was in a serious automobile accident. A motorcyclist crashed into her car and was killed. Abundantly grateful that God had spared her life, she invited Christ into her life as her personal Lord and Savior. This was, for her, a season of personal and private tribulation. Tribulation is not just a coming seven-year period. Such personal tribulation has led many to accept Christ like this woman did. It is our prayer that you have already made your decision to invite Him into your life. If you haven't, or if you are not sure you have, please do so today! Avoid the necessity of unnecessary tribulation. Act now, while you are living in an easy, calm period of reflection.

TODAY'S PRAYER

Dear Lord, I have always believed You exist and that You sent Your Son to die for my sins. I also believe He rose from the dead and is now in heaven with You. I believe that He is coming one day to take all Christians into Your heavenly home. I want to formally invite Him to come into my heart. Forgive my sins, I plead. Save my soul. In Jesus' name I pray, Amen.

30 THE SIGN OF UNIVERSAL GOSPEL PREACHING

> And the Good News about the Kingdom will be
> preached throughout the whole world, so that all
> nations will hear it; and then, finally, the end will
> come. MATTHEW 24:14

ONE of the very thrilling signs of our Lord's return comes from the disciples' question, "What will be the sign of Your coming, and of the end of the age?" Here He gives us a very clear prophecy. It is the prediction of a universal gospel being preached worldwide. This sign will be literally fulfilled during the Tribulation period, before Christ returns with His church to rule for a millennium.

During the Tribulation, the 144,000 witnesses will be preaching all over the world. The Holy Spirit will be poured out on the world just like it was on the Day of Pentecost (Joel 2:28-32). There will even be an angel assigned to communicate the gospel to every creature under heaven. All of this global evangelism will demonstrate how loving God really is. In those seven years He will get His message to every individual on earth.

But the gospel is even now being preached around the world. At this very moment the Good News is being carried in every language by shortwave radio. The Wycliffe Bible Translators are rapidly printing Bibles in the languages of Earth's most primitive tribes. I can remember when the Wycliffe slogan used to be "2,000 tongues to go." Today it is but a few hundred.

In addition, the *JESUS* film of Campus Crusade for Christ has now been translated into more than five hundred languages. Over a half billion souls have seen the film and come to the Savior. With computers, the Internet, and other state-of-the-art technology at our disposal, we will soon be able to communicate the gospel to every person.

That capability was not possible even a generation ago. We are technologically closer to the fulfillment of this fourteenth verse than we have ever been. Our Lord could come for His church at any moment. The faithful witnesses that He will "seal" with His calling during the Tribulation period could use an Internet witness and easily accomplish His worldwide plan.

The fact that it will be done during the Tribulation period in no way removes from us the responsibility of sharing Christ now while our friends and loved ones still have time to receive Him. Just recently, I learned of a man who buys cases of *Left Behind* to distribute as a gospel witness to his friends and loved ones. For his witness I am grateful, but however we do it, Christians must boldly share their faith now more than ever. Nothing in Bible prophecy requires that there be a revival before the Lord returns. Remember the Rapture is a signless event. But it would not be unlike our God, whom the psalmist described as "merciful and gracious" (Psalm 103:8), to send a worldwide revival just before the Rapture. Remember, Jesus said, "It is not my heavenly Father's will that even one of these little ones should perish" (Matthew 18:14).

Today's Prayer

Dear heavenly Father, it is thrilling to live in these days that could well be the last times. I want to be available to share my faith with others during these days. May I offer my lips, my brain, and whatever I have that You might speak through me. Guide my steps and my thoughts that I might be sensitive to anyone to whom You are speaking today. In Jesus' name, Amen.

31 SIGNS OF THE GREAT TRIBULATION

> "The time will come when you will see what Daniel the prophet spoke about: the sacrilegious object that causes desecration standing in the Holy Place"—reader, pay attention! MATTHEW 24:15

IN THE midst of His masterful Olivet discourse, our Lord gave some unmistakable signs that will come before the last three and a half years of the Tribulation. First will come the desecration of the temple, which Daniel predicted almost six hundred years earlier than Jesus' discourse. When the disciples first asked Jesus "What will be the sign of Your coming, and of the end of the age?" (Matthew 24:3, NKJV), they automatically thought of Daniel's prophecy of the desecration of the temple. This, of course, has not happened, which is one reason we know the temple in Jerusalem has yet to be built. It must be desecrated by Antichrist (described also by the apostle Paul in 2 Thessalonians 2:8) after the Rapture and before the Second Coming.

In 2 Thessalonians 2:3-5, Paul gives two other characteristics of the second half of the Tribulation: The Antichrist will establish a lawless regime and will blaspheme the God of heaven, even establishing an idol of himself in the temple. Everyone will be forced to bow down and worship that image.

According to Jesus, this Tribulation period will be the worst time in the history of the world. During the last half of the Tribulation there will be a great battle between God and Satan. It will be the worst struggle in the long conflict of the ages. Satan will be thrown down to the earth and, realizing that he has only a short time to wage war, will use everything at his disposal to deceive the human race.

While some false christs and false teachers will come before the Tribulation begins, during the last three and one-half years they will

PERHAPS

abound. They will deceive the world with supernatural powers and lying wonders "to deceive, if possible, even the elect" (Matthew 24:24, NKJV).

Recently a man was brought by his wife to one of the prophecy conferences where I was speaking. He had read our fiction series and when he saw me, he flippantly said, "LaHaye, I'm going to wait and see if all these things happen as you say the Bible teaches. If I miss the Rapture and wind up in the Tribulation, I will for sure call on the Lord then because I will know it is all true." He obviously has no idea how much false teaching and deception Satan will unleash. What he has read in our fiction series or heard others teach from the Bible will pale in comparison to the supernatural signs and wonders Antichrist will perform to convince him to "believe all these lies" (2 Thessalonians 2:11). If Satan could "almost" deceive the elect, he may certainly deceive this man and the many others like him.

It is for this reason we must double our efforts to reach the lost on this, the front side of the Rapture. This will not only keep them from having to go into the Tribulation, but it will also keep them from being deceived by the Antichrist. One thing we should keep in mind is that as wonderful as it will be for us to be raptured by Jesus, we cannot fully imagine how horrible it will be for the unsaved to live during the Tribulation period, especially the last half of it.

I would like to suggest that you make a list of people you know who need to receive Christ. Pray for them every day. You will be amazed how God will lead either you or someone else to share the gospel with them.

Today's Prayer
Dear Lord, as the horrors of the Tribulation begin to come, I shudder to think that some of my loved ones and friends may miss the Rapture and have to go through the Tribulation. Please bring to my mind all those with whom I must share my faith before it is

too late. Help me make a list of those for whom I should pray. Use me as an instrument to help save them from "the wrath to come." In Jesus' name, Amen.

32 THE GLORIOUS APPEARING

Immediately after those horrible days end, the sun will be darkened, the moon will not give light, the stars will fall from the sky, and the powers of heaven will be shaken. And then at last, the sign of the coming of the Son of Man will appear in the heavens, and there will be deep mourning among all the nations of the earth. And they will see the Son of Man arrive on the clouds of heaven with power and great glory. And he will send forth his angels with the sound of a mighty trumpet blast, and they will gather together his chosen ones from the farthest ends of the earth and heaven.

MATTHEW 24:29-31

JESUS CHRIST is coming again. Evangelical Christians are not the only ones who believe this. While only 41 percent of Americans claim to be born again, 64 percent of all Americans believe in His return. This means that 23 percent more Americans believe He is coming than are actually ready for His return.

Beyond America, many Muslims, who consider Jesus a prophet of "Allah," are actually afraid He will return. During the Middle Ages when they controlled the city of Jerusalem, they sealed the eastern gate of the city to prevent Jesus from coming back. Today's tourists to the Holy Land are still shown that cemented gate. Muslims seem not to realize that when Jesus returns the next time, it will not be as a prophet or a holy man. When He comes again it will be in "power and great glory" and as "King of kings and Lord of lords"! No gate in the world can keep Him from fulfilling His promise to return.

Although there are many promises of Jesus' return, this text, coupled with Revelation 19:11-21, teaches that He will come as "King of kings and Lord of lords" immediately "after those horrible days end." This Glorious Appearing of Jesus will come between the Tribulation and the beginning of His millennial reign. God is going to shake the earth to bring a maximum number of souls to Himself. Then Jesus will descend "with power and great glory" to establish His thousand-year reign.

Verses 29-30 give us six signs of His second coming:

1. "The sun will be darkened."
2. "The moon will not give light."
3. "The stars will fall from the sky, and the powers of heaven will be shaken."
4. "The sign of the coming of the Son of Man will appear in the heavens" (possibly the sign of the cross, for nothing else so clearly designates Jesus' role in human redemption).
5. "There will be deep mourning among all the nations of the earth" (doubtless because of their refusal to accept Him during the tremendous gospel crusades of the Tribulation).
6. "They will see the Son of Man arrive on the clouds of heaven with power and great glory."

What a magnificent event the return of Jesus will be!

For believers it will be a time of incredible blessing. For the majority of those still alive (after the seven long weary years of tribulation) it will be a time of "mourning." They will weep that they have been left behind and have forfeited the many blessings God had prepared for them.

This event at the end of time will be heartbreaking. Millions will have believed the lies of Satan. What lies? The same lies already being told, that Jesus is not really the Son of God, or that He is not "the way, the truth, and the life" (John 14:6). In that moment all will know that their best was not enough. They will know that it took the blood of Christ to cleanse the sins of the whole world.

Recently I read of a lady who had always thought she was a Christian. What had sponsored her false confidence? She had been raised in Sunday school. She had been baptized and had always attended church. Alas, she had never been born again. Overwhelmed by grace, she finally realized the truth. She had never repented of her sins or invited Jesus into her life as Lord. Gladly she came to Christ and could see that she had not only been saved but instantly made ready for His second coming. Are you counting on any area of false security? It is our sincere desire that you, too, know Christ and be prepared for His coming!

TODAY'S PRAYER

Dear heavenly Father, thank You for the wonderful plan You have for my future. I realize there is nothing comparable to what You've planned for me in all the religions of the world. I have never deserved such a future. But thank You for sending Jesus to die for my sins, and raising Him again from the dead. Please use my life to share this great news to those too enchanted by the lies of Satan. Help me to convey the reality of Jesus' coming, and the joy of a certain future. In Jesus' name I pray, Amen.

33 THE CONTRASTING EVENTS OF THE SECOND COMING

I can tell you this directly from the Lord: We who are still living when the Lord returns will not rise to meet him ahead of those who are in their graves. For the Lord himself will come down from heaven with a commanding shout, with the call of the archangel, and with the trumpet call of God. First, all the Christians who have died will rise from their graves. Then, together with them, we who are still alive and remain on the earth will be caught up in the clouds to meet the Lord in the air and remain with him forever.

1 THESSALONIANS 4:15-17

Immediately after those horrible days end, the sun will be darkened, the moon will not give light, the stars will fall from the sky, and the powers of heaven will be shaken. And then at last, the sign of the coming of the Son of Man will appear in the heavens, and there will be deep mourning among all the nations of the earth. And they will see the Son of Man arrive on the clouds of heaven with power and great glory.

MATTHEW 24:29-30

A COLLEGIAN spoke to me at the conclusion of a prophecy conference and asked, "I thought there was only one second coming of Jesus Christ; you make it sound like there are two. How do you reconcile what you call 'the Rapture' with what you call 'the Glorious Appearing'? "

This question is one that occupies the minds of many people. So let us examine two very clear aspects of the Second Coming.

Anyone who examines these relevant passages can see that one of them describes a secret coming of Jesus in the air to gather His church, and the other describes His public descent to the earth to set up His kingdom. Examine the following chart carefully, and you will see there are at least fifteen contrasting events all describing the second coming of Jesus Christ.

The easiest way to reconcile these two events (His secret Rapture

Contrasting Second Coming Events

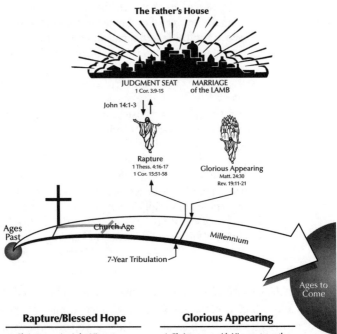

Rapture/Blessed Hope

1. Christ comes in air for His own
2. Rapture of all Christians
3. Christians taken to the Father's House
4. No judgment on earth at Rapture
5. Church taken to heaven at Rapture
6. Rapture imminent—could happen any moment
7. No signs for Rapture
8. For believers only
9. Time of joy
10. Before the "day of wrath" (Tribulation)
11. No mention of Satan
12. The Judgment Seat of Christ
13. Marriage of the Lamb
14. Only His own see Him
15. Tribulation begins

Glorious Appearing

1. Christ comes with His own to earth
2. No one raptured
3. Resurrected saints do not see Father's house
4. Christ judges inhabitants of earth
5. Christ sets up his kingdom on earth
6. Glorious Appearing cannot occur for at least 7 years
7. Many signs for Christ's physical coming
8. Affects all humanity
9. Time of mourning
10. Immediately after Tribulation (Matthew 24)
11. Satan bound in Abyss for 1,000 years
12. No time or place for Judgment Seat
13. His bride descends with Him
14. Every eye will see him
15. 1,000-year kingdom of Christ begins

PERHAPS

and His public descent) is to see them as two phases of the Second Coming. First, the rapture of the church will occur when Christ meets His church in the air and takes His people back to His Father's house for at least seven years. Then His Glorious Appearing will occur when He comes publicly to the earth "with all His saints" to establish His reign (1 Thessalonians 3:13, NKJV).

As we have seen, the first is called "the Rapture," a title it was given in the fourth century when the Greek word meaning "snatched up" was translated into Latin. First Thessalonians 4:14 limits the Rapture to "those who believe that Jesus died and was raised to life again." The dead who believed will rise first in the Rapture, then those who are alive will be "changed—in a moment, in the twinkling of an eye" (1 Corinthians 15:52, NKJV) and "caught up together with them in the clouds to meet the Lord in the air" (1 Thessalonians 4:17). This is an obvious coming of Christ but not one in which He comes down to the earth. In this coming He stops midair and calls His believing church together.

From other passages we have examined (like 1 Thessalonians 1:9; 5:9) we know this Rapture event will occur prior to the "time of wrath" (the Tribulation period) that shall try the whole earth.

Taken together, the Rapture and the Glorious Appearing explain how His coming can be both before and after the Tribulation. It explains why the church is never seen during the entire Tribulation. These two aspects of the Second Coming point out how His coming can be both sudden and unexpected, and yet be preceded by several recognizable events. The Rapture requires no prophecy to be fulfilled and could take place at any moment. His Glorious Appearing will be distinctly different from the Rapture. It will come after the Tribulation is over—seven years later—at the beginning of the thousand-year reign. The Glorious Appearing, by contrast, cannot occur for at least seven years after the Rapture and will be preceded by many signs.

If the final scheme of things seems too complex, the important thing to remember is that we are to be ready when He comes.

Thank You, dear Lord, for making this complex truth so clear. I want to be prepared for the Savior at His coming. I am a Christian, I know, for I have invited Jesus into my heart already. But I want to live in constant readiness for His coming. So if there be any wicked way in my life, please reveal it to me so that I may confess it and live in constant readiness. In Jesus' name I pray, Amen.

34 OUR RESURRECTION FAITH

And he will send forth his angels with the sound of a mighty trumpet blast, and they will gather together his chosen ones from the farthest ends of the earth and heaven.   MATTHEW 24:31

THE CENTRAL miracle of Christianity is the Resurrection. From that doctrine comes our view of the afterlife. The entire Old Testament and the Jewish faith it engendered also believed in a life hereafter. Job, Moses, David, Daniel, and the other prophets refer, in one way or another, to life after death.

In the Gospel of John, the Savior arrives in Bethany four days after Lazarus died. Jesus, wanting to comfort Lazarus's grieving sisters, tells them, "Your brother will rise again!" Martha replies, "I know that he will rise again in the resurrection at the last day" (John 11:23-24, NKJV). Her answer proves that a belief in a bodily resurrection was well established among the Jews.

Many Christians take for granted this blessed doctrine. Yet it is deeply ingrained in the teachings of the New Testament and the early church. The Resurrection is one of the few teachings that nearly all Christians readily agree upon.

In today's text, the entire church has been resurrected. Believers of all ages have been called to life in the Rapture by the Lord's shout from heaven (1 Thessalonians 4:16-17). The Tribulation period is now over, and Jesus is coming in power and great glory with His bride (the church) to judge the nations of the world. The millennial kingdom is about to begin. Even the Old Testament saints are present. From Revelation 20:1-3, we learn that it is at this moment He casts the devil into the bottomless pit. In Revelation 19:20 we see that He throws the Beast and the false prophet into the lake of fire. Then He will resurrect all those believers who were killed during the Tribulation and they, too, will come alive to enjoy the incredible millennial kingdom. All people, from Adam to the last soul killed during the Tribulation period, are alive and accounted for in this final resurrection.

The thousand-year millennium will be made rich when a multi-millennial resurrection of all the dead will gather around the feet of the triumphant Christ. We are indeed a blessed people.

Today's Prayer

Dear heavenly Father, I am awed at the marvelous plan You have for planet Earth. And I thank You for those who led me to You and I thank You for guaranteeing my salvation. Your blessing is eternity's benediction, for You said, "Because I live, you will live also" (John 14:19, NKJV). I know Jesus lives in heaven with You, and I look forward, because of Him, to being there, too. Thank You, in Jesus' name, Amen.

35 LEARN A LESSON FROM THE FIG TREE

Now learn a lesson from the fig tree. When its buds become tender and its leaves begin to sprout, you know without being told that summer

> is near. Just so, when you see the events I've
> described beginning to happen, you can know his
> return is very near, right at the door. I assure you,
> this generation will not pass from the scene
> before all these things take place. Heaven and
> earth will disappear, but my words will remain
> forever. However, no one knows the day or the
> hour when these things will happen, not even the
> angels in heaven or the Son himself. Only the
> Father knows.   MATTHEW 24:32-36

CONSIDER for a moment Christ's last prophetic message given just before He began his priestly work of the Cross. All that He has been saying has been in response to the original question of His disciples, "When will all this take place? And will there be any sign ahead of time to signal your return and the end of the world?" (Matthew 24:3).

Several chapters ago we saw that *the* sign was the First World War, the first "birth pain" of the end times. The gathering of Israel into their land was another sign, among many others. Then the Rapture is scheduled, after which the signing of the seven-year covenant between Israel and the Antichrist. This covenant will be followed by three and a half years of the Antichrist's rule, and then he will desecrate the temple in Jerusalem.

Keeping these events in mind, let us consider Jesus' challenge that we "learn a lesson from the fig tree." Some popular prophecy teachers have erred by interpreting the fig tree as a symbol of Israel's place in God's future plans. This seems unlikely since in a parallel passage in Luke, Jesus adds the words "or any other tree" to His use of the fig tree (Luke 21:29). What Jesus really seems to be saying is that when any of the trees begin to bud, we know that summer is near. He expressly states that no man knows the day or the hour of His coming. Yet He seems to say that as budding trees signal summer, so the obvious signs of the time signal that the Second Coming is near.

Further, He promises that "this generation will not pass from the scene before all these things take place."

There is much speculation and some debate about this statement. It seems to us that He is saying that folks on Earth who live to see the temple desecrated will not die of old age before His Glorious Appearing. From Revelation and other passages in Daniel, we know that this will require only three and a half years (or 1,260 days). So those alive at the desecration of the temple will find Jesus' words a message of hope. They will realize they have only three and a half years of Satan's blasphemy to endure before Christ comes.

God never leaves the world without hope. Whether it is the people living before Christ came or Christians today, the Lord has promised, "I will not leave you nor forsake you" (Deuteronomy 31:8, NKJV).

Recently my wife and I had dinner with the former president of Biola University and some other friends. We realized, in the course of our evening together, that the eight of us combined had given four hundred years of service to our Lord. We were not celebrating our faithfulness to God, but His faithfulness to us. Faithfulness is the essence of His nature.

You may be going through some trial or difficulty in your life that may make you wonder if you are in the Tribulation. We can assure you that you are not, for Christ has not raptured His church yet. Still we want to celebrate the faithfulness of God. All through history there have been Christians who had to suffer for the cause of Christ. Satan has always been active in persecuting the church. Paul warns, "Everyone who wants to live a godly life in Christ Jesus will suffer persecution" (2 Timothy 3:12). But let all who await His coming remember this: He is faithful. Call upon Him, and He will hear you and supply you with the grace to go through whatever trial you are experiencing.

Dear heavenly Father, thank You for Your many years of faithfulness and the many assurances of Your presence in my life. There are times when I need the consciousness of that presence to face today's trials and tribulations. Fill me with Your Holy Spirit today so that I might manifest Your love, joy, peace, long-suffering, and other fruit of the Spirit. Give me joy and a spirit of thanksgiving in the face of adversity as a testimony of Your presence in my life. In Jesus' name I pray.

36 JESUS' MESSAGE TO OUR GENERATION

However, no one knows the day or the hour when these things will happen, not even the angels in heaven or the Son himself. Only the Father knows. When the Son of Man returns, it will be like it was in Noah's day. In those days before the Flood, the people were enjoying banquets and parties and weddings right up to the time Noah entered his boat. People didn't realize what was going to happen until the Flood came and swept them all away. That is the way it will be when the Son of Man comes. Two men will be working together in the field; one will be taken, the other left. Two women will be grinding flour at the mill; one will be taken, the other left. So be prepared, because you don't know what day your Lord is coming. Know this: A homeowner who knew exactly when a burglar was coming would stay alert and not permit the house to be broken into. You also must be ready all the time. For the Son of Man will come when least expected. MATTHEW 24:36-44

OUR LORD'S greatest prophecy was delivered near the end of His ministry on this earth. In fact, this was given only hours before His trial and crucifixion. Jesus introduces an incredible challenge to our generation: "No one knows the day or the hour when these things will happen. Only the Father knows." Almost everyone has heard the warning that Jesus' second coming will occur at a moment of low expectancy. Such a clandestine prophecy cannot refer to the Glorious Appearing, for that will not be a secret and must take place exactly seven years after the Antichrist signs his covenant with Israel.

This Rapture Jesus refers to is a different matter. It has no warning signs.

There are no dates we can use for reference. He will come at a set time known only by the Father. So He challenges us all to be ready and live continually in a state of watchfulness. We must stay prepared, for we "don't know what day [the] Lord is coming."

Jesus used the days before the Flood as a metaphor of His coming. Noah had long warned the people to repent. In fact, he had preached as he built his ark for over a 120-year period. During this time, the people were "marrying and giving in marriage" (Matthew 24:37, NKJV). They had lived wickedly in the midst of Noah's warnings of judgment.

Individuals today hear the same kind of warnings, for Jesus is coming again. But they still refuse to be saved. They have lulled their consciences into a false peace. They believe that since we have had almost two thousand years since Jesus ascended, He can't be expected to come in their lifetimes. Unfortunately for them—like those in the days of Noah—He will come. Those who are not ready (the unsaved) will be left behind. It isn't, however, just the unsaved who need to watch and be ready. I am confident that many carnal Christians living selfish, unconcerned lives will regret their neglect of the Lord if they do not get their lives straightened out and recommit themselves to the coming Savior.

A minister recently told me he once had been a pilot in the U.S. Air Force and had expected to make flying his career. Then God spoke to him about going into the ministry. At first he resisted God's call until finally it dawned on him that Jesus was coming. Suddenly he knew that when Jesus returned he did not want to be doing something other than the perfect will of God for his life. Flying is a legitimate profession for those whom God does not call to minister. But for those He calls to minister His Word, no other profession could ever be legitimate. We must commit ourselves to do whatever He wants. The day is coming when all unfaithful servants (those not doing exactly what Jesus wants them to) will be surprised to find themselves standing suddenly before Him at His coming.

From a practical standpoint, even if Jesus does not come during your lifetime, you will never regret your decision. I know many lifetime servants of God who testify that the best decision they ever made was to let Jesus Christ be Lord of their lives. They have no regrets.

Today's Prayer

Dear heavenly Father, I thank You that You have a specific will for my life. I may not fully understand what that will is, but I have faith in Your love for me. I know that Your plan is the best for me. I yield my total self to You. Take charge of my personal and family circumstances. Rule over all my obligations. From now until Jesus comes for me, I want to be under Your direction. I give myself totally to You. In Jesus' name I pray, Amen.

37 WATCHFUL LIVING IN LIGHT OF HIS COMING

Watch therefore, for you do not know what hour your Lord is coming. But know this, that if the master of the house had known what hour the thief would come, he would have watched and not allowed his house to be broken into. Therefore you also be ready, for the Son of Man is coming at an hour you do not expect. Who then is a faithful and wise servant, whom his master made ruler over his household, to give them food in due season? Blessed is that servant whom his master, when he comes, will find so doing. Assuredly, I say to you that he will make him ruler over all his goods. MATTHEW 24:42-47, NKJV

Watch therefore, for you know neither the day nor the hour in which the Son of Man is coming. For the kingdom of heaven is like a man traveling to a far country, who called his own servants and delivered his goods to them. And to one he gave five talents, to another two, and to another one, to each according to his own ability; and immediately he went on a journey. Then he who had received the five talents went and traded with them, and made another five talents. MATTHEW 25:13-16, NKJV

To those who use well what they are given, even more will be given, and they will have an abundance. MATTHEW 25:29

OUR LORD followed His lengthy discourse on His second coming with an even longer challenge to "watchful living." At the end of his Olivet discourse, He told the tale of the five foolish virgins (those unprepared for His return) and the story of the talents, in which He describes a large householder leaving on a journey (two thousand years ago).

The reason for these parables was to call every Christian to live in the light of His sudden coming. Immediately after He takes us up to His Father's house in the Rapture, the Lord will require that we account for our stewardship of those talents He gave us.

These ingenious illustrations have one essential message: Watch and be ready.

Someone has suggested that when we receive Jesus as our Lord, He opens a bank account in heaven in our name. He challenges us to deposit our good works by the faithful stewardship of our lives. We are to make no excuse as to why we fail to deposit. We are to avoid using the excuse, "I am not very talented; I can't serve the Lord." Beware of all such alibis! God holds us accountable only to use all the talents He gives us. Then when we do so, He will add His Spirit's blessings, and the results will be eternal.

Dr. George W. Truett, pastor of the First Baptist Church of Dallas, told the story of a prominent doctor in that city who regularly attended one of the church's morning services with his Christian wife. On this particular Sunday they were seated in the front row of the balcony. During the invitation the pastor grimaced as he saw a twelve-year-old, mentally retarded girl go to the doctor and begin talking to him. Dr. Truett groaned, believing that this little girl—known to be an outspoken witness for Christ—would probably turn the doctor off. But a brief one stanza later, the doctor, who had been the object of many prayers, came forward to receive Christ.

As they were leaving the church that Sunday, the pastor asked the physician what it was that caused him to come forward to be saved. The doctor said, "It was what little Millie said to me. You see, she has been my patient her entire life. From birth we knew that she would be mentally retarded, but I have grown to love her and she, me. After your sermon she was so concerned for my soul, she came over and said to me, 'Doctor, do you want to go to heaven with us?' I replied, 'No!' Then she sadly responded, 'Then you will have to go to hell!' Suddenly I realized she was right. If I did not receive Jesus, I would be eternally lost. I owe my conversion to Millie's gentle frankness."

Millie could never teach a Sunday school class, preach a sermon, or even give her testimony in public. But she was a bold witness for her Lord and did not hesitate to urge all she knew to accept the Savior. Millie was "watching" for her Lord's coming. She probably didn't know the fine details of Bible prophecy, but she loved the Savior and the souls of individuals. I have a hunch that Millie and many others like her will hear her Lord say one day, "Well done, my good and faithful servant. Enter into the joy of your Lord."

TODAY'S PRAYER

Dear Lord, thank You for the opportunity to serve You in this life and lay up for myself treasures in heaven. Forgive me for the times I have lived to please myself. From this day on I want to be used of You. Give me opportunities to share the truth of the gospel with others. Use whatever talents I have. They are Yours from now until Jesus comes. In His precious name I pray, Amen.

38 REMEMBER "THE LEAST OF THESE"

But when the Son of Man comes in his glory, and all the angels with him, then he will sit upon his glorious throne. All the nations will be gathered in his presence, and he will separate them as a shepherd separates the sheep from the goats. He will place the sheep at his right hand and the goats at his left. Then the King will say to those on the right, "Come, you who are blessed by my Father, inherit the Kingdom prepared for you from the foundation of the world." MATTHEW 25:31-34

CORRIE TEN BOOM, one of Holland's most dynamic Christians, charmed and inspired hundreds of evangelical Christian audiences during the 1960s. Her stories of how she defied the edicts of Hitler to provide a safe haven to Jews have inspired us all. She seemed to express the heart of the Abrahamic covenant: "I will bless those who bless you and curse those who curse you" (Genesis 12:3). One of the reasons America has been blessed of God in these last days is that it has been our national policy to befriend Israel and the Jewish people. No country in the history of the world has provided more freedom for Jews than America. It is no accident America has received the unprecedented blessings of God. The Father will always bless those who are good to His people and will continue to do so until the end of the Tribulation period.

We have already seen in our studies that our Lord Jesus Christ will judge the world at His coming and will make all things right. That is true both for the church before the Tribulation and for all who later go through it.

After the rapture of the church, all believers will be taken to heaven, where we will stand before the judgment seat of Christ. In this text, however, we are focusing on the judgment of the nations at the very end of the seven-year Tribulation. This will be a judgment of good works—the good works done by those who defy the edicts of the Antichrist and respect the Jews.

In Matthew 25:35-46 our Lord summed up the judgment of the righteous in these words, "I assure you, when you did it to one of the least of these my brothers and sisters, you were doing it to me!" (verse 40). Five verses later He severely judges the unrighteous because they did not help Him (verse 45).

The Hebrew prophets, particularly Isaiah and Jeremiah, tell us much about the Kingdom Age over which Christ will personally rule. In Revelation 20, the apostle John tells us six times that the length of the Kingdom Age will be a thousand years. In His Olivet discourse, Jesus tells us that entrance into that Kingdom Age will be by way of salvation and good works. These good works are those kind acts extended to the children of Israel and all believers.

The Tribulation period will feature an unprecedented persecution of both Christians and Jews. This parable points out that those who visit strangers in prison, tend to the sick, and feed the hungry will earn the reward of open access to the kingdom. In fact, Jesus considers that what we do for all these unfortunate brethren, we do for Him. He has made it clear: "I assure you, when you did it to one of the least of these my brothers and sisters, you were doing it to me!" (verse 40).

While this passage refers specifically to the end of the Tribulation and the beginning of the millennial kingdom, He also applies it to God's judgment of all people in every age. Many times I have seen Christians reach out to help others in need.

One of the best advertised avenues of such compassion is the care of orphaned children in the impoverished countries of the world. Many families take on the support of such children for a small cost each month. This text clearly indicates that they will assuredly receive a reward. These don't give to be noticed. They do not give grudgingly. They give because they love Jesus. How Christ must bless their compassion! When we remember the orphans, the homeless, the mentally and physically handicapped, we remember Him. In a country where Christians enjoy unprecedented blessings, we should be careful to provide blessings for others less fortunate. To do so is to ready our hearts for the judgment of the righteous.

Today's Prayer

Dear heavenly Father, thank You for Your unprecedented blessings on this nation. Thank You for our freedom to worship and for the prosperity we have to share with others. Forgive us for our tendencies to be selfish. Entrust us with generosity. Make us desire to reach out to the starving, the broken of spirit, and those in prison. Help me to see that as I serve them, I serve You. In Jesus' name I pray, Amen.

39 HOW DO YOU TREAT OTHERS?

But when the Son of Man comes in his glory, and all the angels with him, then he will sit upon his glorious throne.   MATTHEW 25:31

Then these righteous ones will reply, "Lord, when did we ever see you hungry and feed you? Or thirsty and give you something to drink? Or a stranger and show you hospitality? Or naked and give you clothing? When did we ever see you sick or in prison, and visit you?" And the King will tell them, "I assure you, when you did it to one of the least of these my brothers and sisters, you were doing it to me!" Then the King will turn to those on the left and say, "Away with you, you cursed ones, into the eternal fire prepared for the Devil and his demons! For I was hungry, and you didn't feed me. I was thirsty, and you didn't give me anything to drink. I was a stranger, and you didn't invite me into your home. I was naked, and you gave me no clothing. I was sick and in prison, and you didn't visit me." Then they will reply, "Lord, when did we ever see you hungry or thirsty or a stranger or naked or sick or in prison, and not help you?" And he will answer, "I assure you, when you refused to help the least of these my brothers and sisters, you were refusing to help me." And they will go away into eternal punishment, but the righteous will go into eternal life.   MATTHEW 25:37-46

WHEN BELIEVERS encounter their Lord at the judgment seat of Christ, they will be judged—among other things—by the way they treated other people. Those who have neglected the poor, the sick, and the imprisoned, will be judged according to the Word and wisdom of God. I suspect the final determination will be of some surprise to those who neglected some of the more weightier portions of God's Word. The great and final Judge will measure all callous disregard of human need as though the disregard were against Himself. If that is true of the judgment that occurs in heaven after the Rapture, how much more will it be true in our own easy lives? Americans live in a time of great freedom and blessing. We can see the signs of cultural deterioration as in the days of Noah, but we are still enjoying an era of abundance. Our current ease, however, will be nothing like the three and a half years when the Antichrist will force believers to chose between Christ and himself.

It is not enough in our abundant, easy times for Christians to tithe and feel as though they have done all that is necessary to serve God. We who have received God's plenty should reach out to the needy, because of these words: "I assure you, when you did it to one of the least of these my brothers and sisters, you were doing it to me!" If we turn our back and refuse to reach out to the suffering of this world, Christ considers it an affront to Him and will say in that great judgment, "I assure you, when you refused to help the least of these my brothers and sisters, you were refusing to help me."

One of the mathematical axioms I remember from high school is that things equal to the same thing are equal to each other. Applying this truth to ministry is to suggest that those committed to Jesus will be committed to those He loves. Who are these objects of His love? They are the poor, the sick, the imprisoned, and all who are persecuted for His name. It is a cop-out to say that the primary meaning of this text refers to those living during the Tribulation but not to us. This is a principle that reveals how God will hold His people accountable in every age.

How well I remember the Nicaraguan father of six whose family was confined to a United Nations internment camp in Costa Rica. He had led his family to escape from the Communists in his Nicaraguan homeland by crossing the river into Costa Rica. He was just one step ahead of the vicious Sandinista Communist regime that had taken over his country. We met these courageous souls because my wife and other members of Concerned Women for America ran a relief mission in those camps. They provided food and clothing for those refugees who had managed to escape with only the clothes on their backs. So it was that these brave women gave clothes to every member of this man's family. He was so moved he could barely speak. I will never forget seeing him standing there with a pile of clothes in his arms and tears of gratitude coursing down his face. Then I heard him say to my wife, "Señora, you have taught me today that God has not forgotten me!"

At his words my mind soared high above the jungles of Costa Rica, and I heard Jesus say, "When you did it to one of the least of these my brothers and sisters, you were doing it to me!" When we pass up opportunities to care, He will speak our judgment: "When you refused to help the least of these my brothers and sisters, you were refusing to help me."

On those Sundays when I am not preaching in some other church, we attend a dynamic church near our home. Once each month our pastor closes the service by saying, "As you go out today, there will be ushers at the door to receive a special offering for those in our community who are in need. Everything you give will be used to help others." I always see this as an entreaty born of Jesus' Olivet discourse. Almost everyone puts in something. God's people should do this. We are commanded to reach out and help the poor, the sick, the imprisoned, and the persecuted. Such generosity warms God's heart and will gain His approval in that day.

TODAY'S PRAYER

Dear heavenly Father, forgive me when I seem callous to the needs of others less fortunate than myself. Help me to see them as You see them and to reach out to them as though I am serving

You. You have been so good to me that I want to pass Your every blessing on to others in the name of Jesus, our coming King. Amen.

40 JESUS IS STILL THE ONLY WAY TO HEAVEN

"Don't be troubled. You trust God, now trust in me. There are many rooms in my Father's home, and I am going to prepare a place for you. If this were not so, I would tell you plainly. When everything is ready, I will come and get you, so that you will always be with me where I am. And you know where I am going and how to get there." "No, we don't know, Lord," Thomas said. "We haven't any idea where you are going, so how can we know the way?" Jesus told him, "I am the way, the truth, and the life. No one can come to the Father except through me."

JOHN 14:1-6

SEVERAL YEARS ago I was invited to offer myself as a conservative sacrificial lamb on the Phil Donahue show. One of my books had hit the best-seller list, and Donahue's producers felt that ridiculing a Bible-believing minister would make great entertainment for his liberal, national audience. Mr. Donahue put me on the hot seat with a classic accusation, "Do you mean to say that Jesus Christ is the only way to heaven?" There was no way I could duck his question and avoid the scorn of the three hundred hostile members of his audience.

"Jesus Himself made that issue very clear," I replied, "when He said, 'I am the way, the truth, and the life. No one can come to the Father except through me.'" Of course my answer produced an eruption of jeers and ridicule. Then Mr. Donahue went on to say, "You mean to say that if I do not accept Jesus, I will go to hell?" I responded, "There is no other way to heaven but through Jesus." Now his audience actually booed.

To the Donahue crowd I came off as the loser that day.

But was I really?

The narrow way to heaven has never been a matter of talk-show theology.

Many say, "But I think . . ." and then give their various ideas on how people get into heaven. But on Judgment Day, when Jesus comes for His own, there is only one vote that will really matter. His! And He has already made it clear how He will vote. Millions of Christians during the past two thousand years have been persecuted and killed for saying exactly what I said to Phil Donahue. Compared to them, I got off light. And the truth of all ages remains: Jesus is the *only* way to heaven.

During the first part of the first Christian century, believers were not persecuted for following Christ. The Romans didn't even object to Christians worshiping Jesus, as long as they would be broad-minded enough to worship the emperor also. It was not until Christians refused to worship Nero that the Roman emperors singled them out for violent persecution and death.

Like Nero, the world doesn't resent Christians because we worship Jesus. The resentment comes because they see us as "intolerant" in insisting that Jesus is the only way to God. John 14:6 is one of the primary texts from which we draw this very "narrow-minded" truth. But the principle is also taught in conjunction with the Savior's promise to come again. This promise is firmly planted in His statement that He alone is "the way, the truth, and the life."

Christianity is indeed a narrow way to God. We might prefer it to be broader, but God has set the boundaries of the issue. Since Christ alone could atone for the sins of the whole world, it was *His* blood alone that could provide the way. No other way to God has ever been found nor ever will be. Christ is the way, the only way. Seek no other. He is both the joy of our journey and the goal of our hope. Jesus forever! Jesus alone!

Today's Prayer

Dear heavenly Father, thank You for sending Your Son, Jesus, to die for my sins and for raising Him up in the resurrection. Thank You for introducing me to the wonderful news that Jesus is the only way to You and the only entrance to heaven. If I have never invited You into my heart personally, I want to do so now. I definitely want Jesus to forgive my sins, save my soul, and include me in the blessed Rapture. In Jesus' name I pray, Amen.

41 ANTICIPATING HIS COMING

It was not long after he said this that he was taken up into the sky while they were watching, and he disappeared into a cloud. As they were straining their eyes to see him, two white-robed men suddenly stood there among them. They said, "Men of Galilee, why are you standing here staring at the sky? Jesus has been taken away from you into heaven. And someday, just as you saw him go, he will return!" ACTS 1:9-11

WHEN ANGELS speak, they speak for God. They speak for all time. It was no accident that the first message from heaven to the forlorn disciples beholding the Ascension was this: "Jesus has been taken away from you into heaven. And someday, just as you saw him go, he will return!" His going will be like His coming: physical, visible, and in the body. He could be clearly seen by the multitude as He was received up into heaven in the clouds. When He comes again it will also be in the clouds. When predicting His second coming, Jesus said it would be in "power and great glory" (Matthew 24:30).

There are many who seem to ignore this principle. But the promise stands. As He went, so He will come. We can be dogmatic about the fact that He has not yet come as He went. Many false teachers have arisen through the years, suggesting that He has already come. One such cult, as unbelievable as it may seem, would have us believe He has already come. They are the preterits who suggest He came during the reign of Nero just before the fall of Jerusalem in A.D. 70, thus fulfilling the book of Revelation. But all false teachers fail at this point. Jesus has not come, for no one has seen Him come as His disciples once saw Him go (Acts 1:9-11).

However, the day is coming when He will appear physically and visibly in the clouds, just as He was seen going physically up to heaven. There is no question about it! But before He does, He will rapture His church and take her to His Father's house. There we who believe will be judged and given our rewards. Then, when the Tribulation is past, Satan will be chained in the bottomless pit. Christ will come exactly as He left—physically. We will then be with Him in "power and great glory." We will rule and reign with Him for a thousand years.

In November, I went to the mall with my wife and was amazed to see Christmas decorations everywhere. She said, "It looks like Christmas is coming," to which I replied, "Yes, but first we must have Thanksgiving." As Thanksgiving precedes Christmas, so the Rapture comes before Christ's visible return.

Dietrich Bonhoeffer, a Lutheran pastor in Germany during the Hitler regime, was imprisoned for being one of the few outspoken Christian voices against the Fürher's inhumane policies. While in prison, this brilliant theologian wrote several books that will remain a blessing for all time. Tragically, just two weeks before the U.S. troops liberated his camp, he was executed. One of the few creature comforts he was afforded during the long months of his imprisonment was an occasional visit from his fiancée, whom he loved deeply. During one of her visits he asked her not to come to see him too suddenly or unannounced. His anticipation of her coming was nearly as meaningful as her arrival. It gave him so much to look forward to.

So it is with the coming of Jesus. Anticipating each day as though this were the day our Lord returns has a motivating effect on our lives.

TODAY'S PRAYER

Dear heavenly Father, thank You for the constant reminders in Scripture that Jesus is coming soon. This world is so much with us that we face the constant temptation to become overly earthly-minded. Forgive us for living as if we had an entire lifetime to serve. In reality, Jesus, You could come at any time. Help us to seek out the many sinners You send our way. Help us to share our hope in Christ with all of them. In Jesus' name I pray, Amen.

42 WHY CHRISTIANS SHOULD NOT JUDGE ONE ANOTHER

Who are you to judge another's servant? To his own master he stands or falls. Indeed, he will be made to stand, for God is able to make him stand.

ROMANS 14:4, NKJV

But why do you judge your brother? Or why do you show contempt for your brother? For we shall all stand before the judgment seat of Christ. For it is written: "As I live, says the Lord, every knee shall bow to Me, and every tongue shall confess to God." So then each of us shall give account of

> himself to God. Therefore let us not judge one
> another anymore, but rather resolve this, not to
> put a stumbling block or a cause to fall in our
> brother's way.   ROMANS 14:10-13, NKJV

JUDGING the behavior of our fellow Christians is a common disobedience. The Scripture teaches us to be critical thinkers on matters of doctrine. We are commanded by the Bible not even to fellowship with heretics and false teachers. But the Bible encourages us to be charitable to all concerning mere behavioral differences. In this Romans passage, the apostle Paul notes that there are differences of opinion on how to observe certain holy days, and much division on whether or not to eat meat butchered for the purpose of pagan sacrifices.

These same kinds of differences exist today. While the ethics of eating meat offered to idols no longer exists, other issues do. Several times I have sat in a restaurant with other Christians who ask, "Would it offend you if I ordered wine with my meal?"

"No," I say, "that is your personal choice." My wife and I do not drink anything alcoholic for several reasons. We would never want weaker Christians to see us drinking and think it is right for them. Still, I have no right to impose my personal convictions on other believers or judge them for their private preferences. I do take Paul's admonition in verse 4 very seriously, "Who are you to judge another's servant? To his own master he stands or falls." In other words, Paul reasons, why bring discord among brethren by judging another's behavior? After all, when Christ returns, He will judge us all at His judgment seat.

We have already studied the judgment seat of Christ—the first post-Rapture tribunal—which exists only for believers. This will be a high court of rewards for the obedient. But it will also be a judgment of loss for those Christians whose behavior has caused others to sin. All Christians must give an account to God for their behavior. There are many kinds of Christian sins that will be judged at Christ's judgment seat. Consider all those who have caused divisions over minor ideas, created church splits, turned people away from the gospel, and alienated believers from each other. Consider what happens when Christians lose their temper. Their anger leads to hatred and then they grieve the Holy Spirit. Harboring unconfessed sin can also cause us to lose rewards we had otherwise earned (2 John 1:8).

If you despise anyone, forgive that person instantly, even if they are clearly in the wrong. Harboring mental bitterness toward anyone can destroy you. Consider these four reasons why you must forgive all:

First, holding a grudge is the root sin that not only leads to bitterness and anger, but also grieves the Holy Spirit (Ephesians 4:29-32).

Second, bitterness that leads to wrath and anger is like a cancer that ruins your relationships with those you love and destroys the healthy tissue of loving discipleship.

Third, bitterness, wrath, and anger will keep you from becoming a mature Christian.

Fourth, these virtues of the flesh will cause you to lose your rewards at the judgment seat of Christ.

The heart of our text for today is seen in Romans 14:12: "So then each of us shall give account of himself to God." From Romans 14:10 we know that will happen at the judgment seat of Christ. Paul counsels us to live every day as if it were our last. Then we will have no regrets, nor will we lose any earned rewards because we harbored bitterness in our hearts.

Those Christians who are concerned about how they will give an account of themselves to God have little time to get upset about the behavior of others. Conversely, those who spend too much time being critical of others usually pay too little heed to their own behavior. Once I gently confronted a Christian who had a critical and angry spirit. She found fault with everyone in the church, from the organist to the custodian. And horrors! She even at times found fault with my sermons! When I had had my say, her reply amazed me. "You don't understand. I have the gift of criticism." When I asked where the Bible mentioned such a gift, she said, "I'm not sure, but if it doesn't it should!"

We may smile at such poor souls and wonder how they get that way. The answer is "very gradually!" Beware!

Today's Prayer

Dear heavenly Father, I must confess that sometimes I let the "speck" of my brother's behavior become a "log" in my own eye (Matthew 7:3). Then I refuse to deal with my own behavior. Forgive me and help me to trust You to judge others' behavior. Above all, may I not let any other person ruin my relationship with You. In His name I pray, Amen.

43 ONLY GOD CAN JUDGE MANKIND

So look at Apollos and me as mere servants of Christ who have been put in charge of explaining God's secrets. Now, a person who is put in charge as a manager must be faithful. What about me? Have I been faithful? Well, it matters very little what you or anyone else thinks. I don't even trust my own judgment on this point. My conscience is clear, but that isn't what matters. It is the Lord himself who will examine me and decide. So be careful not to jump to conclusions before the Lord returns as to whether or not someone is faithful. When the Lord comes, he will bring our deepest secrets to light and will reveal our private motives. And then God will give to everyone whatever praise is due.   1 Corinthians 4:1-5

MY SON-IN-LAW, a dedicated minister of many years, recently asked me to help unravel a convoluted conflict between quarreling members of his church. It was easy to see the source of the problem. Pride and ego were so rampant among both groups that neither was willing to say with the Prodigal Son, "Forgive me, Father, for I have sinned against heaven and in your sight" (Luke 15:21, NKJV).

Discord between Christians is easily resolved when either side of the argument is willing to say, "It's my fault; please forgive me." The blame game all too often becomes a partisan struggle in the church. Instead of looking inward, we are prone to point our finger toward others.

There is a day coming when the Lord, the righteous Judge, will summon us to the table to get to the heart of every matter. Even in Paul's day, Christians were taking sides. The Corinthian church was full of partisan groups. Some claimed allegiance to Apollos, an early church evangelist. Some loved the apostle Paul more because he was a deeper teacher.

Paul counseled the Corinthians to see that both he and Apollos were "servants of Christ who have been put in charge of explaining God's secrets." The issue was not who they were, but if they each would be found faithful when the Lord came. We have already seen in previous studies that our Lord is going to judge us for our attitudes, our motivations, and our intentions. In verse 5, Paul points out that He will "bring our deepest secrets to light and will reveal our private motives."

In truth, God is the great heart inspector. When Jesus comes to judge the believers in the Rapture, it will be the most penetrating evaluation we have ever had—an examination of the "thoughts and intents of the heart" (Hebrews 4:12, NKJV). Remember the unwritten beatitude, "Blessed are the flexible for they shall not be bent out of shape." The Lord will set all things right when He comes!

A heartbroken divorcé told me that his wife had left him for another man and had taken his three children with her. He was so financially strapped with alimony and child support he didn't dare think of finding another person with whom he might share his life. He ached inside as he struggled with loneliness and discouragement. His wife, on the other hand, married again and went to another church across town. She continued to blame him for all their woes and was accepted with open arms among a loving new church family. He was left with the ache and stigma of being divorced.

What should a Christian do in such a situation? I was more than once faced with this question. A Christian wife in our congregation said she had fallen in love with another woman's husband. Both families got divorces and then she remarried. The Christian wife brought her three children into the new marriage, and she and her new husband had two more children. Finally, after some years, she repented of her sin and recommitted her life to God. She then asked me what she should do. After much prayer for wisdom, I urged her to go back to her first husband, who was still single, and confess her sin to him. Then I told her she should ask for his forgiveness and commit herself to being more cooperative with her former husband's rights to see his children. I told her to voluntarily reduce her child support payments and go with her former husband to their former pastor and confess her wrongdoing. This, I told her, would help restore her husband's status in his church. Then I urged her to confess her wrongdoing to her husband's first wife and accept the blame for ruining that marriage. Finally, I told her to go to her new pastor and acknowledge her sin of misrepresenting herself to the new congregation.

Even with all of this, she could not undo the heartbreaking results of her sins. But after she finally confessed to all involved, she did find peace. Only time will tell the lasting effects her behavior will have on her children. However, I have found that when we do right, "where sin abounded, grace abounded much more" (Romans 5:20, NKJV).

The average church today is filled with heartbreaking stories like this. But our God "heals the brokenhearted, binding up their wounds" (Psalm 147:3) if we do the right thing, even after doing the wrong thing. But it always begins on our knees in repentance and the confession of our guilt and wrongdoing. And, in addition, it removes our sin "as far as the east is from the west" (Psalm 103:12, NKJV) so that it will be remembered against us no more. Consequently, it is always best to judge our own sins today because we can be sure that when Jesus comes He will do it for us. After all, 1 Corinthians 11:31 says, "If we examine ourselves, we will not be examined by God and judged in this way."

Today's Prayer

Dear heavenly Father, thank You for always being willing to forgive my sins and restore my fellowship with You. If there be any "hidden things of darkness" or evil "counsels of the [heart]" (1 Corinthians 4:5, NKJV), reveal them to me so I can truly repent and confess them. And if my sins have offended or hurt others, please give me the courage to confess them and repair whatever damage I can. I sincerely want to be ready for my Lord when He comes. In His name I pray, Amen.

44 REMEMBERING HIM TILL HE COMES

For I received from the Lord that which I also delivered to you: that the Lord Jesus on the same night in which He was betrayed took bread; and when He had given thanks, He broke it and said, "Take, eat; this is My body which is broken for you; do this in remembrance of Me." In the same manner He also took the cup after supper, saying,

"This cup is the new covenant in My blood. This
do, as often as you drink it, in remembrance of
Me." For as often as you eat this bread and drink
this cup, you proclaim the Lord's death till He
comes. Therefore whoever eats this bread or
drinks this cup of the Lord in an unworthy
manner will be guilty of the body and blood of the
Lord. But let a man examine himself, and so let
him eat of the bread and drink of the cup. For he
who eats and drinks in an unworthy manner eats
and drinks judgment to himself, not discerning
the Lord's body. For this reason many are weak
and sick among you, and many sleep. For if we
would judge ourselves, we would not be judged.

1 CORINTHIANS 11:23-31, NKJV

COMMUNION is a special time for God's people. There is always
something special about commemorating our Lord's death. It is in remembrance of Him that God's people draw closer together than at
any other time. Somehow as we put the bread in our mouth we relive
the memory of Jesus' willingness to give His life so that He could taste
death for all of us. When we put the cup to our lips, we remember that
His blood was willingly shed for our sins. Communion reminds us
that everything we have in this life or the one to come is because of
Him. Differences between Christians seem insignificant at such moments. Here we are reminded that all of us owe everything to Him.

This custom of remembering His sacrifice for our salvation reminds us of the "new covenant." God has given us a new relationship
to Him in which we are no longer required to sacrifice the blood of
animals. Jesus has now paid the ultimate price for our salvation. Each
time we take part in the Lord's Supper, we testify that we have participated in His new covenant. We have entered into an intimate relationship with Him by faith and have called on His name to be saved.
In John 3:3, Jesus calls our salvation experience being "born again."

Physically we can only be born once. Spiritually we can only be "born again" once. But by taking Communion we are remembering our salvation experience and witnessing to others that we have had it.

Paul, in quoting Jesus, said we are to "proclaim [testify to] the Lord's death till He comes." In a vital sense, when we partake of Communion, we are testifying that we believe in the two most important events in the Bible, the first and second comings of Jesus. As Christians we have accepted the historical fact of His first coming. But in Communion we are also testifying that we believe He is coming again. In some sense, it is but an interim ordinance. There will be no need for Communion in heaven to testify to His death until He comes, for He will have already come.

Paul gets to the very heart of the matter in warning, "Let a man examine himself, and so let him eat of the bread and drink of the cup." Further, he warns us that "he who eats and drinks in an unworthy manner eats and drinks judgment to himself, not discerning the Lord's body." That is why when I lead Communion services, I always give members of the congregation a few moments to examine themselves spiritually. I want to give them time to confess all known sin so that they do not partake unworthily of the Lord's Supper and bring judgment upon themselves. God in His marvelous grace has given His church this special service in which we should examine our hearts to see if there is any sin in our lives so we can confess it and go on in communion with Him.

After one Communion service a man asked to talk with me privately. The first thing he said was, "I did not take Communion today because I don't believe I have ever become a Christian. I was raised in a Christian home and have taken Communion many times, but I have never been saved." Then and there we knelt together, and he confessed his sin in the name of Jesus, acknowledging that Christ had died and adding, "Lord Jesus, come into my heart so I can honestly take Communion."

When we stood again, I noticed the Communion service was still in place, so I said, "Let's fulfill that prayer request you just made." So all alone in the empty church the two of us observed the Lord's Supper, and for the first time this man testified to the Lord's death "till He comes."

Today's Prayer

Dear heavenly Father, thank You for sending Your only Son to die on the cross for my sins and the sins of the whole world. Forgive anything I have done that would cause me to be unworthy of Your love and mercy. If I have offended or sinned against any other person, I also want to confess and apologize for this offense. I want nothing to stand between us as I come to the Lord's Table. Here I want to offer a pure witness—a cleansed partaking of grace until He comes. In Your name I pray, Amen.

45 CHRISTIAN RESURRECTION AT HIS COMING

I passed on to you what was most important and what had also been passed on to me—that Christ died for our sins, just as the Scriptures said. He was buried, and he was raised from the dead on the third day, as the Scriptures said. He was seen by Peter and then by the twelve apostles. After that, he was seen by more than five hundred of his followers at one time, most of whom are still alive, though some have died by now. Then he was seen by James and later by all the apostles. Last of all, I saw him, too, long after the others, as though I had been born at the wrong time.

1 Corinthians 15:3-8

> Everyone dies because all of us are related to
> Adam, the first man. But all who are related to
> Christ, the other man, will be given new life. But
> there is an order to this resurrection: Christ was
> raised first; then when Christ comes back, all his
> people will be raised. After that the end will come,
> when he will turn the Kingdom over to God the
> Father, having put down all enemies of every kind.
> For Christ must reign until he humbles all his
> enemies beneath his feet. And the last enemy to
> be destroyed is death.   1 CORINTHIANS 15:22-26

THE EXPECTATION of resurrection is one of the unique teachings of the Judeo-Christian faith. It has long been a common teaching among Jews. It is also taught in the New Testament and in early Christian history. It is one of the reasons the early church did not accept the pagan custom of cremation; they wanted the bodies of their loved ones to be as much intact as possible as they awaited the Resurrection.

How could any of us ever forget Jesus' promise, "Because I live, you will live also" (John 14:19, NKJV)? Because He rose from the dead, we too will one day rise. Our passage for today is based on Paul's most distinct definition of the gospel. In verses 3-8, he reminds us that Christ died for our sins, was buried, and rose again the third day, then was seen alive by many witnesses.

For more than 1,700 years, few skeptics ever questioned the resurrection of Jesus Christ. It was accepted as fact. All great scholars of the faith knew that without this miracle there could be no Christianity. But in the mid-eighteenth century, David Hume, a Scottish philosopher, taught the theory that there is neither a God nor a supernatural realm. If the supernatural does not exist, then obviously Jesus did not perform any miracles. Further, He did not rise from the dead. Subsequent philosophers following Hume also tried to destroy Christianity.

These philosophers were right about one thing: It is impossible to explain Christianity's existence without the bodily resurrection of Jesus. If He had not risen, there would be no Christianity! Further, if there is no resurrection, all twelve apostles died for their belief in vain. And if there is no resurrected Christ, what was it that transformed Saul of Tarsus from being the worst destroyer of the church into its greatest missionary? The world has no real answer for this question, unless it accepts the fact that there is a supernatural God who raised His Son from the dead.

Paul puts it this way: If there is no resurrection, then we "are of all men the most pitiable" (1 Corinthians 15:29, NKJV).

The history of the church Christ died for will culminate in the second coming of Jesus. "Christ was raised first; then when Christ comes back, all his people will be raised" (verse 23). When does this take place? At the end of all things, when Christ delivers the kingdom to the Father, "having put down all enemies of every kind."

Prophetically speaking, everything in heaven and on earth is on hold until Jesus comes again. Although He does not distinguish here between His coming for the church and His coming to set up His kingdom, Paul does point out that when He comes He will triumph over the ever-present specter of death. What confidence is ours! Our own resurrection is in very sure hands. The Creator of the universe, the Giver of life, is the keeper of our destiny.

There is one great agreement that serves to unite all believers. From the time of Adam to the Millennium, all who would be saved have one thing in common: We must all accept God through faith in His Son to gain eternal life. Whether we believe we are to be resurrected at the time of the Rapture or at the end of the Tribulation— whether at the beginning of the Millennium or its conclusion—all resurrections are based on one thing: personal faith in Jesus.

The uniqueness of Christianity lies in its assurance of resurrection. This confident expectation is guaranteed by Jesus Himself, without whose resurrection there would be no Christianity. His being raised is the authenticating event that assures all other resurrections.

TODAY'S PRAYER

Dear Lord, I thank You for the elaborate plan You had of sending Your Son, Jesus, to purchase my salvation. I thank You that You raised Jesus from the dead. This gives me confidence that You will also raise us from the dead when Christ comes again. Thank You for all those who shared their faith with me in times past. But in case I have never called on You before, let me do so in the name of Jesus. Forgive my sin and save my soul. I want to be certain I am among "those who are Christ's at His coming" (1 Corinthians 15:23, NKJV). In His name I pray, Amen.

46 THE MYSTERY OF THE RAPTURE

Now this I say, brethren, that flesh and blood cannot inherit the kingdom of God; nor does corruption inherit incorruption. Behold, I tell you a mystery: We shall not all sleep, but we shall all be changed—in a moment, in the twinkling of an eye, at the last trumpet. For the trumpet will sound, and the dead will be raised incorruptible, and we shall be changed. For this corruptible must put on incorruption, and this mortal must put on immortality. So when this corruptible has put on incorruption, and this mortal has put on immortality, then shall be brought to pass the saying that is written: "Death is swallowed up in victory. O Death, where is your sting? O Hades, where is your victory?" The sting of death is sin, and the strength of sin is the law. But thanks be to

God, who gives us the victory through our Lord
Jesus Christ. Therefore, my beloved brethren, be
steadfast, immovable, always abounding in the
work of the Lord, knowing that your labor is not in
vain in the Lord.   1 CORINTHIANS 15:50-58, NKJV

THE RAPTURE of the church is the next great event on the prophetic calendar of God. We have already seen the details of that rapture in 1 Thessalonians 4:13-18. As the Rapture begins, all the dead
members of the body of Christ for the past two thousand years will be
resurrected to meet the living saints in the clouds. This exciting and
distinct event will be followed by the Tribulation and His Glorious
Appearing as He sets up His kingdom.

This text is the second most definitive passage in Scripture on the
mystery of the Rapture. We should keep in mind that the word "mystery" in the Bible does not signify something we cannot understand.
It means it is a concept that cannot be understood apart from the Bible. But the Word of God never sets out to baffle its readers. Even the
Rapture is fully explained in the Word.

It is fitting that Paul mentions the Rapture here in his discussion
of the Resurrection. Indeed the Rapture is one kind of resurrection—
the resurrection of the entire church in a single moment. Most Christians at the time of the Rapture will be dead and in their graves. Paul
says they are asleep. Their souls and spirits are with the Lord. Only
the elements of their "corruptible" bodies are still in the grave. Peter's
and Paul's bodies have been in the grave now more than nineteen
hundred years. But one of these days "the last trumpet" will sound
for the church. Then "the dead will be raised incorruptible, and we
shall be changed." The bodies of these dead apostles, like the bodies
of millions of other saints, will be instantly made "incorruptible"
(that is, like Christ's glorified body). Then their heavenly souls and
spirits will rejoin their earthly bodies as they rise out of the grave.

The believers living at that time are the "we" of verse 51. This refers to all the Christians who are alive when Christ shouts and the trumpet sounds. Then "we who are still alive" (1 Thessalonians 4:17)—if we are alive when it happens—will have our corruptible earthly bodies made fit for heaven.

Bill Bright suggests that half the people who have ever lived are now alive and on the earth. If this is so, we can assume that there have been a total of twelve billion people who have ever lived on Earth. Some missiologists estimate that there are more than half a billion "born again" people who currently live on Earth (about 10 percent) and are ready for the Lord's return. If these figures are true, then it is reasonable to assume that about half a billion Christians from throughout the church age are in their graves awaiting the Day of the Lord. Hopefully, then, there are approximately one billion people who will be involved in the Rapture.

One thing is certain, when the Rapture occurs, the world will know we are missing. We can only hope that many will, in that moment, turn to Christ. Having missed the Rapture, they will have to go through the awful days of the Tribulation. But even that kind of trial is better than the alternative of being cast alive into the lake of fire.

This rapture of believers will not be the first time someone has been "snatched up." Enoch, a pre-Flood prophet according to the book of Jude, was such a godly man, he prophesied the second coming of Christ. Genesis 5:24 tells us that after walking with God for three hundred years, "suddenly, he disappeared because God took him." Enoch was instantly made "incorruptible" and taken up to heaven with God.

Another example of such an individual rapture is found in 2 Kings 2:11, where the godly prophet Elijah was taken up into heaven by a whirlwind. These are the only two men in Scripture who escaped death by being raptured. So although the rapture of the church is a mystery, it does have precedent in Enoch and Elijah.

Paul leaves a final word about the Rapture, saying, "Therefore, my beloved brethren, be steadfast, immovable, always abounding in the work of the Lord, knowing that your labor is not in vain in the Lord."

Since the Rapture is going to take place suddenly and unexpectedly, there will be no opportunity to get ready for it. Therefore, I have two questions for you: First, what two things *do you not want* Jesus to find you doing when He comes? And second, what two things *do you want* Him to find you doing?

TODAY'S PRAYER

Dear heavenly Father, thank You for making the mystery of Jesus' coming to rapture His church so clear. I am truly privileged to be a part of it! Thank You for those who first told me I needed the Savior. Please make me sensitive to the spiritual needs of those around me and help me to keep sharing my faith with others so they, too, will be included in the Rapture. Use my lips to testify to Your grace every hour that I live and await Your coming. In Jesus' name I pray, Amen.

47 DON'T LOSE HEART—JESUS IS COMING!

And so, since God in his mercy has given us this wonderful ministry, we never give up. We reject all shameful and underhanded methods. We do not try to trick anyone, and we do not distort the word of God. We tell the truth before God, and all who are honest know that.   2 CORINTHIANS 4:1-2

We know that the same God who raised our Lord Jesus will also raise us with Jesus and present us to himself along with you. All of these things are for your benefit. And as God's grace brings more and more people to Christ, there will be great thanksgiving, and God will receive more and more glory. That is why we never give up. Though our bodies are dying, our spirits are being renewed every day. For our present troubles are quite small and won't last very long. Yet they produce for us an immeasurably great glory that will last forever! So we don't look at the troubles we can see right now; rather, we look forward to what we have not yet seen. For the troubles we see will soon be over, but the joys to come will last forever.

2 CORINTHIANS 4:14-18

DISCOURAGEMENT is one of the principal tools Satan uses to defeat Christians. If we allow him to take our eyes off Jesus and His coming, Satan can render us useless to God. He knows that discouragement opens the door to self-pity, which can plunge anyone into deep depression and nullify our witness for Christ.

Paul here challenges us not to give up. In fact, in both verse 1 and verse 16 he says the same thing: "Never give up." Then he says the problems of this world are "quite small and won't last very long." He advises us not to let the temporary cares and afflictions of this life be magnified out of proportion. They must never dominate our thinking, or they will cause us to lose heart.

Have you noticed how watching the news or reading the paper can build an odd negativity into life? Probably the worst thing we can do is to watch the news just before going to bed. The late-night news is an endless recitation of muggings, murder, rape, and mayhem. This forces the viewer to go to bed nightly in a mind-set of gloom, doom, and despair.

How much better it would be to read the second-coming promises of God at bedtime. Then we could project on the screen of our mind the biblical realities of the Rapture. The daily joy of Christ produces an "exceeding and eternal weight of glory" (2 Corinthians 4:17, NKJV). Remembering nightly that the Lord Jesus will also raise us up with Him can produce a joyous resurrection-rapture as a habit of life.

Al and Sue Graham are Wycliffe missionaries who have spent forty years in the jungles of Brazil translating the Scriptures for tribespeople who originally didn't want them and resisted their entrance to the village. But today, thousands of those people are believers and are awaiting the coming of Jesus along with the rest of us. In fact, only eternity will reveal how many former unbelievers now know Jesus as their Lord and Savior because the Grahams were willing to trade the good life in America for the rigors of life in the bush.

Did they ever become discouraged? Of course! Did they ever miss their parents or their children, whom they had to send to boarding school? Of course! But they renewed themselves daily in the promise of His coming. During all their years in the bush there hung before them the constant reminder that Jesus was going to come.

Jim Elliot, one of the five missionaries who gave their lives to see an entire tribe of Auca Indians in Ecuador come to Jesus, left behind this classic statement: *He is no fool who gives what he cannot keep to gain what he cannot lose.* When Jesus comes, He will set all things straight. He will reward those who have given their lives to share the gospel with others, and that reward will be eternal.

My family and I have been lifetime football fans. For a while I had the privilege of teaching a Bible study for the San Diego Chargers. In one game against Kansas City, they had been behind for the entire game. John Hadel was the quarterback and Lance Allworth was his wide receiver. It was a high-scoring game, but late in the game the Chargers were down by three points. On the last play of the game, John threw a long pass into the end zone and Lance leaped four feet into the air to catch it, winning for the Chargers in the last two seconds of the game.

I have often compared the second coming of Jesus to that football game. Historically, Christians have seemed defeated most of the time during the two thousand years that have elapsed since our Lord ascended to heaven. Believers have suffered persecution, ridicule, rejection, martyrdom, and even crucifixion. It sometimes looks as though we will never catch up and win the game. But don't lose heart; keep looking unto Jesus. He is coming! We will win!

TODAY'S PRAYER

Dear heavenly Father, thank You for the blessed hope of Jesus' coming. It is a constant reminder that, as the song "Turn Your Eyes Upon Jesus" says, one day the things of this earth will "grow strangely dim, in the light of [Your] glory and grace." I look forward to that day and pray that I will not let the burdens of this earth drag me down to discouragement. In Jesus' name I pray, Amen.

48 CONFIDENT IN THE RAPTURE

God himself has prepared us for this, and as a guarantee he has given us his Holy Spirit. So we are always confident, even though we know that as long as we live in these bodies we are not at home with the Lord. That is why we live by believing and not by seeing. Yes, we are fully confident, and we would rather be away from these bodies, for then we will be at home with the Lord. So our aim is to please him always, whether we are here in this body or away from this body.

2 CORINTHIANS 5:5-9

FOR SEVERAL years now I have been trying to convince my pastor friends that there is no more motivational teaching in the Bible than the second coming of Jesus. It makes us more sensitive to living holy lives in an unholy age. Anticipating Jesus' coming also increases our evangelistic fervor and missionary zeal.

Paul was very practical in pointing out one other benefit of preaching the Lord's return. It gives us, Christ's church, a confidence that the next life will definitely be better than the one we are now living. Twice Paul uses the expression "we are confident" and then states that our confidence is based on faith.

In 2 Corinthians 4, the apostle gives us a long list of all the persecutions he had gone through for the gospel's sake. Then in 2 Corinthians 5:2 he writes, "We grow weary in our present bodies, and we long for the day when we will put on our heavenly bodies like new clothing." How was Paul so sure he would someday have a new resurrected body? "God," he said, "has given us the Spirit in our hearts as a guarantee" (2 Corinthians 1:22, NKJV). Paul knew he was a Christian by the powerful, indwelling Holy Spirit who daily transformed his life and motivations. Yet his body ached with the pain of all he had endured. The pain reminded him that "as long as we live in these bodies we are not at home with the Lord" (verse 6). Then in verse 8 he states, "We would rather be away from these bodies, for then we will be at home with the Lord." Our old body (or perhaps in your case, your young body) will be replaced by a new resurrected body when our Lord comes.

This confidence was made real to me while I was on a missionary tour of India. I had been invited to preach at Katarah, a leper colony. I shall remember forever an old blind man who said, "Leprosy was the best thing that ever happened to me. Because of my leprosy I lost my sight. Because of my blindness I was brought here to Katarah. Here I learned about Jesus. Now I know that the first person I will ever see will be my Savior when He comes."

Now that old man is "asleep" in Jesus. In the aged earth of India his body lies awaiting that wonderful shout from heaven. Then he will be resurrected in a brand-new eternal body with 20/20 vision and so he will "remain with [the Lord] forever" (1 Thessalonians 4:17).

Do you have that same confidence? If you do, Paul has one final challenge for you: "Please him always."

Today's Prayer

Dear Lord, thank You for the confidence I have in Christ that one day this temporary body will be replaced by a perfect eternal body. Help me to live every day desiring to please You. Forgive the wasted years when I lived to please myself. Help me to consider each new day as if it were about to end in heaven. In Jesus' name I pray, Amen.

49 CONSTRAINED BY LOVE AND JUDGMENT

For we must all appear before the judgment seat of Christ, that each one may receive the things done in the body, according to what he has done, whether good or bad. Knowing, therefore, the terror of the Lord, we persuade men; but we are well known to God, and I also trust are well known in your consciences.　2 Corinthians 5:10-11, NKJV

Whatever we do, it is because Christ's love controls us. Since we believe that Christ died for everyone, we also believe that we have all died to the old life we used to live. He died for everyone so that those who receive his new life will no longer live to please themselves. Instead, they will live to please Christ, who died and was raised for them.
2 Corinthians 5:14-15

> We are Christ's ambassadors, and God is using us
> to speak to you. We urge you, as though Christ
> himself were here pleading with you, "Be recon-
> ciled to God!" For God made Christ, who never
> sinned, to be the offering for our sin, so that we
> could be made right with God through Christ.
>
> 2 CORINTHIANS 5:20-21

THE APOSTLE Paul must have been the most motivated Christian in the first century. In addition to being the premier missionary-church builder, he was the best of personal soul-winners. As a writer, he left behind thirteen epistles that have helped to change the world.

What motivated him? Actually there were many things. But the three motivators of his life are found in this passage. Let's consider them one at a time.

The first motivation of the apostle was the judgment seat of Christ. We will all face this judgment when Jesus comes to rapture His church (verse 10). "For we must all appear before the judgment seat of Christ." Our appearance at this heavenly court will not be for our salvation. This is a settled matter for the redeemed. Still, all Christians from Pentecost to the Rapture will face it. The grounds for this judgment will be the things we have done since our salvation. The Greek text here does not suggest that this will be a judgment of our sin. It will be an evaluation of our deeds. We will have to answer whether our works were done for good motives or selfish ones. Christ will reward us for those things we have done out of a pure heart. He is no fool who invests both his life and assets in the eternal work of Christ.

The second motivator of the apostle was the love of Christ. "Whatever we do, it is because Christ's love controls us" (or challenges or drives us—verse 14). Who can read the account of the apostle Paul in Acts 13–28 and not realize that he supremely loved the Christ he once met on the Damascus road? Think of how he was stoned and left for dead at Lystra by the enemies of Christ. Even after that, the love of Christ motivated him to get up and walk to the next city to preach.

Third, he was motivated by the "terror of the Lord." This motivation is clear in verse 11: "Knowing, therefore, the terror of the Lord, we persuade men." In this day of "easy believism," we have lost respect for the awesomeness of God. We concentrate too much on the love and mercy of God, giving some the impression that God is but a doting old grandfather, overlooking our carnality and indifference. Not so! The same Bible that teaches us the love of God revealed in Christ also teaches us that God is going to judge sinners for their wickedness and rebellion, their apathy and negligence.

Paul always held God in holy awe and reverence. This awe amounted to feelings of fear that he would drop his cup of responsibility and disappoint his Father in heaven. Thus he wrote, "Knowing, therefore, the terror of the Lord, we persuade men." He knew that when Jesus comes again to this earth to set up His kingdom, He will judge all those who have rejected Him. We can understand His judging those who openly rebelled and blasphemed Him, but we tend to overlook those who ignore Him—those who sometimes go to church and who appear to hold God in respect. Still, they behave as though they are not in need of His salvation and guidance. As one man told me, "I have never really done anything worthy of being thrown into an eternal hell." He was as most saw him a nice man, a good husband, and a patriotic citizen. His sin was that he considered himself above repentance. He was in effect saying, "For me Jesus' death on the cross was really unnecessary."

Knowing the "terror of the Lord," Paul persuaded men. This call to persuasion is our business, too. Paul says in verse 20, "We are Christ's ambassadors, and God is using us to speak to you. We urge you, as though Christ himself were here pleading with you, 'Be reconciled to God!' "

Every time we share our faith with others, we urge them to "be reconciled to God." The only way they can do this is to receive Him "who never sinned," who became sin for them that they might be made right with God through Christ. As "Christ's ambassadors," we know the terror of the Lord, the constraint of the love of Christ, and the necessity of facing the judgment seat of Christ. Because of all these compulsions, we must share our faith with others. Like the ambassadors of any foreign power, our message is not our own and may be rejected. Still, our responsibility is to convey the message regardless of its reception.

I wish I could say that sharing Christ was easy, but it is not true. Recently I tried to share Christ with a man on an airplane. The man then spent the next thirty minutes ridiculing my faith. His overbearing personality and his loud voice left me humiliated. Still, I did not take his ridicule personally. He wasn't really mad at me. He hated God, whose ambassador I am.

TODAY'S PRAYER

Dear Lord, give me a passion like the apostle Paul to serve whenever I can as Your ambassador. Give me Paul's motivation to let the world know that Jesus is coming soon. More than anything, I want to bring others into the kingdom with me. Help my desire to produce fruit for the kingdom. In Jesus' name I pray, Amen.

50 WHEN ALL WORSHIP JESUS!

Because of this, God raised him up to the heights of heaven and gave him a name that is above every other name, so that at the name of Jesus every knee will bow, in heaven and on earth and under the earth, and every tongue will confess that Jesus Christ is Lord, to the glory of God the Father.   PHILIPPIANS 2:9-11

MANY of the passages that deal with the fulfillment of prophecy are used to encourage holy living in an unholy age. Here we have one of the most sublime exaltations of Jesus to be found in the Scriptures.

It should be remembered that whenever Isaiah mentions the coming of Jesus, Christ is seen as the suffering servant. The second-coming texts by contrast present Christ as coming in power and great glory. The book of Revelation always presents Jesus as coming in power and glory as the object of transmillennial obedience and worship.

Like most Christians, I have read and reread the Gospels, particularly the Gospel of John. But in these narrations of Jesus' first coming, our Lord is always presented as the suffering Savior who left His first estate in heaven. There, in the presence of God, He was a monarch of power above all the angels in rank. He left His throne to take on human form. In this lower state, He "tasted death for every man" (Hebrews 2:9, KJV), "even the death of the cross" (Philippians 2:8, NKJV).

Paul uses Christ's humility to encourage Christians everywhere not to think more highly of themselves than they ought. But the reason I love Revelation so much is that it always presents Jesus as He now is and will forever be: the object of all adoration and worship.

Paul makes this clear in our text when he teaches that "at the name of Jesus every knee will bow, in heaven and on earth and under the earth, and every tongue will confess that Jesus Christ is Lord, to the glory of God the Father."

This event is not the same for all. For Christians this bowing will be at the judgment seat of Christ (Romans 14:10). For the unsaved, the bowing will come at the end of the millennial kingdom when the unsaved stand before God in the Great White Throne Judgment (Revelation 20:1-11).

You might wonder why God will force all humankind to confess with their mouths while kneeling. This will complete a universal acknowledgment that even though most refused to submit to Him while on this earth, they will do so on the Day of judgment. Unfortunately their confession will then be too late. They will be cast into the lake of fire, which is called "the second death" (Revelation 20:14). That means that all atheists and skeptics and blasphemers will at last admit their eternal mistake. But it isn't just the blatant atheists and ridiculers of Jesus who will be judged. All who never worshiped Him will also meet this fate.

During my two-year experience in the air force, the blasphemous use of Jesus' name became most odious to me. Even to this day I cannot resist correcting those who curse in His name. I recently heard a man on an airplane take God's name in vain. I said to him, "Did you know that the Bible teaches that someday you will bend your knee before Jesus and confess His name as Lord before God?"

"Where does it say that?" he asked.

So I showed him this text.

"It's just a habit," he said. "I don't mean anything by it." That was untrue, of course. At the very least, he had no respect for the Lord Jesus Christ. This lack of respect will land him in big trouble on Judgment Day. There he must give an account of "every idle word" that has ever come out of his mouth (Matthew 12:36). "Out of the abundance of the heart the mouth speaks" (Matthew 12:34, NKJV).

When I share the gospel, I try to point out that on Judgment Day everyone will bend his or her knee before Jesus, who sits on the throne of God (John 5:22). On that day "every tongue will confess that Jesus Christ is Lord" (Philippians 2:11). That is the inevitable truth of the Bible! Better to confess now than then, for doing so now will change your eternal destiny.

TODAY'S PRAYER
Dear heavenly Father, I willingly confess before You that Jesus, Your Son, is my Lord and Savior. Forgive me for any time

that I have used His name improperly. I love Him and respect
Him above all others. Like Thomas I can say, He is "my Lord and
my God!" (John 20:28). Help me to share my faith with others so
that all who need to bend their knees and confess with their
mouths will do it now and avoid having to do it in eternity. In
Jesus' name I pray, Amen.

51 STANDING FAST IN YOUR HEAVENLY CITIZENSHIP

For our citizenship is in heaven, from which we also
eagerly wait for the Savior, the Lord Jesus Christ,
who will transform our lowly body that it may be
conformed to His glorious body, according to the
working by which He is able even to subdue all
things to Himself. Therefore, my beloved and
longed-for brethren, my joy and crown, so stand
fast in the Lord, beloved. PHILIPPIANS 3:20–4:1, NKJV

TO RETURN from travel abroad is to appreciate being an American.
The long line at the U.S. Immigration window marked "foreigners"
designates all those who do not have a U.S. passport. The shorter,
fast-moving line is labeled "U.S. Citizens Only." We have only to
show our blue-gray passport, gilded with the U.S. coat of arms, and
we are welcomed home. Our passports are usually treated with respect in other countries as well. Most people worldwide sense that it
is a privilege to be an American.

We Christians are citizens of heaven. Our new-birth status
should enable us to "stand fast in the Lord," as kingdom citizens with
passport status. Our heavenly citizenship entitles us to passage into
the Father's house. Then our lowly bodies will be transformed and
"conformed to His glorious body."

The coming resurrection of our bodies is the final immigration glory of kingdom citizens. It just hasn't taken place yet. But the very prophecy should open to us all the promises of God: the Rapture, the Resurrection, the judgment seat of Christ, the seven-year visit to the Father's house, the marriage of the Lamb, the marriage supper of the Lamb, returning with Christ in His Glorious Appearing, ruling and reigning with Him for a thousand years, and finally eternity in heaven.

Several years ago, my sixteen-year-old grandson and I hiked up to prayer rock at Hume Lake Christian Camp. I still have a picture of him silhouetted against the beautiful valley and mountains below. We worshiped our Lord up there, just the two of us. Then I asked him what he thought his future might be.

"I don't know," he said, "but I sure hope it is exciting."

Neither of us could know at that moment that the exciting future he hoped for would include a devastating motorcycle ride. That ride resulted in his cartwheeling through the air at sixty-five miles per hour. When he landed, three vertebrae in his neck had been broken. Fortunately, God had a registered nurse at the scene who would not let anyone move him until he could be flown to a hospital. There he lay in traction for four months while he healed. Today he is 98 percent recovered! A true miracle! Thanks be unto God!

None of us know what awaits us on this earth. But the moment that Christ shouts from heaven and raptures us up to His Father's house, we will embark on a most exciting journey. Our final destination is what led Paul to quote Isaiah, saying, "Eye has not seen, nor ear heard, nor have entered into the heart of man the things which God has prepared for those who love Him" (1 Corinthians 2:9, NKJV).

The future for the citizen of heaven is truly beyond our comprehension. It is little wonder that Paul challenges Christians from every age to "stand fast in the Lord." No matter what temptations, trials, or setbacks we face, we are to "stand fast in the Lord." We must love and study the Word of God to hone our upward perspective. Too few churches today teach the marvelous prophetic truths that reveal the wonderful things God has planned for His children. Reading God's Word regularly will keep fresh in our minds God's hope and expectation for the future.

Such positive thoughts will keep us standing fast in the Lord without apology or equivocation. Someday, then, we will see the fulfillment of God's incredible promises. The most exciting and glorious days of our lives are just ahead. Study and anticipate. Contemplate the glory. End every prayer with, "Even so, come quickly, Lord Jesus."

TODAY'S PRAYER

Dear heavenly Father, thank You for making known to me all the blessings You have planned for my future. I am the first to admit that I do not deserve these blessings, but I thank You that they were part of the great gift of Your salvation. Help me to stand for the faith of Jesus without apology, compromise, or grumbling. Fill me with Your Holy Spirit so that I can share my faith with all who need to become citizens of heaven. In His name I pray, Amen.

52 THE SECOND-COMING VICTORY

So you see, just as death came into the world through a man, Adam, now the resurrection from the dead has begun through another man, Christ. Everyone dies because all of us are related to Adam, the first man. But all who are related to Christ, the other man, will be given new life. But there is an order to this resurrection: Christ was raised first; then when Christ comes back, all his people will be raised. After that the end will come, when he will turn the Kingdom over to God the Father, having put down all enemies of every kind. For Christ must reign until he humbles all his enemies beneath his feet. And the last enemy to be destroyed is death.   1 Corinthians 15:21-26

Foolish one, what you sow is not made alive unless it dies. And what you sow, you do not sow that body that shall be, but mere grain—perhaps wheat or some other grain. But God gives it a body as He pleases, and to each seed its own body. All flesh is not the same flesh, but there is one kind of flesh of men, another flesh of animals, another of fish, and another of birds. There are also celestial bodies and terrestrial bodies; but the glory of the celestial is one, and the glory of the terrestrial is another. There is one glory of the sun, another glory of the moon, and another glory of the stars; for one star differs from another star in glory. So also is the resurrection of the dead. The body is sown in corruption, it is raised in incorruption. It is sown in dishonor, it is raised in glory. It is sown in weakness, it is raised in power. It is sown a natural body, it is raised a spiritual body. There is a natural body, and there is a spiritual body.
1 Corinthians 15:36-44, NKJV

So when this corruptible has put on incorruption, and this mortal has put on immortality, then shall be brought to pass the saying that is written: "Death is swallowed up in victory. O Death, where is your sting? O Hades, where is your victory?" The sting of death is sin, and the strength of sin is the law. But thanks be to God, who gives us the victory through our Lord Jesus Christ. Therefore, my beloved brethren, be steadfast, immovable, always abounding in the work of the Lord, knowing that your labor is not in vain in the Lord.   1 Corinthians 15:54-58, NKJV

A SKEPTIC once asked me, "How is a Christian sailor buried at sea going to be resurrected?" Before I could answer he jeeringly added, "Suppose his body is eaten by fish, which in turn is caught by fishermen and brought to a cannery where it is processed, then eaten by humans and naturally eliminated? How will God ever resurrect that sailor's body?"

Like most skeptics, his concept of God was too small! While the ways of God are "past finding out" (Romans 11:33, NKJV), we do have some insights on how such a resurrection might take place. Consider the many martyrs whose bones and flesh were destroyed by fire and the elements of their bodies seemingly lost to the smoke. The Resurrection includes even those whose bodies, buried centuries ago, have decomposed. It includes those whose bodies have been displaced by massive digging equipment as well as those lost in other radical forms of decomposition.

God is well able to take care of such things. But for those who must have some scientific explanation, let us remember this: matter is neither created nor destroyed. While a body may turn to dust or ashes, the elements of that person will never leave the universe. It would be a simple thing for God, who created the entire universe in the first place, to call together the elements of all the people who have ever lived, in a new resurrected form. Millions of Christians are now dead, and only an infinite, omnipotent God could keep track of all their elements and reassemble them on Resurrection Day. If He could speak a word and call this world with all its intricate detail into existence, He can certainly bring us back to life in a new and improved form.

The apostle Paul refers to our present "corruptible" body being "changed—in a moment, in the twinkling of an eye, . . . and the dead [being] raised incorruptible," so that we shall all be changed (1 Corinthians 15:51-52, NKJV). On the day of resurrection, our degenerating bodies with all their elements will be transformed in a split second of time from every corner of the earth where they may have been scattered.

Though the complexity of death will always trouble us as humans, in this passage it is considered just a "sting." It hurts for a time to lay our loved ones to rest, but if they are Christians it is never an eternal good-bye. Dying is a temporary parting that will be replaced when death, our last enemy, is destroyed. And when will that take place? At Christ's coming!

Before Christ comes to set up His kingdom, He will rapture His church. Since the church has been growing over these past two thousand years of history, multiplied millions of followers have been resting in their graves while their souls and spirits are with the Lord. That will be changed instantly on resurrection day when again their previous personhoods will be reestablished in new, living, glorified bodies, made like Christ's body after He rose from the grave. "So shall we ever be with the Lord," said Paul in 1 Thessalonians 4:17 (KJV), recalling our victory through Jesus Christ!

This concept of resurrection gives us a bit of an appreciation for all that Jesus did on the cross. It was there He paid the debt for our sin, taking our judgment on Himself in order to give us eternal life.

To all God's children Paul says one more time, "Therefore, my beloved brethren, be steadfast, immovable, always abounding in the work of the Lord, knowing that your labor is not in vain in the Lord."

One cold winter day, a carpenter in our first pastorate in Minneapolis was putting up wallboard in the gymnasium. He and I were the only people in the church. From the warm office where I sat, I could hear him pounding at his work. Finally I went down to talk to him and found him hammering while wearing wool gloves. When I asked why he was working on such a cold day, he said, "Pastor, I can't teach a Sunday school class, but I can build rooms where someone else can do it. I am working here to invest in something eternal." That was almost forty-five years ago. That workman has been in heaven for many years now, but his works do follow him. Last year I visited that church building and stopped in that same Sunday school room. There were at least seventy junior-aged boys and girls learning about Jesus. I am confident my carpenter friend did not labor in vain.

Today's Prayer

Dear heavenly Father, thank You not only for saving me but also for giving me an opportunity to invest my life in something eternal. Help me to use every opportunity to make my life count eternally. I want to live significantly, particularly in view of the fact that Jesus is coming soon. In His name I pray, Amen.

53 SIGNS OF THE LATTER TIMES

Now the Holy Spirit tells us clearly that in the last times some will turn away from what we believe; they will follow lying spirits and teachings that come from demons. These teachers are hypocrites and liars. They pretend to be religious, but their consciences are dead. They will say it is wrong to be married and wrong to eat certain foods. But God created those foods to be eaten with thanksgiving by people who know and believe the truth. Since everything God created is good, we should not reject any of it. We may receive it gladly, with thankful hearts. For we know it is made holy by the word of God and prayer. If you explain this to the brothers and sisters, you will be doing your duty as a worthy servant of Christ Jesus, one who is fed by the message of faith and the true teaching you have followed. Do not waste time arguing over godless ideas and old wives'

> tales. Spend your time and energy in training
> yourself for spiritual fitness. Physical exercise has
> some value, but spiritual exercise is much more
> important, for it promises a reward in both this
> life and the next. This is true, and everyone should
> accept it.   1 TIMOTHY 4:1-9

ON A RARE occasion my wife gets me to go to a shopping mall. On one such occasion, we had not been in the mall long when a good-looking young man was suddenly in my face trying to sell me a religious magazine. The first thing I spotted about him was the glassy, almost hypnotic glaze of his eyes. Then I noticed he was wearing a name tag identifying him as a member of a cult. I knew enough about his particular cult to know that its founder claims to be the Messiah. I said to the young man, "It is impossible for your founder to be the Messiah, because Jesus Christ is the only Messiah." When he tried to protest, I quoted Scriptures. "I am the way, the truth, and the life. No one can come to the Father except through me" (John 14:6). My wife jumped into the conversation, saying, "Your founder did not die for your sins; he cannot save you. Only Jesus can do that." The young man's eyes suddenly filled with tears. He confessed that he had been raised as a Christian and soon admitted to being grossly deceived.

The New Testament warned this deception would be common in the latter times. The church has always attracted false teachers, false prophets, and imitators of Christ. But there seems to be an increase in those who "follow lying spirits and teachings that come from demons." To live in a fallen spirit world is to ignore the real world. Long ago, the cult of theosophy got its direct revelation through "channelers" from the spirit world. Alice Bailey, the writer of most of their doctrines, admitted she was used by the spirit world to communicate to our world. Brigham Young and many others too numerous to mention claimed to have inspiration from otherworldly sources. Jesus said, "When the Spirit of truth comes, he will guide you into all truth" (John 16:13). It is imperative today to test all teachers, particularly teachers claiming to have new truth, by the Word of God. When the Holy Spirit instructs us on anything, that instruction will agree with the Bible which He also inspired. God is not the author of confusion! He will not contradict His Word.

Dr. Harry Ironsides, one of my heroes in the battle for truth, used to say, "Beware of any teaching that is new, for it likely is not true." Our message does not change; it is the message "which was once for all delivered to the saints" (Jude 1:3, NKJV).

A lady going out of church one Sunday said to me, "You preach a message that is four hundred years old! I'll never come back to this church!" I said, "No, my dear, my message is over nineteen hundred years old. It is the same message that Jesus, Paul, and Peter taught." Somehow she was not impressed, but such individuals are more easily deceived because they more easily give ear to the new truth of demons and deceivers.

In the context of this passage, we must remember that false teachers in Paul's time often forbade marriage or omitted it and advocated free sex or polygamy instead of the marriage relationship God ordained. Similarly, cults often gather around sexual permissiveness. They also promote legalisms, abstaining from certain foods as though what a person puts into the physical body is more important than what is put into the eternal soul.

The apostle gives us the same challenge we have seen many times in our study of the second-coming passages: "training yourself for spiritual fitness." Wherever we look in the Scripture, we find ourselves challenged to holy living in the light of Jesus' coming. If there are things in your life that are displeasing to God, surrender them at once and begin to live holy in this unholy age. Don't lower the standards of morality and decency. Live for this truth: *Jesus is coming*, and it may be very soon.

Dear heavenly Father, thank You for Your wonderful plan for my life. I want to live a holy life pleasing to You. Help me to seek those things that are above, where Christ sits on His throne. Help me to realize that the decisions I make in this life I will be responsible for in the life to come. Help me to distinguish error from truth that I may rightly discern the word of truth from the error of false messiahs that seem to be ever increasing. In Jesus' name I pray, Amen.

54 NINEFOLD HOLINESS AT HIS APPEARING

Yet true religion with contentment is great wealth. After all, we didn't bring anything with us when we came into the world, and we certainly cannot carry anything with us when we die. So if we have enough food and clothing, let us be content. But people who long to be rich fall into temptation and are trapped by many foolish and harmful desires that plunge them into ruin and destruction. For the love of money is at the root of all kinds of evil. And some people, craving money, have wandered from the faith and pierced themselves with many sorrows. But you, Timothy, belong to God; so run from all these evil things, and follow what is right and good. Pursue a godly life, along with faith, love, perseverance, and gentleness. Fight the good fight for what we believe. Hold tightly to the eternal life that God has given you, which you have confessed so well before many witnesses. And I command you before God, who gives life to all, and before Christ Jesus, who gave a good testimony before Pontius Pilate, that you obey his commands with all purity. Then no one can find fault with you from now until our Lord Jesus Christ returns. For at the right time Christ will be revealed from heaven by the blessed and only almighty God, the King of kings and Lord of lords. He alone can never die, and he lives in light so brilliant that no human can approach him. No one has ever seen him, nor ever will. To him be honor and power forever. Amen.

1 TIMOTHY 6:6-16

IN A single afternoon recently I counseled five troubled people, each in one-hour interviews. I felt their various problems deeply and was soul-weary from the weight of all they carried. My first counselee for the afternoon was ruining his life through hostility and overaggression. Another was depressed. Another was bound up in immorality; one was dominated by fear. But one thing they all had in common was that each of them believed their problems were hopeless. Fortunately, the Holy Spirit is available to all such troubled saints.

Although it is tempting to examine the prophetic significance of this passage, I would rather expose the great practical instruction it contains. This passage looks at the fruit of the Spirit and commands all troubled people—like the "hopeless" souls I counseled—to have victory in *nine* distinct areas of life.

1. God said that we are to be content with what we have and *flee greediness* (verses 6-10). The love of money inevitably leads to greed, which destroys our lives and our testimonies and fails to prepare us to meet our Lord at His coming.
2. The Spirit would have us *follow what is right and good* (verse 11). This simply means that we are to crave right living. We should

be good citizens, pay our taxes, tell the truth, and live with integrity.

3. We are to *pursue a godly life.* This is a higher step in our spiritual maturity. We are to obey God in all things, including the purity of our minds and holy living.

4. We are also to *pursue faith.* Into every life comes some testing. God means it for our good. At times He allows these trials to strengthen our endurance. James 1:2 says, "Whenever trouble comes your way, let it be an opportunity for joy." Complaining about our woes only makes matters worse.

5. We are to *pursue love.* Love comes easy for some people, but most of us have to work at it. We all want others to love us. And while we are willing to love those who are easy to love, God wants us to learn to love the unlovely. Fortunately, love comes from God, so when you find anyone who is difficult to love, ask God for a little help. Wisely the Bible counsels us that "love covers a multitude of sins" (1 Peter 4:8). So when you truly love someone, you will no longer see his or her flaws.

6. God demands that his children *persevere.* Some of us need this challenge more than others. One of my favorite scriptural challenges is this: "Ye have need of patience" (Hebrews 10:36, KJV). I admire those who are patient by nature, probably because the virtue comes harder for me. My grandmother used to say that patience was next to godliness. It could well be true since God is its source.

7. The Spirit wants his children to *pursue gentleness.* Gentleness comes as the result of having a meek spirit. Have you noticed how easily proud people run over others? Not so with the gentle. Seek gentleness, therefore, and ask God to give you a humble spirit.

8. God calls each of us to *fight the good fight for what we believe.* Know your Bible well enough that you can defend your faith.

This is essential in a day when many false teachers are rising. More than ever we need to pray for doctrinal boldness in our wishy-washy culture.

9. We are to *hold tightly to the eternal life that God has given us.* The amazing thing about studying the Bible is that the more you know it, the more you love and trust its author. The more you trust its author, the more you "hold tightly to . . . eternal life."

A lady on a plane recently said to me, "Oh, I was saved once, but I don't know if I still am." As I questioned her, I learned that she rarely attended church, never read the Bible, and prayed only when she was in trouble. There are many people who claim to love Jesus and have accepted Him, but He is not real to them. You will never really know God or have the assurance that you have laid "hold tightly to . . . eternal life" unless the Bible is a regular part of your life.

Actually, what Paul is telling Timothy here is the same thing he told the Galatians (in 5:16-24). Christians should walk under the control of the Spirit and display these nine fruits of the Spirit. I learned through years in the counseling room that each of these nine fruits of the Spirit is more than adequate for any of our human weaknesses. Whatever your worst sin, walk in the Spirit through the reading and study of the Word of God. Yield yourself totally to Him. Then "no one can find fault with you from now until our Lord Jesus Christ returns."

Today's Prayer

Dear heavenly Father, thank You for this challenge to be more consistent in my devotional feeding on Your Word. Many times I have promised to be more faithful, but this time I really mean it. Help me to feed my soul on Your Word for a minimum of five days a week. I want to be ready when Jesus comes, and I know a regular diet of Your Word must be a part of that readiness. In Jesus' name I pray, Amen.

55 YOUR QUOTIENT OF MERCY WILL BE REVEALED

But that is why God had mercy on me, so that Christ Jesus could use me as a prime example of his great patience with even the worst sinners. Then others will realize that they, too, can believe in him and receive eternal life. Glory and honor to God forever and ever. He is the eternal King, the unseen one who never dies; he alone is God. Amen. Timothy, my son, here are my instructions for you, based on the prophetic words spoken about you earlier. May they give you the confidence to fight well in the Lord's battles.   1 TIMOTHY 1:16-18

ONE OF the Beatitudes challenges us: "Blessed are the merciful, for they shall obtain mercy" (Matthew 5:7, NKJV). Here Christ is establishing a kingdom without an army, country, or military force of any kind. Instead of calling His followers to arms, He says the way to blessing is to be merciful, pure of heart, and peaceful, and to endure persecution for righteousness. This would not seem the way to usher in a worldwide kingdom. Still, it is the recipe for eternal victory.

When He comes, He will judge His followers by their behavior. In addition to faithfulness from the heart, He requires that His followers be men and women of character and integrity, living holy lives. He also requires that we walk in mercy.

Evidently Onesiphorus, a Greek businessman who may have been a Roman citizen, was a dedicated Christian. Some assume he accepted Christ during one of Paul's missionary journeys. The unique feature of the man's life was that he showed mercy to Paul by ministering to him, first at Ephesus, probably during the eighteen months Paul had served as a pastor there. But then "when he came to Rome," said Paul, "he searched everywhere until he found me" (2 Timothy 1:17).

It was not easy to find Paul, for even though he was a citizen, he had to wait an interminable period of time for his case to come up in the Roman courts. The government had provided little in the way of creature comforts. Consequently, prisoners like Paul were at the mercy of their friends and loved ones to bring them warm clothes and other comforts. Onesiphorus obviously helped with some of these acts of mercy. As a result Paul prayed that on the Day of judgment God would grant Onesiphorus mercy in proportion to the mercy he had shown.

Our Lord has promised us that anything we do in His name will be remembered at the judgment seat of Christ. "He who receives a prophet in the name of a prophet shall receive a prophet's reward. He who receives a righteous man in the name of a righteous man shall receive a righteous man's reward" (Matthew 10:41, NKJV). There is, then, both a "prophet's reward" and "a righteous man's reward," and those who provide acts of mercy for such individuals will share in these rewards.

Our God is eager to reward us. He wants us to accumulate vast holdings in eternity by using our talents and gifts for His glory. Sometimes they are big acts that can be seen of men. More often they are simple acts of mercy done for those who can never repay us. When we show mercy for the Lord's sake, He will remember us and grant us mercy as we have shown it to others.

When I graduated from high school, I went to Moody Bible Institute for a semester and studied under Dr. Wilbur M. Smith. His teaching helped mold my Bible knowledge for the next fifty years. I thought I had saved enough money to pay for the entire semester, but just before final exams, I discovered that I was running short. In the mail I received a fifty-dollar check from our church Sunday-school superintendent and a note telling me, "The Lord prompted me to send you this money." It was the first time anything like that had ever happened to me. Not only did that act of mercy meet my needs at the time, I found myself praying, like Paul, that God would grant this man and his wife even more mercy than their act of mercy had blessed me.

Today's Prayer

Dear heavenly Father, I marvel that You are attuned to showing mercy in Jesus' name to others. I must confess, I have not always been as thoughtful of others' needs as I should be. Help me to be more sensitive to the needs of the people You allow to pass my way, and give me the willingness to reach out in mercy to help supply those needs. In Jesus' name, Amen.

56 ARE THESE THE LAST DAYS?

You should also know this, Timothy, that in the last days there will be very difficult times. For people will love only themselves and their money. They will be boastful and proud, scoffing at God, disobedient to their parents, and ungrateful. They will consider nothing sacred. They will be unloving and unforgiving; they will slander others and have no self-control; they will be cruel and have no interest in what is good. They will betray their friends, be reckless, be puffed up with pride, and love pleasure rather than God. They will act as if they are religious, but they will reject the power that could make them godly. You must stay away from people like that. 2 TIMOTHY 3:1-5

ABOUT THE time we think things can't get any worse, they do. The moral standards of our culture seem to have sunk to an all-time low. I remember when the first discussion of pedophilia, "the last taboo," occurred in print. The article suggested that child molestation would someday be made legal in our country. That remark struck me as being insane. Recent reports revealed that a national psychological organization began circulating a report that pedophilia was not proving to be as harmful to children as previously thought. Some so-called experts were actually calling for legislation that would make it legal.

Normal people shudder when this sort of suggestion is offered by "authorities" and "experts" in the field. Such ideas almost always come from those steeped in secular thought. Plumbers, construction workers, and factory workers rarely come up with suggestions to legalize pedophilia. These notions originate among the most educated people of our times, thanks to secular humanism.

There was a day when adultery was considered shameful. Today it is assumed that "everyone does it." Violent crime (the constant fare of TV and movies) has struck many communities with ever-increasing intensity among even younger children. Twelve-year-olds steal weapons, go to school, and shoot their fellow students. Yet elitist Americans refuse to acknowledge that we have a morally sick society. This country was once based on biblical and Christian principles. In fact, the greatness of America during the first 250 years of our existence must be credited to such founding principles.

But much of that is changing. In the 1980s the secular cry was, "We don't want the religious right to impose its moral values on us." The ACLU and others began working to impose their antimoral values on the rest of us. The moral laws of our land became suspect. Secular forces in education, media, and entertainment began to work to elect politicians who would change our laws, outlawing prayer and Bible reading from our once great schools. Abortion was made legal in the name of science. The high Christian view of love degenerated into free love and recreational sex. "Christian America" became "Secular America."

None of this caught God by surprise. Our text tells us that just such "difficult times" would be a sign of the approaching "last days." One secular writer coined the expression "the end of history," which is what the Bible calls "the end of this age" (Matthew 13:40, NKJV). Notice the list of eighteen negative characteristics of those who will live in the last days: they will "love only themselves and their money. They will be boastful and proud, scoffing at God, disobedient to their parents, and ungrateful. They will consider nothing sacred. They will be unloving and unforgiving; they will slander others and have no self-control; they will be cruel and have no interest in what is good. They will betray their friends, be reckless, be puffed up with pride, and love pleasure rather than God."

Make a list of these eighteen characteristics of the last days and write them on the left-hand side of a sheet of paper. Then on the right side of the same sheet of paper list the characteristics of our times. Such elementary comparisons will show you that if we are not already there, we must certainly be close.

What is Paul's challenge to those living under such conditions? "You must stay away from people like that." In other words, don't spend your time with such individuals, or you will become just like them. Charlie "Tremendous" Jones made this classic statement: "You are today the result of the books you have read and the people you have associated with during the last ten years." Jones' statement jibes with another classic statement: "You are today the result of what you have been becoming." As we approach the last days, the Bible is clear: The world is going to descend into moral chaos and depravity. Then will come the rapture of the church.

TODAY'S PRAYER
Dear heavenly Father, help me to pick my friends and associates carefully so that my moral values will help them and theirs will

help me. Help me always to turn from close association from anyone who would keep me from being prepared for that wonderful day when Jesus raptures His church. In His name I pray, Amen.

57 FOR THOSE WHO LOVE HIS APPEARING

And so I solemnly urge you before God and before Christ Jesus—who will someday judge the living and the dead when he appears to set up his Kingdom: Preach the word of God. Be persistent, whether the time is favorable or not. Patiently correct, rebuke, and encourage your people with good teaching. For a time is coming when people will no longer listen to right teaching. They will follow their own desires and will look for teachers who will tell them whatever they want to hear. They will reject the truth and follow strange myths. But you should keep a clear mind in every situation. Don't be afraid of suffering for the Lord. Work at bringing others to Christ. Complete the ministry God has given you. As for me, my life has already been poured out as an offering to God. The time of my death is near. I have fought a good fight, I have finished the race, and I have remained faithful. And now the prize awaits me—the crown of righteousness that the Lord, the righteous Judge, will give me on that great day of his return. And the prize is not just for me but for all who eagerly look forward to his glorious return. 2 TIMOTHY 4:1-8

PAUL the apostle had many friends. These included Dr. Luke, Barnabas, Titus, Onesimus, Silas, and John Mark. But among all those Paul led to Christ and encouraged to serve Him, he had the greatest affection for Timothy. The most godly servants of Christ always seem to reach out to some specific disciple to whom they entrust the gospel message. Usually they are not content to merely lead their successor to Christ. They desire to mold this follower into one who can hand the torch of the gospel to the next generation.

One of the things Paul stressed with his young disciples was the importance of them viewing their lives in the light of Christ's coming. This message to Timothy, whom he called "my own son in the faith" (1 Timothy 1:2, KJV), is one example. Written from a Roman prison not long before he was beheaded for his faith, Paul charged his "son" to faithful service "before God and before Christ Jesus—who will someday judge the living and the dead when he appears to set up his Kingdom."

Note how he refers to both aspects of Christ's return and the judgments associated with them. Christ will judge "the living" at His appearing. All Christians must appear before the judgment seat of Christ. There they will either be given rewards for their faithful service or suffer loss for failing to serve others during this life.

The second group Paul mentions are "the dead." These are the unsaved, who in another epistle Paul describes as those who are dead while they live (1 Timothy 5:6, NKJV). These have physical life but have not received the Savior; they are dead even while they live.

Paul is about to lay a challenge on Timothy and thus on all of us who follow Christ. Paul knew he was about to be executed, and he wanted to challenge Timothy to serve Christ after he was gone. Paul left five challenges to all who desire to be ready for Christ's appearing.

1. His first instruction was to *preach the word!* Timothy was never to teach human philosophy or any worldly theories. He was to "rebuke" those who were wrong and "encourage" others to

conform their ways to Christ, lest they lose interest in "good teaching."

2. Second, Paul told Timothy to *keep a clear mind*. "The devil walks about like a roaring lion, seeking whom he may devour" (1 Peter 5:8, NKJV), and faithful pastors need to watch over the flock and warn them of pitfalls and errors.

3. Third, Paul advised Timothy *not to be afraid of suffering for the Lord*, which sometimes comes from the world and sometimes from self-willed church members.

4. Fourth, Paul said to *work at bringing others to Christ*. This should be the objective of all believers.

5. Finally, Paul counseled Timothy to *complete the ministry God had given him*. This applies to you too. Use your talents to the maximum degree for as long as you live. If you are a singer, never stop singing to the glory of God. If you are a teacher, teach on. If you have the gift of mercy, keep on being merciful. "Whatever you do, do all to the glory of God" (1 Corinthians 10:31, NKJV).

The Lord is coming, and Paul wanted Timothy to be able to give an account of the way he had used his talents throughout his life. You too have received the Savior and become one of His servants. Before you were saved you served only yourself. Now that you are a Christian, Paul challenges you to serve Him until the day He comes for you.

I have been a minister of the gospel for fifty-two years. Thirty-seven of those years I served as the pastor of three churches. I still travel and speak at forty or more churches and prophecy conferences every year. I will always be a pastor at heart. Even now I think of you, dear readers, as members of my ever-growing congregation. My desire from the Lord for you is that when you stand before the Lord Jesus and watch as He tests your works, you will hear Him say, "Well done, good and faithful servant; you have been faithful over a few things, I will make you ruler over many things. Enter into the joy of your lord" (Matthew 25:23, NKJV).

Dear heavenly Father, I consider it a great privilege to be Your child and Your servant. Forgive me for those times when I have let the cares and deceitfulness of this world close in on me and sap my energy and my ministry. I do love the appearing of Jesus and want to keep my eyes fixed on things above, not on things of this earth. Help me today not to be so "busy-minded" that I am not open and sensitive to those around me who need the coming Savior. In His name I pray, Amen.

58 THE CROWN OF RIGHTEOUSNESS

And now the prize awaits me—the crown of righteousness that the Lord, the righteous Judge, will give me on that great day of his return. And the prize is not just for me but for all who eagerly look forward to his glorious return. 2 TIMOTHY 4:8

I CONSIDER this passage to be the most treasured promise in all the Scriptures for believers. Everyone who believes will receive a crown of righteousness at Christ's appearing. The apostle Paul influenced Christianity more than any other man in history. He also advanced the kingdom of God further than anyone else, and he remains the best example of how to live the Christian life.

The resurrection of Christ is the most incredible evidence of His deity. Further, the miracle of the Resurrection is responsible for the great transformation that took place in Paul's life on the Damascus road. The Resurrection changed him from the arch-destroyer of the early church to its greatest builder. Skeptics who do not believe in the resurrection of Christ can neither comprehend nor find an explanation for the transformation of the great apostle.

Like the Resurrection, the Second Coming has an amazing effect on all believers. In getting ready for it we all desire to "keep [ourselves] pure, just as Christ is pure" (1 John 3:3). This desire to be pure at His coming may be one reason He designed His coming to be "as a thief in the night" (1 Thessalonians 5:2). Those who love His appearing must live so that His any-moment return will find them living pure.

Those who love Him and are awaiting His return will have no trouble serving Him. I have seen several elderly servants of the Lord express a desire to keep on serving Him right up to the time of their death.

Recently one of the speakers at a prophecy conference told of being with Dr. John Walvoord, chancellor and professor emeritus of systematic theology at Dallas Theological Seminary. At eighty-nine, after teaching the prophetic word for sixty-nine years and suffering a broken hip (and other physical complications), Dr. Walvoord asked a friend if he would be on call in case he needed him as a substitute to serve at a moment's notice. That way he could continue to schedule speaking engagements. Doubtless he too is a candidate for the crown of righteousness, for he obviously loves Christ's appearing.

What is this crown of righteousness?

It is the regalia of those believers who will "reign with Him a thousand years" (Revelation 20:6, NKJV). Crowns are symbols of leadership. Kings wear them, not servants. So the crown of righteousness which a Christian earns by loving the appearing of Christ is something that will last at least a thousand years and characterize our lives all through eternity.

Dr. M. R. DeHaan once said, "To come to Christ costs you nothing, but to serve Christ costs you everything." Any sacrifice made because we love His appearing will be long forgotten when we receive the crown of righteousness that lasts forever.

Dear Lord, it is enough that You sent Your Son to die for my sin. You have challenged me to live a righteous life devoted to Your faithful service. You have promised me a crown of righteousness in that day because I live each day motivated by my love of the appearance of Jesus. Please burn the promise of His coming into my mind, so the choices I make and the things I do will really count for eternity! In Jesus' name I pray, Amen.

59 PECULIAR PEOPLE HAVE PECULIAR VISION

For the grace of God has been revealed, bringing salvation to all people. And we are instructed to turn from godless living and sinful pleasures. We should live in this evil world with self-control, right conduct, and devotion to God, while we look forward to that wonderful event when the glory of our great God and Savior, Jesus Christ, will be revealed. He gave his life to free us from every kind of sin, to cleanse us, and to make us his very own people, totally committed to doing what is right.   TITUS 2:11-14

YOU DON'T have to look peculiar to let the direction of your life affect the way you live. We have already mentioned our experience with the *People* magazine writer who insisted that their picture of us catch us looking off into the heavens as if we were awaiting the coming of Jesus. Paul challenged Pastor Titus and his people to look for "the blessed hope" (the Rapture) and "the Glorious Appearing" (Jesus' coming in power and great glory—Titus 2:13, NKJV). This was to motivate them to live the life of those who had been redeemed from iniquity. The Christian who is legitimately excited about the Second Coming is always actively engaged in serving the Lord in this life.

In talking to many people at prophecy conferences, I have discovered that most of them were already serving as Sunday-school teachers, Bible-study teachers, youth workers, soul-winners, deacons, and so forth. The prophecy conferee doesn't have any more time than anyone else might to attend. But their love for Christ's return and their interest in learning more about His coming are passions in their lives. They know they will be judged by their works to determine the rewards they will have. They understand that now is the time to "store [their] treasures in heaven" (Matthew 6:19) so that it can affect their eternal lifestyle.

When I was a boy, we rented two rooms of a family's home. The landlady took care of my infant brother while my widowed mother worked in a factory. The landlady and her husband were Christians and went to church Sunday mornings. Other than that there were few evidences that they were believers. One night this man showed us his special box containing bric-a-brac that he had found on his way through life. He had gathered old coins, jewelry, rings, bolts, and a small lock. Even as a high school sophomore, I thought his treasures were just junk. But what struck me was how animated the man became contemplating all his "treasures." My mother's comment later was, "Hoping to pick up stuff off the ground, the man never looked up to see the trees or any part of God's creation."

Contrast this poor soul with Mr. Jolliffe, a factory worker I came to know. This man loved Jesus and treasured the blessed hope of His coming. He was my Boy Scout leader in our church troop. He also was the youth sponsor of our high school youth department. He was like a surrogate father to me after my own father died. He taught me how to get along with other boys and how to survive in the woods, and most of all, he was a man I could look up to and imitate as I grew up. That man influenced my life from sixth through twelfth grade! He never seemed to care much about yard work or working on his old car. He cared about young people. I can name several missionaries and ministers who came out of his youth group.

After my return from summer camp, the first person I told about dedicating my life to God was this wonderful Scout leader, Mr. Jolliffe. His eyes filled with tears, and he gave me a bear hug I can still feel. I knew even at age fifteen that I had made the right decision because Mr. Jolliffe approved. I'm going to be an interested bystander at the judgment seat of Christ when Mr. Jolliffe receives his rewards. I hope the Lord calls on me as a character witness on his behalf. He was always "committed to doing what is right."

TODAY'S PRAYER

Dear Lord, thank You for helping me to see that one day this world and everything in it are going to be burned up. Help me always to remember that life is short, eternity is forever, and I need to keep looking for His coming when making the decisions of life. In Jesus' name, Amen.

60 THE KINGDOM AT HIS APPEARING

And so I solemnly urge you before God and before Christ Jesus—who will someday judge the living and the dead when he appears to set up his Kingdom. 2 TIMOTHY 4:1

In the past few years a number of scholars and authors have begun to use an interesting expression: *the end of history.* Their use of the term is often a reflection of their doomsday view of the geopolitical landscape. We are, as some suppose, the most educated generation in history. Measured by the number of wars and deaths, we are also quite likely the most barbaric generation. It is estimated that approximately 180 million people have been killed by their fellow human beings in this century alone.

Any honest historian can see that this world is on a collision course with annihilation. Germ warfare and the existence of nuclear bombs make this world a frightening planet to call home. Considering the possibility that such weapons might fall into the hands of terrorists, it's hard to be hopeful about the future.

But Christians are fortunate to have the inside track on the future. We have what Peter calls a "sure word of prophecy" (2 Peter 1:19, KJV) to guide us. This sure word paints an optimistic picture. We can have confidence. This world is not going to self-destruct. It may go through some difficult times in the ugly continuum of humanity's inhumanity. Our own country is one of the most humanitarian countries in the history of the world, yet we are far from free of international self-interest.

While these are fearful times, no one is going to destroy the earth. God has revealed in His prophetic Word that He has great plans for this world and all who live in it. After the rapture of the church takes place, many people will continue to live on this earth. The majority will be left behind at the Rapture because they have not personally received Jesus as their Savior. Then most of those left will follow the Antichrist during the seven years of the Tribulation. Yet "a vast crowd, too great to count, from every nation and tribe and people and language" (Revelation 7:9), will respond to the faithful teaching of the 144,000 Jewish witnesses God will raise up to preach His gospel.

Unquestionably, then, as bad as things may look, man is not going to destroy himself from the earth because billions will be on the earth during the seven-year Tribulation. But that isn't all. Following the Tribulation, Jesus is going to come and judge the nations and begin His kingdom. The Hebrew prophets frequently mentioned this future kingdom over which the Messiah would reign. It was also mentioned by our Lord when He was on Earth. It is addressed in very specific terms in Revelation 20 where the Bible states six times that this kingdom will last "one thousand years."

Believe it or not, the future is very bright. No matter what the doomsayers say, God has a wonderful plan for this world, and it will all begin with the coming of Christ to establish His kingdom.

The real question is, are you ready for His coming? Are you a Christian? If you are, you will be taken in the Rapture and enjoy the splendors of the Father's house for at least seven years. Then you will return with Christ to this earth in His Glorious Appearing. You will then "reign with Him a thousand years" (Revelation 20:6, NKJV). What could be better than this?

But if you are not a Christian, now is the time to call on the name of the Lord and be saved. He paid the price of your salvation. It comes at no cost to you. You have but to receive it. Make haste! Receive this gift and join us in the Rapture. You need not be left behind when Jesus claims His church.

TODAY'S PRAYER

Dear heavenly Father, thank You for Your wonderful plan for my future and the future of all those who love "His appearing and His kingdom" (Titus 4:1, NKJV). Thank You for giving us a brief glimpse of that future. I am blessed to be Your child and want to be used of You today. Use me I pray, in Jesus' name, Amen.

61 HIS APPEARING AND HIS KINGDOM

And so I solemnly urge you before God and before Christ Jesus—who will someday judge the living and the dead when he appears to set up his Kingdom. 2 TIMOTHY 4:1

THIS IS the second day in a row we have meditated upon this one passage of Scripture. Can you doubt its importance? At the end of Paul's life, he gave these words as his last challenge to his young son in the faith. He appealed to Timothy to live his life in view of the fact that Jesus would ultimately judge us for the way we have lived our lives. This will happen at "His appearing and His Kingdom" (Titus 4:1, NKJV).

Having served his Savior and Lord all his life, Paul knew that the time of his departure was at hand. He said, "I have fought a good fight, I have finished the race, and I have remained faithful" (2 Timothy 4:7), and he knew that the crown of righteousness was awaiting him.

What Paul is doing here is challenging Timothy, and all of us who read the Word, to maximize our service so that we can reap kingdom-sized blessings at the appearing of Jesus. In addition to wanting to save us, Christ also wants to bless us both in this life and the one to come. Christians sometimes choose to live self-centered lives. But we can also invest our lives in eternity. To live this kind of life is to be blessed in the Day of judgment when He appears.

In a vital sense, Christ makes us stewards of our own lives after we are converted. He intends us to invest our lives for Him rather than to live them for ourselves. We all have differing talents, abilities, and opportunities. Paul likens our lives to vessels in a "wealthy home" (2 Timothy 2:20). There are many kinds of these vessels. Some are of gold and silver, some are of wood and clay, but they are all vessels of honor when dedicated to Him for His use.

We are not to be neurotic because we are a vessel of wood and not a vessel of gold or silver. We are to be what His service demands. God often passed up very gifted vessels in the church in favor of ordinary wood or clay vessels that were willing to serve in holiness before Him. But God will never use a dirty vessel. Christians must walk in humility and holiness to be clean. They can perform beyond their natural ability when they live the kind of life God can use and bless.

True, there are to be some inequities in this life, where the undeserving or "puffed up" Christians get more glory than they deserve. The deserving are sometimes overlooked. But the last chapter hasn't been written. Just wait until Jesus appears and sets up His kingdom! They who served humbly in this life will receive their rewards at His appearing. Some of the most obscure servants of Christ today will be exalted in the judgment while many who are self-exalted today will be passed over.

Learn to leverage your life. You are probably familiar with the principle of "leverage" in the financial realm. You invest your money in a house, and ten years later it becomes worth twice what you invested; that's leveraging. God wants to use our vessels during this life to advance His spiritual kingdom. As you follow His leading on a day-by-day basis, He will use your life to accomplish far more with His blessing than you could ever have accomplished without it.

TODAY'S PRAYER

Dear heavenly Father, thank You for the opportunity to serve You in this life. And thank You that our Lord Jesus challenged us to live faithful lives of service today because one day He is going to return and reward His servants. We will not be rewarded for talent or productivity, but for our dedication and obedience. If there is anything in my life that stands in the way of my being filled and used by Your Spirit, please reveal it to me so I can be a vessel fit for Your use. In Jesus' name I pray, Amen.

62 GOD REALLY WANTS YOU IN HIS KINGDOM

And so I solemnly urge you before God and before Christ Jesus—who will someday judge the living and the dead when he appears to set up his Kingdom.

2 TIMOTHY 4:1

THE HOLY SPIRIT inspired the apostle Paul to merge Christ's appearing and His kingdom for a specific reason. He wants us to live in such a way that we will earn the privilege of serving Him during Christ's reign. We have tried several times in this book to remind you that we will "reign with Him one thousand years" (Revelation 20:6, NKJV), but our ultimate reign will be in direct proportion to the way we have served Him here on Earth.

Jesus said, "You were faithful over a few things, I will make you ruler over many things" (Matthew 25:21, NKJV). He meant that he who is faithful in serving the Lord here will be rewarded with an honored position in His millennial kingdom. I have not found any Scripture that says we will also serve Christ in heaven, but who would object? Serving Christ in any world is a privilege.

Personally, we have found life's greatest enjoyments have always come when we are serving our Lord. Admittedly, Beverly and I are both sports enthusiasts and have had some very good times watching the Super Bowl. But honestly, neither my wife nor I can remember the scores of particular games, and in most cases, even who won. It was great fun at the time, but in the passage of time it became merely another life experience.

Our greatest pleasure is seeing our own children walk in truth or seeing those we have led to Christ influence others to surrender to Him. Sports trophies tarnish in time and someday will be burned up. But all work done in the name of the Lord is eternal.

Dr. Henry Brandt was the first Christian psychologist who tested all the theories of humanistic psychology by the Word of God. He was the first psychologist who recommended that pastors quit referring their difficult cases to secular psychologists or psychiatrists. He advocated conforming our behavior and attitudes to the principles found in the Word of God. To refer Christians to atheist psychologists is like saying Jesus Christ doesn't have the answers to problems in the Christian's life. Dr. Brandt himself has long studied the Scriptures. His lectures always present biblical solutions to life's greatest difficulties.

In his eighties, after a long and distinguished career as a Christian counselor, Dr. Brandt contracted Parkinson's disease. Sometimes he can't stop his hands from trembling while speaking, so he hooks his thumbs in his belt and carries on. When I called him to wish him a happy eighty-fourth birthday, I found he was spending a month in Africa ministering to pastors. He has kept eternity's values in view and is looking forward to Christ's appearing and His kingdom.

You might wonder why more Christians don't have Dr. Brandt's perspective on life. Actually, there are several reasons. One is that many are captive to the cares and deceitfulness of this world. Others are controlled by "the sin that so easily hinders our progress" (Hebrews 12:1).

On a recent Sunday in our church, our pastor challenged the congregation to make generous faith commitments for three years to raise 16 million dollars to pay for the next phase of our building program. In the course of his remarks he said, "There are enough cars in this church parking lot today that if they were sold, the proceeds would provide the needed 16 million dollars." The next Sunday he reported that a man came into his office that week, dropped the keys and title to his Ferrari on the pastor's desk, and said, "This car means the world to me. In fact, it means too much to me, so I am giving it to the Lord. Please sell it and apply it to the new church building."

Anything that stands between us and giving our whole heart to the Lord is not worth it! The first commandment to worship the Lord is the key to serving him. Jesus commanded us to "love the Lord our God with all your heart, all your soul, and all your mind" (Matthew 22:37). No earthly thing, be it an idol, a car, or any other god, is worth cheating ourselves out of the opportunity to serve Him. Christ has prepared a home in heaven for us. His appearing and His king-

- Checkout Receipt -

Patron
Barcode:
Number of items: 2

Barcode: 31449002791566
Title: The Gospel of Ruth :
loving God enough to break the
rules
Due: 11/13/2019

Barcode: 31449004877355
Title: Perhaps today : living
every day in the light of Christ's
return
Due: 11/13/2019

10/23/2019 5:02 PM

dom are near. Are you living in fiscal, physical, psychological, and spiritual readiness to meet him?

TODAY'S PRAYER

Dear heavenly Father, it is so easy to get our eyes off that which is eternal and look too longingly at the things of this world. Help me to live every day in the light of Jesus' coming and the establishment of His kingdom. I do want to be used of Your Spirit to help others prepare for His coming. In Jesus' name, Amen.

63 ADORNING THE DOCTRINE OF HIS COMING

Exhort bondservants to be obedient to their own masters, to be well pleasing in all things, not answering back, not pilfering, but showing all good fidelity, that they may adorn the doctrine of God our Savior in all things. For the grace of God that brings salvation has appeared to all men, teaching us that, denying ungodliness and worldly lusts, we should live soberly, righteously, and godly in the present age, looking for the blessed hope and glorious appearing of our great God and Savior Jesus Christ, who gave Himself for us, that He might redeem us from every lawless deed and purify for Himself His own special people, zealous for good works. Speak these things, exhort, and rebuke with all authority. Let no one despise you.

TITUS 2:9-15, NKJV

THE LITTLE book of Titus is filled with practical admonitions for Christian living. It only mentions the coming of the Lord once. When it does, however, it distinguishes between the Rapture and the Glorious Appearing in a very significant manner.

Titus, like Timothy, was one of Paul's "sons in the faith." He had been put in charge of about a hundred churches on the island of Crete where many former pagans had come to faith in Christ. So Paul's advice here came as a senior Christian to a younger pastor.

Titus 2:10 contains an interesting expression that we need to emulate today. Paul told Titus to urge Christian slaves "to be obedient to their own masters, to be well pleasing in all things, not answering back, not pilfering, but showing all good fidelity." Why should slaves go this extra mile? So "that they may adorn the doctrine of God our Savior in all things."

Adorning the doctrine of God is to clothe oneself with honesty and integrity. The Bible says that God cannot lie. God does not have to try to be honest. By definition He is the truth. Like Him, we should adorn ourselves with "fidelity," which moves the world to consider the genuine nature of our salvation experience. In the case of the people of Crete, they are reputed to have been lazy, dishonest thieves. Thus new converts were exhorted to live lives of integrity as a badge that they had become espoused to God in a new and personal relationship.

Paul encourages all Christians to deny themselves all "ungodliness and worldly lusts." He says that they "should live soberly, righteously, and godly in the present age, looking for the blessed hope and glorious appearing of our great God and Savior Jesus Christ." This is indeed a powerful challenge for us to live holy lives in view of the Rapture, which Paul calls "the blessed hope."

Living the Christian life is not an easy task. In fact, it is impossible without the transforming power of the indwelling Holy Spirit. Even then, it takes time to overcome our previous lifestyle and begin living one that "may adorn the doctrine of God."

To motivate these young believers, Paul held out both the

"blessed hope" and the "glorious appearing of our great God and Savior Jesus Christ." There are two things that must be said about Jesus' coming:

First, it is legitimate to challenge Christians to make whatever sacrifices they must to be ready for His coming. We have said repeatedly in this book that no Christian will ever be sorry *after* the Rapture that he or she made personal sacrifices to live the Christian life. Usually temptations subside in time and it becomes more natural to live a Christian lifestyle and "adorn the doctrine of God." But even after years of walking in the Spirit, we must discipline ourselves to keep our eyes on the ever-possible rapture of the church. Let its prospect purify your lifestyle.

Second, the Rapture did not occur during these Christians' lifetimes! They were all dead by the end of the first century. And here we are nineteen centuries later, still challenging people to live holy lives in the light of His coming.

He is still going to come one of these days, and we do not want you to be like the foolish virgins Jesus talked about who ran out of oil before the bridegroom appeared. We must be ready to go to the Father's house and to experience the marriage of the Lamb. We must "adorn the doctrine of God" all the days of our lives, for we never know the day or the hour.

Today's Prayer

Dear heavenly Father, thank You for saving me and giving me a challenge to live a life of integrity and godliness. I know I cannot live that life independent of Your power, so I ask for Your Spirit to fill my life that I may "adorn the doctrine of God." May I be always careful to speak the truth in love and deny ungodly lusts. Help me ever to look "unto Jesus, the author and finisher of our faith" (Hebrews 12:2, NKJV) and the One who will soon come to take me home. In His name I pray, Amen.

64 FIFTEEN DIFFERENCES BETWEEN THE RAPTURE AND GLORIOUS APPEARING

Looking for the blessed hope and glorious appearing of our great God and Savior Jesus Christ, who gave Himself for us, that He might redeem us from every lawless deed and purify for Himself His own special people, zealous for good works. TITUS 2:13-14, NKJV

THE END of time is certain! The second coming of Jesus is mentioned 318 times in the Bible. When these passages are closely examined, it is easy to separate the description of the Rapture from His second coming—two events separated by seven years of time.

In our text for today, Paul gives these two events different names. The first stage he calls "blessed hope." Christians have long referred to this stage as the "Rapture," a word derived from the Latin meaning "snatching" of all believers from the earth.

The second stage of Christ's coming Paul calls "the glorious appearing." This is the only place in the Bible where both events are mentioned in a single verse. In 2 Thessalonians 2, the first of these two events is called "our gathering together unto him" (verse 1, KJV) and the second event is called "the splendor of his coming" (verse 8).

In my commentary on the book of Revelation, called *Revelation Unveiled*, I point out that these two stages are pictured in Revelation 4:1-2. Here John is snatched up into heaven before the Tribulation period begins. Then in Revelation 19:11-21, the church returns with Christ in power and great glory after the Tribulation. The church, which is mentioned seventeen times in the first three chapters of the book of Revelation, is not mentioned at all after John is taken up into heaven in 4:1-2. The reason the church is not mentioned in these next fifteen chapters of Revelation is that the church is not on Earth during the Tribulation.

The chart on page 88 reveals the fifteen differences between the rapture of the church and Christ's Glorious Appearing. These two events of the Second Coming make it clear that there are no discrepancies in the Bible's teaching. They are two distinct events for two separate kinds of people whose existence is separated by the seven-year Tribulation period.

Please study these differences again carefully. We think you will agree that these two very different stages of Christ's return cannot be speaking of the same event. The Rapture could come at any moment, but Christ's Glorious Appearing could not take place today! It cannot take place for at least seven years! Yet the coming of Jesus is taught in many places in the Scriptures as being a constant, any-moment possibility. The only way to reconcile these contrasting teachings is to see them as separate. The first is prior to the seven years of tribulation predicted for Israel and mentioned by the Hebrew prophets almost fifty times as "the time of Jacob's trouble," the "day of wrath," or many other similar terms. The second occurrence speaks of the visible return when Christ comes in power to set up His kingdom.

Taken together, these two events of the second coming of Christ can be used as very motivational teaching. Whenever the church has taught this any-moment awareness of the blessed hope, it has produced a spirit of evangelistic zeal, holy living, and a missionary concern. The first three centuries of the church's history were saturated in this hope. Then the church stopped taking the Bible literally and for more than eleven hundred years the message of the return of Christ died out. After the Protestant Reformation had emerged and scholars translated the Bible into the language of the common people, the blessed hope and the Glorious Appearing were returned to the church.

Throughout history this blessed hope has had a purifying, evangelistic, and missionary effect on the church. During the past thirty years, however, there has been a shameful decline in preaching the Second Coming. One notable exception is the Southern Baptist churches, which make up the largest Protestant denomination in the nation. In recent years they have done something nearly impossible. They have turned from a liberal, moderate theological position to a well-publicized conservative takeover. Now most of these churches again preach the blessed hope and the Glorious Appearing of Christ's return.

No wonder they have added more than one million members in the last three years. Second-coming teaching transforms dull doctrinal thinking. The rapture of the church is exciting doctrine. Just this week I received a letter from one reader saying, "I am not sure I was a Christian before reading your Left Behind series, but I know I am now. I will never again live a lackadaisical, unconcerned life. I have rededicated my life so that I won't be left behind when Jesus comes. I am now ready for His coming, and I want to help others get ready too."

TODAY'S PRAYER

Dear heavenly Father, thank You so much for teaching me the difference between the two stages of Christ's return. Help me never to lose sight of the possibility that Christ could come at any moment. I want my life to be so pure that He can use me as a vessel for evangelism and missions. May I do my part to make the Rapture as all-inclusive as it can be. In Jesus' name, Amen.

65 THE ZEAL OF LOOKING FORWARD

For the grace of God has been revealed, bringing salvation to all people. And we are instructed to turn from godless living and sinful pleasures. We should live in this evil world with self-control, right conduct, and devotion to God, while we look

forward to that wonderful event when the glory of
our great God and Savior, Jesus Christ, will be
revealed. He gave his life to free us from every
kind of sin, to cleanse us, and to make us his very
own people.   TITUS 2:11-14

DR. MAXWELL MALTZ, a famous psychiatrist and motivational
speaker, often said, "The human mind is a goal-striving mechanism."
He taught that it is important to keep our goals in mind or we will
lack motivation and zest for living. Those who keep goals and objectives uppermost in their minds find that their thought processes automatically move to accomplish those goals. I am not a detailed or
analytical person by natural temperament, so I have had to discipline
my mind to keep a series of well-defined goals out in front of me. I
pray about these goals repeatedly. I am sure the Lord, through His
Holy Spirit, has to goad the gremlins of my mind to keep me doing
those things necessary in order to achieve His will.

The Bible speaks of goal-oriented living in Proverbs 29:18:
"Where there is no vision, the people perish" (KJV). Many times in the
counseling room, part of my role as a Christian counselor is to listen
to some despairing soul pour out hopelessness and discontent. Then
I try to help the struggler to reestablish life's goals and objectives.
That is particularly true for those forced to deal with the death of a
loved one or a major defeat. Someone has well said, "Human beings
have been known to live forty days without food and four days without water but only four minutes without hope." That may be a bit ex-
aggerated, but it is true that we all must have hope in this life or
something major within us dies.

God knew this, which is why He gave us both the blessed hope
and the promise of His Glorious Appearing. These final events serve
as a constant reminder that there is a better world on the way. God
guarantees that He will share it with us one day. For two thousand

years, that hope has inspired millions of Christians to look beyond their immediate troubles and smothering circumstances. They anticipate the day when they will see Jesus and join Him forever. Surely this is goal enough to motivate any Christian.

God leaves us in this world to achieve some holy purpose after we become Christians. If He took us to heaven immediately after we were born again, we would all go into heaven much cleaner and more righteous. Instead, He leaves us here on this earth to struggle with the flesh, the world, and the devil, knowing full well we will lose some of those struggles. There is a purpose, however, in His plan. He wants us to be committed to doing what is right.

I have never known God to refuse to use any Christians who give themselves fully to Him. But this yielding of the self must be a willing surrender to His will and a forsaking of fleshly desires. I have seen many miss God's perfect will for their lives because they were unwilling to forsake their pet sins or surrender private habits that were displeasing to God.

I remember an attractive and stylish lady in our church who accepted Christ the same night her husband did. When they got home they took all the liquor stashed in their bar and dumped it down the drain. Christ changed their entire lives, and they began leading many of their unsaved friends to Him. Then God began speaking to them about Christian service on a full-time basis. Mary told me that every time she got down to pray, she broke out in a sweat. She wanted to surrender to God to do anything He asked of her. Still, she had irrational fears He would call her to be a missionary. Every time she prayed, all she could see in her mind was a thatched hut with a mud floor and with no electricity or running water. She hated the idea of being a missionary. Then one day she got realistic. She looked up, saw Him who had redeemed her on the cross, and yielded. She then looked forward to His blessed hope and Glorious Appearing and surrendered all to Him.

Once she made herself available to go to Africa, God began to use her right here in America. God never made her live in a thatched hut. He just wanted her to be willing to go. She has now served the Lord for over thirty years, speaking to women's groups all over the country. She has taught thousands to share their faith in Christ.

Our vision begins when we clean up our lives to become "vessels ... for honor" (2 Timothy 2:20, NKJV). And it isn't all that difficult to get the right perspective. When we honestly look upon Him who "gave his life to free us from every kind of sin," we can clearly see Him who is coming to Rapture us. In the double understanding of His current reign and His coming reign, our lives begin to fit together. When we look at life this way, there is nothing worth doing that we may have once considered too great a sacrifice.

TODAY'S PRAYER

Dear heavenly Father, as I look back at all Jesus has done for me and look forward at all He has planned, I can do no less than surrender all my dreams and cares to His keeping. Use me any way You want. Ask me to do anything You want me to do. Then help me to resolve to anticipate Your coming with my hands immersed in the most noble of work—the work of the kingdom. In Jesus' name I pray, Amen.

66 CHRIST'S THRONE IS FOREVER

"You love what is right and hate what is wrong. Therefore God, your God, has anointed you, pouring out the oil of joy on you more than on anyone else." And, "Lord, in the beginning you laid the foundation of the earth, and the heavens are the work of your hands. Even they will perish, but you remain forever. They will wear out like old

clothing. You will roll them up like an old coat.
They will fade away like old clothing. But you are
always the same; you will never grow old."

HEBREWS 1:9-12

IN ANCIENT royal courts when subjects addressed their sovereign leaders, they cried, "O king, live forever." It was used in addressing monarchs from Egypt and Babylon. Now all those rulers whom their vassals told to live forever are dead and buried. No one lives forever.

Jesus is the one notable exception. When Jesus, the Son of God, is ensconced on His throne at the beginning of the Millennium, He will indeed rule forever. His rule will not be just a thousand-year reign of peace, it will be a stable order that God has planned for those who love Him. The biblical name of this place is heaven.

That is what the writer of the book of Hebrews had in mind when he spoke of Jesus stepping down from His throne to make Himself "a little lower than the angels" (Hebrews 2:9, NKJV) and become a man. Jesus did this so that He could die for the sins of the world. Then a brief three days later, He rose again from the grave. Jesus later ascended to heaven promising that one day He would come back and assume His throne as King of the universe.

The book of Hebrews presents Christ as better than any person in the Old Testament. Further, He is a better sacrifice, a better covenant, a better way of salvation, and certainly a more excellent king. His title tells it all. The Christ of the Millennium will be called "King of kings and Lord of lords!" (Revelation 19:16).

Even now there is a hush in heaven. Angels wait in anticipation. The entire universe, galaxies, and praying souls everywhere look forward to His coming. We who love Him listen daily for His shout from heaven. We are eager to see Christ come. "Then, . . . we who are still alive and remain on the earth will be caught up in the clouds to meet the Lord in the air and remain with him forever" (1 Thessalonians 4:17).

PERHAPS

Seven years after King Jesus comes to take His church up to His Father's house, He will return to be the center of the most magnificent ceremony in the history of the world. His throne will be forever; His scepter will usher in an era of blessing unlike anything that has ever existed. All the angels will be His "ministering spirits" (Hebrews 1:14, NKJV), and His enemies will be deleted from every human dream. He will rule *forever*.

During the Korean War, I was a young pastor in a small church near Minneapolis. A part-time custodian and his wife were among the most dedicated families in the congregation. They were the parents of three girls and a boy. After their son was drafted into the army, they asked me to come to their home on Saturday morning to pray with them as their boy left their close-knit family for the first time.

The night before I went to this humble home to pray, I received an emergency message that led me to go to one of the richest homes in our community. In contrast to the custodian's family, these people owned an enormous house on Lake Minnetonka and kept a yacht tied to their private dock. When I got inside their lavish home I walked through the thick carpet only to sense icicles of hostility that hung in the air. I was not surprised to find that this couple was getting a divorce. I wasn't able to do much for them. Their material needs were few, but their spiritual needs were great. They had everything except God, and because they lacked Him, they had nothing.

The next morning I drove up the muddy driveway to the custodian's home. In contrast to the wealthy, quarreling couple from the night before, this poor family was seated around a dilapidated table. They had few chairs. They turned an old orange crate on end so I would have a place to sit at my end of the table. The most expensive things they owned were the framed pictures of their family hanging on the walls. The custodian worked in a factory and cleaned the church as his second job.

Suddenly I saw the truth. It was these who were rich. The wife looked at her husband with love in her eyes, and he looked at her the same way. I could tell by the way the three girls hugged their older brother that the family could have written a book on love and marriage. Still, they were about to experience their first major change.

When I finished praying, there was not a dry eye among them. They all laid hands on their son and brother and committed him to God. It is a sight I have never forgotten. They all loved Jesus, and because of Him, they loved each other. I knew that one day they would be together again forever where there would be no war or separation. It would all start when Jesus came to reign as King of kings and Lord of lords.

TODAY'S PRAYER

Dear heavenly Father, thank You for enriching my life with the love that only God can provide. It has affected my whole family, and certainly my attitude toward them. And I thank You that one day Jesus is coming back. All the inequities and injustices of this life will be remedied, and we will enjoy His reigning presence forever. Amen.

67 OUR DIVINE APPOINTMENT

And just as it is destined that each person dies only once and after that comes judgment, so also Christ died only once as a sacrifice to take away the sins of many people. He will come again but not to deal with our sins again. This time he will bring salvation to all those who are eagerly waiting for him.　　　　　HEBREWS 9:27-28

DANIEL WEBSTER was a great American, a scholar, and a Christian. One evening he was invited to lecture to a group of congressmen. After dinner, the group engaged in small talk that did not interest the speaker. So the chairman tried to engage Webster in conversation. Getting his attention he said, "Mr. Webster, tell me, what is the greatest thought that has ever passed through your mind?"

"My accountability to God!" the brilliant guest replied.

This awareness is what makes us different from the animals. This is our task: to recognize that we are accountable to God. He put us here and will someday judge us for the way we have treated both Him and our fellow human beings. This thought should be written in bold type on the tablets of our heart.

"It is destined that each person dies only once and after that comes judgment" should come as no surprise. Our consciences tell us the same thing. Many a sinner has gone into eternity screaming for fear of having to meet God on Judgment Day. Voltaire, the French skeptic who set out to prove Christianity was a hoax, is quoted as saying that "it took twelve men to establish Christianity; I will prove that it will take but one man to destroy it." One hundred years later the home where he made that statement was filled with Bibles for distribution throughout Europe. In that same house, just before Voltaire died, he said, "Now, Oh Christ, it is time for You to demand Your accounting." What a horrible way to die!

This message of hope from the book of Hebrews offers a distinct contrast to Voltaire: "Christ died only once as a sacrifice to take away the sins of many people" and that "to all those who are eagerly waiting for him" He "will come again but not to deal with our sins again." The obvious meaning of this verse is this: Just as Jesus came the first time to die on the cross as our only means of receiving forgiveness for our sins, He is coming a second time to save us by taking us to those eternal realms He has been preparing for us.

Who would ever question Jesus' first coming? The most authenticated life in the ancient world is that of Jesus of Nazareth. He influenced the world so much that all of history is dated B.C. (Before

Christ) and A.D. (*Anno Domini*, or "in the year of the Lord"). Of the entire twelve billion people who have ever lived, Jesus Christ has influenced this world like no one else. Every other leader in the world who has ever influenced mankind had a lifetime to do it. But Jesus influenced this world in only three and a half years of ministry!

How could this be? Very simply, He died for our sins according to the Scripture and rose again the third day. We know that Jesus rose from the dead, for Christianity would never have been heard of had He not done so. Actually, the resurrection of Jesus is what turned the cowardly disciples into courageous evangelists who in turn inverted the world.

Jesus' first coming to Earth to die for the sins of the whole world is a certified historical fact. Yet His second coming will be even more sure! There are at least three times as many recorded prophecies of His second coming than His first. It is three times more certain. Since it is so certain, let us trust fully in Him.

I have a good friend who has spent almost six years in a federal penitentiary for a crime he did not commit. It's a long story, but if he could have afforded a good attorney instead of having an incompetent counsel appointed by the state to defend him, he would not have spent a day in prison. He needed an earthly advocate.

We who belong in the family of God have an advocate, "Jesus Christ the righteous" (1 John 2:1, NKJV), who has paid the penalty to forgive our sins by what He did on the cross. He wants to save us and be our personal attorney and Savior. But remember, He is available only to those who call on His name. If you have the slightest doubt that you have ever personally invited Him into your life, do it now.

Today's Prayer

Dear heavenly Father, thank You for sending Jesus, Your Son, to die on the cross for my sins. I know I am a sinner and that only He, the resurrected Christ, can forgive and save me. Jesus, I invite You into my life to become my Savior and Lord. I give my life to You. In Jesus' name I pray, Amen.

68 IN ANTICIPATION OF HIS COMING

Do not throw away this confident trust in the Lord, no matter what happens. Remember the great reward it brings you! Patient endurance is what you need now, so you will continue to do God's will. Then you will receive all that he has promised. "For in just a little while, the Coming One will come and not delay. And a righteous person will live by faith. But I will have no pleasure in anyone who turns away." But we are not like those who turn their backs on God and seal their fate. We have faith that assures our salvation.

HEBREWS 10:35-39

"LORD, hurry up and give me patience!" This has been my constant prayer. Patience is a virtue that I've always found hard to wait on. All through my adolescence my mother was forever saying, "Tim, when are you going to learn to be patient?" During my three-month term at Moody Bible Institute, before I joined the air force, my roommate nagged me constantly, saying, "You need patience, Tim. God has you where you are for a reason." After the war I couldn't wait to be discharged and go to college. Once I met Beverly I couldn't wait until we got married. Then I fidgeted all through the university until I became a pastor. I pastored a country church while only a junior in college. When I started memorizing Scripture en route to discipling men, I came upon a verse that has become a daily reminder to wait on the Lord. "Patient endurance is what you need now, so you will continue to do God's will. Then you will receive all that he has promised." The following verse ties it in with the Second Coming by saying, "For in just a little while, the Coming One will come and not delay."

We should wait patiently because Jesus is coming, and waiting on His coming should influence everything we do. Some might object, saying that Christians have been waiting patiently for two thousand years, and He still has not returned.

Nonetheless, it is our responsibility to wait patiently until He does come. The Greek word "patient" might better be translated "endurance." It doesn't mean we shouldn't get excited about His coming. But we should never become overly anxious and lose our calm dependency as we yearn for Him. It really means we should live each day expecting it to be the day of His coming.

To do this, we must make the Bible a part of our daily lives. Just as we feed our body each day to give it energy and health, we should feed our soul on "the bread of life" (John 6:35). The Word of God keeps the hope of His return alive in our hearts. Perhaps that is why God continually reminds us of Jesus' return all through the Bible. There are more than three hundred references to the return of Christ scattered through the twenty-seven books of the New Testament. The Second Coming is mentioned at least once by each of its writers.

There are two other virtues that result from a daily feeding on God's Word. First, verse 35 points out that we must avoid casting off our "confident trust." The more we read and study the Word of God, the more we build that confidence. The Christians I meet who are easily lured to consider every false doctrine are those who spend very little time in the Bible. Most know barely enough to be saved and far too little to make their confidence sure.

Second, those who fail to read the Bible become impatient in waiting for Jesus' return. They often lose faith and turn away from the great hope.

A friend of mine in the insurance business used to come down to the church gym, and we would work out together two or three times a week during our lunch hours. We talked about everything. Gradually, as the church grew and my travels increased, our times together declined and except for occasional meetings at church we lost close touch with each other. About five years after I resigned my ministry at the church, I heard that on his fiftieth birthday he quit his job and left his wife, blaming his marital boredom on a midlife crisis. He brashly announced on his birthday that he needed "a new job, a new wife, and a new life!" When I heard this I remembered he was a great reader of self-help and motivational books but read very little from the Bible.

He has now had several jobs and multiple wives. He is living a miserable life because he fed his soul on the wrong kind of information. Had he been reading the Psalms, the Gospels, or the Epistles of Paul, he might have been challenged to righteousness by the many promises of the Second Coming.

God obviously has "no pleasure" in him today, and he has no pleasure in himself. He has made himself and everyone else around him miserable. I once taught him how to keep a daily journal of God's blessings to him. But he quit that practice, replacing it with worldly ideas. We are called to a better hope. We are called to read the Word of God and keep focused as we patiently wait for Jesus' coming.

Today's Prayer

Dear heavenly Father, thank You for the promise of Jesus' coming! When I am impatient, help me to trust You more and read Your Word. I want to grow in confidence and faith in Your promises. Everything I hold dear for the future is dependent on Jesus' coming. May my hope of a splendid tomorrow characterize the way I live today! In Jesus' name I pray, Amen.

69 GLORY FOREVER AND EVER

> And now, may the God of peace, who brought
> again from the dead our Lord Jesus, equip you
> with all you need for doing his will. May he
> produce in you, through the power of Jesus Christ,
> all that is pleasing to him. Jesus is the great Shep-
> herd of the sheep by an everlasting covenant,
> signed with his blood. To him be glory forever and
> ever. Amen.   HEBREWS 13:20-21

UNTIL we have received Jesus Christ as our Lord and Savior, we cannot give Him the glory He really deserves. Certainly this world does
not honor Him properly. The media, the entertainment industry, our
humanistic educational system—all these things seem at times to be
hostile and blasphemous toward Him.

But one day that will all change. When Jesus comes again He will
receive "glory forever" (Romans 11:36, NKJV). In other Scriptures we
find that He will be adored and worshiped even by the angels.
Among even the most reluctant mortals, "every knee will bow, . . .
and every tongue will confess that Jesus Christ is Lord, to the glory of
God the Father" (Philippians 2:10-11). That is interesting because in
another part of Scripture, God says, "I will not give my glory to anyone else" (Isaiah 42:8).

Notice how the writer of Hebrews develops one thought in this
text. He refers to God the Father as "the God of peace" who resurrected our Lord Jesus from the dead. From the Godhead comes the
most important event in the history of the world: the bodily resurrection of Jesus. Without this resurrection there would be no Christianity. It is this event that transforms Christ's story into saving truth.
Without His resurrection no one would have ever heard of Him. His
life in Nazareth was so obscure that had He not risen from the dead,

He would not be listed in the history books of the world today. But because of this event Jesus has been given the most prominent position in all accurate history. Further, His resurrection inspired His disciples to change the world.

Our own immortality has come to be because God raised Jesus from the dead. Our redemption comes from God's stamp of approval on Jesus' cross. At the end of Christ's sacrificial life He cried, "It is finished!" (John 19:30). The death He died for our sins finally completed God's redemption plan. His cross made it possible for mankind to have forgiveness and salvation. Because of the cross, billions of people can be cleansed and eternally saved.

But how do we know that what occurred two thousand years ago was really approved by God? It is all very simple. "The God of peace" raised Him from the dead. If Jesus had committed any sin, His death would not have been an adequate sacrifice for the sins of the whole world. Had He been a blemished sacrifice, His body would still be decaying in some Judean hillside.

But hallelujah! The God of peace has raised Him from the dead! His was indeed such a perfect sacrifice that we can be forgiven for all time through His redemptive work on the cross. That is why evangelicals so often use an empty cross as the symbol of Christianity. It is Christ's testimony that "He is risen, as He said" (Matthew 28:6, NKJV). We also worship on the first day of the week, using Sunday as a weekly reminder of that Sunday when Jesus rose from the dead.

Consider the significance of what He did on that cross. The writer of Hebrews called Him "the great Shepherd of the sheep" and referred to the covenant of salvation He provided us as "an everlasting covenant, signed with his blood." Everything in this life is temporary—marriage, family, home, and money. Our covenant of salvation is the only enduring treasure we own, and the One who made it all possible is that "great Shepherd of the sheep."

On the basis of what Christ has done for us, what He is now doing, and what He will one day complete for us, this Bible writer challenges us to live lives that are pleasing to Him. We must always give Him the glory He alone is entitled to. Living every day for His pleasure is the winning formula to prepare us for the life that's on the way.

Remember this proverb: "You can spend your life any way you like, but you can only spend it once." Thirty years from now (if the Lord tarries) it may be too late to turn your life over to Him. Better to turn it over to Him now. Then when He is glorified in God's great forever, you will share with Him and there will be no regrets.

Today's Prayer

Dear heavenly Father, thank You for raising Jesus from the dead so I can benefit forever from His sacrifice. Thank You for giving me the opportunity of spending my life any way I want. I choose this day to give it all to You! Do with me as You will. Direct my steps as You have promised. Come quickly that I may behold You face-to-face. In His name I pray, Amen.

70 THE CROWN OF LIFE

> God blesses the people who patiently endure testing. Afterward they will receive the crown of life that God has promised to those who love him.
>
> JAMES 1:12

THE BOOK of James was one of the earliest books of the New Testament to be written. It is a highly practical book of only five short chapters, yet it mentions the Second Coming three times and refers to "the last days" once.

The writer, James, thought by many to be the brother of Jesus, was the first to mention the martyr's crown, which he calls "the crown of life." It is a special crown reserved for those who suffer persecution and perhaps even martyrdom for the cause of Christ. The existence of such a crown is confirmed by our Lord Himself many years later through the apostle John who was on the Isle of Patmos, "for the testimony of Jesus Christ" (Revelation 1:9, NKJV). In Revelation 2:10, Jesus cautioned one of the seven churches not to "be afraid of what you are about to suffer." Then He reminds them of this: "The Devil will throw some of you into prison and put you to the test. You will be persecuted for 'ten days.' Remain faithful even when facing death, and I will give you the crown of life."

This crown of life to which both Jesus and James refer is only one of five crowns that the Bible tells us will be a part of the rewards God confers upon faithful believers in eternity. The other four crowns are these: the crown of righteousness, the crown of glory, the crown of rejoicing, and the imperishable crown. Each one seems to be earned differently, and each seems to indicate a different reward.

When both references to the crown of life are examined, it is apparent that one of the first things our Lord does after He raptures His church is to bring us before the judgment seat of Christ. Some Christians will have no rewards, for their works will all be burned up. Those works burned are either evil works or good works done with an evil motive. Those whose works pass the test of fire will receive crowns. One such crown is this special crown of life for those who have suffered for the cause of Christ. Some who became martyrs died suddenly, some torturously. History indicates there have been millions of these martyrdoms, from crucifixions to burnings to beheadings. Many were tortured in the Spanish Inquisition. Throughout history those who hate Christians seem to know no bounds in the kind of torture they inflict.

While we read of their imprisonments, persecutions, and martyrdoms, we have not as yet seen their rewards. But the day will come when all the inequities of this life will be rectified by the just Judge, who will grant believers their crowns according to their faithful service.

One of the *LIFE* magazine covers that moved the entire world in the 1950s pictured the five missionaries killed by the Auca Indians in Ecuador. I can still see in my mind the bodies of those five young men lying in the river pierced with spears. What a horrible way to die. Yet from the eternal side, they will one day be resurrected and stand before their Lord and receive a crown of life that never fades. Somehow in the eternal plan of God, the sacrifice of these men inspired a virtual army of volunteers to go to the uttermost part of the earth in service to their Lord.

My mind rushes to the thousands of Christians savagely killed and maimed by the lions in Roman amphitheaters long ago. Their crime? They refused to bow down and worship Caesar. Doubtless some on that day cowered before their oppressors and feigned a rejection of Christ. Like those who were martyred, they will also be saved. But they will not receive the martyr's crown their Lord wanted them to have.

The crown of life is the Lord's promise to those who stand fast. We don't know where that promise was first given. The only other record in Scripture comes from John while on the Isle of Patmos. Evidently Jesus had already taught this principle to His disciples while still on this earth.

The motivation for such valiant sacrifice, James says, is to be our love for Him. If you were forced to suffer or be threatened with dying for your faith, would you have the courage to be true? God has promised to supply our every need—not in advance but as we need it. We may doubt whether or not we have dying grace today because we don't need it at the moment. If and when we do, He will provide it.

When we visited the Great Wall of China, my wife and I had a dedicated Christian for a guide. This young woman had been a high-level Communist until she heard the gospel over shortwave radio out of Hong Kong. Miss Gee (not her real name) later introduced Bev to a shop owner. Miss Gee was buying a T-shirt for Bev as a reminder of that wonderful experience. We couldn't understand the long conversation our guide had with the shopkeeper because it was in Chinese.

But afterwards we asked Miss Gee about it and she said, "I told her you were an American and that you and I were sisters, that we had both received Jesus and been brought into His family. I told her that if she would repent of her sins and call upon Jesus she could be saved and become our sister too."

We were startled! We knew all this shop owner had to do was call to one of the ever-present Communist soldiers and they would arrest Miss Gee and take her to prison. When we asked her why she had not remained more guarded she responded, "Why should I keep silent? Christ died on the cross for my sins and saved me. I love Him with all of my heart!"

When Jesus comes we will not be surprised to see Miss Gee receive the crown of life that fades not away. She has won her special place during the Millennium and beyond. She will glory one day as she "[reigns] with him a thousand years" (Revelation 20:6).

TODAY'S PRAYER

Dear heavenly Father, I am humbled at the sacrificial love demonstrated by many of Your faithful servants. Help me not to forget that the blessings we enjoy as Christians came from the sacrifice of those who've gone before us. I am also thankful that they will be rewarded for that sacrifice when Jesus comes. I have never personally sacrificed anything of real value for You. But I love You, and with Your help I want to be faithful in boldly sharing my faith. In Jesus' name I pray, Amen.

71 ESTABLISH YOUR HEART; THE LORD IS COMING!

Dear brothers and sisters, you must be patient as you wait for the Lord's return. Consider the farmers who eagerly look for the rains in the fall

and in the spring. They patiently wait for the
precious harvest to ripen. You, too, must be
patient. And take courage, for the coming of the
Lord is near. Don't grumble about each other, my
brothers and sisters, or God will judge you. For
look! The great Judge is coming. He is standing at
the door! For examples of patience in suffering,
dear brothers and sisters, look at the prophets
who spoke in the name of the Lord. We give great
honor to those who endure under suffering. Job is
an example of a man who endured patiently. From
his experience we see how the Lord's plan finally
ended in good, for he is full of tenderness and
mercy.   JAMES 5:7-11

PATIENCE is not a new word to those who study the Word of God
relating to the Second Coming. How many times we have prayed,
"How long, O Lord, will You permit Your name to be trampled in the
mud and Your servants to be persecuted?" How long indeed? As long
as it takes! We have to realize that our particular wants and desires are
not His primary interest. We are living in the midst of the long war
against God. It has been rightly dubbed the "Conflict of the Ages." It
is a battle between God and Satan for the souls of men. That battle
underlies much of what we find in the Bible.

Why God has permitted this battle to go on so long is a matter of
debate. No one knows for sure. It seems that for reasons known only to
Him, His desire is for a maximum number of souls to voluntarily
choose to be saved. Until then we have to be patient by establishing
our hearts; that is, we must ground our hearts in the Word of God that
repeatedly challenges us to remember "the coming of the Lord is near."

One element of that patient waiting for His return is found in the
first seven verses of this text. James warns us there will be an increase
in misery among the rich in the last days. Capital and labor problems
will be a characteristic of that period. We are not to let the riches of

some cause us to get our eyes off the goal of waiting patiently for His coming. He then uses the farmer as an illustration. The farmer plows his ground, plants his seed, and waits patiently for the harvest. He gets nothing from the planting process, or even the waiting; in fact, they cost him money. He profits nothing until the harvest.

If you have ever been on a farm, you know that things get pretty frantic in mid- to late August (depending on location and weather), for the harvest cannot be reaped before the crop is ripe. But if the farmer waits too long, frost (or even too much rain) can ruin the crop. There is just a small window of time when the harvest is ripe and must be gathered in. Until then the farmer must wait patiently.

In these last days we think we are living in, we too must wait patiently, establishing our hearts, for the coming of the Lord is near. Just because He has not come yet does not mean He won't. His Holy Spirit, through the efforts of His church, is busy gathering in as many souls as possible before His coming.

There is nothing in Scripture that indicates that there will be a big ingathering of souls just before the Rapture, but frankly, knowing the loving heart of God as revealed by the prophets, I wouldn't be surprised if the world is swept by revival even before the Rapture. We know there will be a great gathering after the Rapture. Then He will seal the 144,000 Jewish witnesses, the two supernatural witnesses, and the angel with the everlasting gospel. During the Tribulation they will harvest "a vast crowd, too great to count, from every nation and tribe and people and language" (Revelation 7:9).

In fact, that is the reason Jerry Jenkins and I have carefully sought the leading of the Holy Spirit in the writing of our Left Behind novels. In each volume we have inserted what we call a *believable conversion story that is reproducible in the heart of the reader.* So far, the result has been better than anything we could ask or think, for we receive hundreds of letters and e-mail messages telling us that some of our readers are coming to Christ every day. Our books are only a small part of the tools God is using as He harvests the souls of men today.

One other challenge the apostle James gives us needs to be mentioned. In verse 9 he says, "Don't grumble about each other, my brothers and sisters, or God will judge you. For look! The great Judge is coming. He is standing at the door!" Treat others, particularly believers, the way you want Jesus, the Judge, to find you. For He is coming!

Today's Prayer

Dear heavenly Father, please forgive me for getting impatient in waiting for Jesus to return. Help me to give thanks that You have tarried. The longer we wait, the more individuals will have time to hear the gospel and receive You as Lord and Savior. Help me to rightly divide my time, talent, and possessions in the light of His coming. Then, when He comes, He will be pleased with my availability to help advance Your kingdom. In Jesus' name, Amen.

72. RESERVED IN HEAVEN FOR YOU

Blessed be the God and Father of our Lord Jesus Christ, who according to His abundant mercy has begotten us again to a living hope through the resurrection of Jesus Christ from the dead, to an inheritance incorruptible and undefiled and that does not fade away, reserved in heaven for you, who are kept by the power of God through faith for salvation ready to be revealed in the last time. In this you greatly rejoice, though now for a little while, if need be, you have been grieved by various trials, that the genuineness of your faith, being much more precious than gold that perishes, though it is tested by fire, may be found to praise, honor, and glory at the revelation of Jesus Christ.   1 Peter 1:3-7, NKJV

NO ROOM in the inn? I couldn't believe it! I felt like Mary or Joseph in Bethlehem two thousand years ago.

I had just deplaned in Dallas to attend a pre-Trib research conference and was checking into the hotel when the clerk said, "I am sorry, Dr. LaHaye, but we have no record of your reservation and the hotel is already overbooked. We have no room for you."

In thirty-five years of traveling all over the world I had never had that happen. "Surely you can find one little room for me to sleep in," I begged. She was resolute. So I even tried to pressure her by saying, "I am the chairman of this conference." I even implied the conference couldn't go on without me. Nothing worked. She wouldn't bend. "No room!" she insisted.

Fortunately for me, an evangelist friend of mine from San Diego happened to be walking by the registration desk and heard of my plight. He graciously invited me to share his room with him. I came out a bit better than Mary and Joseph did.

There will never be a no-vacancy sign when the Lord calls us home. He has promised us that we have an eternal "inheritance incorruptible and undefiled . . . reserved in heaven for [us]." What a blessed assurance! Our reservation is guaranteed. How? By the resurrection of Jesus Christ from the dead! Christ promises, "Because I live, you will live also" (John 14:19, NKJV).

Several times through the years I have had a clerk tell me I had no reservation, but when I showed my confirmation number, I always got a room. One time I was told at a car-rental agency they had no more cars. Fortunately, I had a confirmation number so they gave me a Lincoln Town Car for the same price as the compact I had reserved. When it comes to heaven, Jesus holds the keys! Revelation 1:18 indicates He even holds the keys "of death and the grave." If we have received Jesus, our mansion in heaven is assured by Him.

In this text Peter encourages us to look beyond the sufferings and inequities of our lives so we may experience grace in the world to come. We can "greatly rejoice" by looking forward to the Glorious Appearing of Jesus. Then he adds that even though we have not seen Jesus ourselves, we still love Him. By faith in what He has done on Calvary, we will be with Him forever. Peter calls it "joy inexpressible and full of glory" (1 Peter 1:8, NKJV). What a definition! Inexpressible joy!

Maybe that is why the devil has hoodwinked so many preachers into remaining mute on the subject of the Second Coming. It is difficult for me to understand why any minister would fail to preach from the 28 percent of the Bible in which prophecy is found. One thing is certain: Those early churches were on fire with the message of Jesus' coming. It evidently filled them with "inexpressible joy."

We sometimes take the teaching of His return for granted. To really appreciate it, compare God's wonderful plan for your future with the often hopeless religions of the world. There really is no comparison. Hinduism offers a nebulous state of nirvana to those who live a succession of good lives in their reincarnated states. These ponderous rebirths may take thousands of years and many lifetimes. Buddhism offers nothing concrete, and the Muslims offer their eternal gratification to a man.

Christianity offers the sublime plan of God that includes the Rapture, the Glorious Appearing, the millennial kingdom, and heaven forever. No religion in the world can compare with that! No wonder it produces—as the King James Version puts it—"joy unspeakable and full of glory"! Jesus is coming! Never lose sight of that fact, and trust in Him in whom "all fulness dwell[s]" forever and ever and ever and ever (Colossians 1:19, KJV). Amen!

Today's Prayer

Dear heavenly Father, my heart is filled with praise and joy unspeakable and full of glory every time I think of the return of Jesus. Help me not to get bogged down with the thoughts and cares of this world and the "deceitfulness of riches" (Matthew 13:22) that "war against the soul" (1 Peter 2:11, NKJV). Rather, let me keep my eyes on the wonderful future You have planned for those who love You and worship Your Son. In Jesus' name I pray, Amen.

73

PRAISE, HONOR, AND GLORY AT HIS COMING

So be truly glad! There is wonderful joy ahead, even though it is necessary for you to endure many trials for a while. These trials are only to test your faith, to show that it is strong and pure. It is being tested as fire tests and purifies gold—and your faith is far more precious to God than mere gold. So if your faith remains strong after being tried by fiery trials, it will bring you much praise and glory and honor on the day when Jesus Christ is revealed to the whole world. You love him even though you have never seen him. Though you do not see him, you trust him; and even now you are happy with a glorious, inexpressible joy. Your reward for trusting him will be the salvation of your souls. This salvation was something the prophets wanted to know more about. They prophesied about this gracious salvation prepared for you, even though they had many questions as to what it all could mean. They wondered what the Spirit of Christ within them was talking about when he told them in advance about Christ's suffering and his great glory afterward. They wondered when and to whom all this would happen. They were told that these things would not happen during their lifetime, but many years later, during yours. And now this Good News has been announced by those who preached to you in the power of the Holy Spirit sent from heaven. It is all so wonderful that even the angels are eagerly watching these things happen. So think clearly and exercise self-control. Look forward to the special blessings that will come to you at the return of Jesus Christ. Obey God because you are his children. Don't slip back into your old ways of doing evil; you didn't know any better then. But now you must be holy in everything you do, just as God—who chose you to be his children—is holy. For he himself has said, "You must be holy because I am holy."   1 PETER 1:6-16

IT HAS been my privilege through the years to receive a number of honors that I treasure: mementos, plaques, honorary and earned degrees, and the wonderful congregational awards one receives over fifty years of public ministry. The awards I prize the most include my ten gold, platinum, and medallion book awards and my doctorate of literature degree from Liberty University. But none of these comes close to the three awards Peter mentions in this passage. These awards are available to all Christians when we stand before Jesus.

In fact, Peter says of these awards that they are "more precious than gold that perishes, though it is tested by fire" (1 Peter 1:7, NKJV). This probably refers to the "fire test" that Paul writes about in 1 Corinthians 3:9-15 where he gives us the details of the judgment seat of Christ. Peter had evidently read Paul's epistles, for he said in 2 Peter 3:15-16, "as our beloved brother Paul wrote to you with the wisdom God gave him—speaking of these things in all of his letters." We know that 1 Corinthians was written about twenty-five years prior to Peter's books, so it is more than likely that he was referring to the same judgment seat of Christ that Paul earlier referred to.

We have already seen that Paul mentions crowns as symbols of reward. In fact, we will later examine the one crown Peter mentions, the pastor's or teacher's crown, which we call the "elder's crown," or the "crown of glory that does not fade away" (1 Peter 5:4, NKJV). Each crown depicts some kind of reward for faithful service. But here Peter sets forth three distinct awards that are available to all believers. Let's examine each of them:

- *Praise* is a reward. In 1 Corinthians 4:5, Paul teaches that at the judgment, "God will give to everyone whatever praise is due." Just getting there and being included in that "gathering together unto Him" (which is what the Rapture is) will earn us the praise of God. We already know that all we have to do to be included in the Rapture is to "believe that Jesus died and rose again, even so God will bring with Him those who sleep in Jesus" (1 Thessalonians 4:14, NKJV).

  Measured in the light of the long conflict between Satan and God for human souls, God will give praise to every Christian who simply calls on the name of the Lord to be saved.

- *Honor* seems to be a separate and distinct award given to a special category of people who serve Him. Jesus said, "All those who want to be my disciples must come and follow me, because my servants must be where I am. And if they follow me, the Father will *honor* them" (John 12:26, emphasis mine). Obviously, this is not a general reward given to everyone; it is a special reward given to those Christians who faithfully serve Him. Some, of course, will be missionaries no one has ever heard of but Jesus. Still, Christ knows all things, and he will be aware of those faithful ones.

  Having pastored a great missionary-minded church, I know some faithful servants of Christ who have served the Lord in some remote area where their life's work went unnoticed. But at the judgment seat of Jesus, they will be rewarded with divine honor. We are not told what that honor entails, but we are assured it will be "more precious than gold that perishes, though it is tested by fire" (1 Peter 1:7, NKJV). The results of that reward will go on throughout the Millennium and into eternity.

During my forty years of ministry in three churches, I saw many Christians who will never receive that reward. When they came to the obstacles or temptations in their lives, they did not choose to obey the Lord and serve Him. They refused to follow Christ in favor of other easier, more gratifying things they deemed more important. Unfortunately, some Christians have never intentionally done much in Christian service. Faith costs nothing, for Jesus paid for our gift of salvation. Serving Christ is a different matter. It does cost. It costs the denial of one's self, one's time, and one's temporary interests. Think of the Sunday-school teachers who week after week and year after year study their Bible to teach a good lesson, shepherd their class members, and try to reach their lost friends. In the judgment they will receive honor—forever.

- *Glory* is evidently the most important of the three rewards Peter lists here. It is mentioned in connection with being a "witness to the sufferings of Christ" (1 Peter 5:1). All Christians have not been called upon to suffer for Christ. Others have suffered severely, even to death. But all who suffer for His sake will be rewarded with *glory* in direct proportion to their suffering. Then sacrifice will be rectified where it really counts: at the judgment seat of Christ!

There have been hundreds of martyrs. Polycarp, a second-century leader and writer of the early church, was burned at the stake because he refused to deny his Lord. He was tied to a stake and wood was placed at his feet and set afire. His last words were, "He has been faithful to me all my life; why should I now deny Him who is my Christ?" By the time the ropes that held him had burned and fallen away, his spirit had left his body. He went immediately into the presence of his Lord. He, like hundreds of thousands of others, is a candidate for the "inheritance which is imperishable" (1 Peter 1:4, NASB).

74

WHY SCOFFERS SCOFF

This is my second letter to you, dear friends, and in both of them I have tried to stimulate your wholesome thinking and refresh your memory. I want you to remember and understand what the holy prophets said long ago and what our Lord and Savior commanded through your apostles. First, I want to remind you that in the last days there will be scoffers who will laugh at the truth and do every evil thing they desire. This will be their argument: "Jesus promised to come back, did he? Then where is he? Why, as far back as anyone can remember, everything has remained exactly the same since the world was first created." They deliberately forget that God made the heavens by the word of his command, and he brought the earth up from the water and surrounded it with water. Then he used the water

to destroy the world with a mighty flood. And God
has also commanded that the heavens and the earth
will be consumed by fire on the day of judgment,
when ungodly people will perish.   2 PETER 3:1-7

SECOND PETER was written near the end of Peter's life. It rings with
such finality that it seems to be Peter's own conclusion to the New Testament. Thirty years later, however, the aged apostle John wrote his Apocalypse which, in time, became the final book of the New Testament.

In this chapter, the apostle Peter reaches back to the words spoken by prophets and to "what our Lord and Savior commanded through your apostles." Peter brings up one of the significant signs of the last days. He says that as these days arrive scoffers will "do every evil thing they desire."

For more than one hundred years, the writings of Charles Darwin and his disciples have filled the academic community. The entire secular world has fallen under the thrall of evolutionist thinking. How often we hear secular scholars teaching that the world has been here millions or even billions of years! This scientific lie has been told so often since the Scopes Trial of 1925 that it is now assumed to be a fact.

A perfect example was our guide during a recent trip to the Grand Canyon. Looking at the gaping gorge that cascaded into the depths before us, he explained that the age of the earth was related to the depth of that gorge. He told us that geologists, having measured the erosion rate of the past one hundred years, had extrapolated the age of the canyon. The canyon, he said, was millions of years old.

"How do you know the erosion rate has always been the same as it is today?" I asked.

"Scientists tell us so," he replied.

"Oh? How do they know? Were they here to observe it? The chasm at Mount Saint Helen's was blown out of the mountain in a single day."

The young man was not convinced. Peter said that in the last days, scoffers will scoff. Further, he said they would "do every evil thing they desire" and "deliberately forget that God made the heavens by the word of his command, and he brought the earth up from the water and surrounded it with water. Then he used the water to destroy the world with a mighty flood." In other words, the worldwide flood which happened only forty-five hundred years ago changed how we measure time in geography! The evidence for a worldwide flood is so obvious that only the willfully ignorant (or those driven by humanistic thinking) refuse to see it.

To appreciate this we must go back in history and realize that until the seventeenth century there were few, if any, skeptics (or as Peter called them, "scoffers"). Flood stories permeate most cultures and religions of the world. The worldwide flood was generally believed until the rise of atheists in the mid-seventeenth century. Today, their progeny continue to dream up fanciful stories to explain how fish fossils of many varieties are found on the top of mountains fifteen thousand feet above sea level. These scientists are willfully ignorant. They refuse to accept the obvious truth: There is a God who keeps His word.

What are the hallmarks of the skeptics of our day? First, they live to the gratification of their own lusts and willful ignorance. Not all those who reject God are leading the world into immorality, but many are. Peter indicated that some in the last days would reject the promise of His coming because of lust, others because of willfulness. In either case they refuse to believe there is a God who keeps His word and will come again. They don't realize that their hedonistic unbelief is a sign we are living in the last days.

Second, verse 7 gives the real reason they have allowed their willfulness to overrule their common sense. Because that same Word of God teaches that just as He once brought the Flood in judgment on the sins of mankind, He will also judge the world of the future. They refuse to accept the abundant evidence that God exists because they do not want to face the fact that He will judge them for the way they have lived their lives.

As Peter said in verse 8, "you must not forget, dear friends, that a day is like a thousand years to the Lord, and a thousand years is like a day." As we see these prophecies, they happened two thousand years ago. But as God sees His promises, they were given just two days ago. He is coming and He will judge all who refuse to believe in Him.

TODAY'S PRAYER

Dear heavenly Father, thank You for the many evidences You have given to encourage our faith. Jesus is coming again. We have Your Word, the evidences of the Flood, the stars that declare Your glory, the Lord Jesus' unmatchable life, and His resurrection. All these convince us that You are going to send a king to establish a righteous kingdom. We are honored to be invited to share in Your kingdom. Help us live our lives in faith and obedience until He comes. In Jesus' name I pray, Amen.

75 WHEN THE DAY STAR ARISES IN YOUR HEART

We have also a more sure word of prophecy; whereunto ye do well that ye take heed, as unto a light that shineth in a dark place, until the day dawn, and the day star arise in your hearts: Knowing this first, that no prophecy of the scripture is of any private interpretation. For the prophecy came not in old time by the will of man: but holy men of God spake as they were moved by the Holy Ghost.   2 PETER 1:19-21, KJV

A FLIGHT attendant could hardly wait until our plane took off before she introduced herself and enthusiastically blurted out her kind affirmation: "God has changed my life since I read your Left Behind series." Then she described a familiar story. "I love my pastor. He is a good Bible teacher, but he never preaches on prophecy. Until I read your books I was never motivated to really share my faith. Now I have gotten as many of our crew members as possible to read your series. I talk openly to them about accepting Christ. Already three of my associates and relatives have received the Lord."

Compliments of this sort never take me by surprise. Nothing is more motivating to Christians than believing that Jesus could come at any moment. Recently, after giving a message on prophecy, I met a man who described himself as a "compulsive witness." He said, however, that until he grasped the truth about the Second Coming he was tongue-tied by fear. But just the thought that Jesus could come at any moment has helped him overcome his timidity, and he is now openly witnessing for Christ.

This passage takes the subject one step further. After making it clear that prophecy in Scripture is not just an accessory teaching but a central doctrine of the church, the apostle predicts it will also cause a "day star [to rise] in your hearts." Scholars are not totally agreed about this phenomenon, but the best interpretation I have read indicates that those who have studied Bible prophecy carefully believe we are living in the last days. Those who do believe will have "the day star arise in [their] hearts." This means they will experience the joyous anticipation that Christ could come in their lifetime. Studying the prophecies can give us such a spirit of anticipation that we may even anticipate the joy of the Lord coming for us should we have to die before He comes. This could be a second way the Lord has of preparing those who really know His Word to "walk through the valley of the shadow of death" (Psalm 23:4, NKJV).

On the other hand, it could be that those who know the prophetic word will be touched by the Holy Spirit and have the day star arise in their hearts—the star of anticipating the Rapture.

Before you write this off as impossible, consider Simeon and Anna, two first-century saints who anticipated the first coming of Jesus. Luke tells us, "Now there was a man named Simeon who lived in Jerusalem. He was a righteous man and very devout. He was filled with the Holy Spirit, and he eagerly expected the Messiah to come and rescue Israel. The Holy Spirit had revealed to him that he would not die until he had seen the Lord's Messiah" (Luke 2:25-26). Could that have been the day star rising in his heart? After all, the Holy Spirit had led him into worship at the exact time that Mary and Joseph brought the Christ child into the temple. Consequently, he had the privilege of holding the baby Jesus in his arms and then making prophecies concerning Him.

Luke wrote that Anna was an old prophetess who did not depart from the temple, but served God with fasting and prayer night and day. She also came into the temple at the same instant Jesus did and she, too, gave thanks to the Lord. She spoke of the child Jesus to all those who looked for the Redeemer of Israel. Obviously, some kind of day star arose in her heart as well. She actually saw and touched the Savior of the world at His first coming.

Part of the force of the day-star formula is whether or not we are the generation that will be included in the Rapture. We have more reason to believe that Christ should come in our lifetime than any generation before us. In our book *Are We Living in the End Times?* we give many of those signs of the Lord's return that were fulfilled during the twentieth century. The rapid increase in travel and the growth of knowledge would indicate that we are the first generation who could literally fulfill Revelation 11:9. This is the prophecy that the two witnesses will be killed and lie in the streets for three days and be seen by all the peoples of the world. That could not have happened even forty years ago. However, today such an event would be as possible as CNN.

As far as the best Bible scholars can tell, there are no signs that need to be fulfilled before the Rapture. Christ could come at any moment and nothing needs to happen to make it possible. Consequently, our age may contain many modern Simeons and Annas—godly saints well versed in the prophetic Scriptures—who will have the day star dawn in their hearts.

TODAY'S PRAYER

Dear heavenly Father, thank You for giving us the prophetic Word of Scripture that prepares us to live in anticipation of the coming of Jesus. May I walk holy before You so Your Holy Spirit can speak to me as I study the Scriptures to learn about end-time events. Of one thing I am certain: I do not want any habit, practice, or sin in my life to keep the day star from arising in my heart. Let me be a part of that generation that shall take part in the rapture of the church. In Jesus' name I pray, Amen.

76 BEWARE OF FALSE PROPHETS

Above all, you must understand that no prophecy in Scripture ever came from the prophets themselves or because they wanted to prophesy. It was the Holy Spirit who moved the prophets to speak from God. But there were also false prophets in Israel, just as there will be false teachers among you. They will cleverly teach their destructive heresies about God and even turn against their Master who bought them. Theirs will be a swift and terrible end. Many will follow their evil teaching and shameful immorality. And because of them, Christ and his true way will be slandered.

2 PETER 1:20–2:2

THERE HAS always been truth in the world and there have always been false prophets to adulterate it. Even in Jesus' day, the apostles had to contend with them. Borrowing from integrity and honest faith, these heretics have always tried to found religions that lead souls astray. These false teachers are abundant in our generation. Ten times as many people inhabit Earth as existed during the first century. More people, more false prophets! Jesus and His disciples warned us about this increase during the last days and right on into the Tribulation period.

Satan is in the deception business. For millennia he has watered down all truth just as he did to Eve. In Eden he cast doubt on the truth of God's Word by asking, "Did God really say . . . ?" (Genesis 3:1) or by contradicting the words of God in saying, "You won't die" (Genesis 3:4). In the end times, Satan will increase his lies through false prophets who will confuse people by secretly bringing in destructive heresies, and "even turn against their Master who bought them."

Today the founders of heresies, like those involved in the Jesus Seminar, get widespread coverage on the front of tabloids and news magazines. Twice every year, the seventy-two scholars of the Jesus Seminar meet for a three-day session to determine what parts of Scripture are actually Jesus' words. These presumptuous "scholars," two thousand years removed from the life and times of Jesus, are arrogant enough to think that they can decide for the "less informed" which Scriptures can be relied upon.

Many so-called scholars deny the essential deity of our Lord and His resurrection. Most of these are academics who have forgotten the most basic premise of all logic: If you start out on a wrong premise, you will always end up with a wrong conclusion. Anyone who starts out with the false premise that Jesus Christ is not the virgin-born, only begotten, resurrected Son of God will always come to faulty conclusions about God and the Bible.

Anyone who heeds the teachings of such false prophets is destined to be misled by them. Sadly, they must also share their eternal fate. The apostle Peter is not timid in warning what will happen to those who mislead others about who Jesus is. "These false teachers . . . laugh at the terrifying powers they know so little about, and they will be destroyed along with them. Their destruction is their reward for the harm they have done" (2 Peter 2:12-13).

It is evident that Peter, thinking of false teachers in his own day, pronounced God's heady judgment upon them.

There isn't much that can be done to redeem those committed to false teachings. Few, if any, ever repent of their heresies. Their arrogance makes them too stiff of knee to fall before Jesus and worship Him. But we who are committed to biblical truth can do something. We can fill the people of God with the truth of God. For this reason I have spent much of my life writing books on prophecy. People saturated in truth are less likely to accept heresy.

Recently a man wrote this in a letter to us, "I have been a Christian all my adult life and have read the entire Bible through three different times, all except for the book of Revelation. My pastors across the years counseled me to avoid reading the book because no one can understand it. Since reading your Left Behind novels, I have read the book of Revelation four times and I love it!" How foolish this man's early counsel was. All the books of the Bible are there for us to read and understand. This is particularly true of the Apocalypse. Indeed, Revelation 1:3 offers a blessing to all those who read it. It exalts Jesus Christ like no other book in the world.

Today's Prayer

Dear heavenly Father, thank You for making so much of the Bible prophetic in nature. Without these prophecies we would know nothing about the wonderful plan You have for our future. Help me to develop a keen interest in studying prophecy. Only through great prophetic passages can I ever arrive at the true pic-

ture of the second coming of Your Son. Please give me an increasing appetite to know Your Word. In Jesus' name I pray, Amen.

77 THE LORD KEEPS HIS PROMISES

But, beloved, do not forget this one thing, that with the Lord one day is as a thousand years, and a thousand years as one day. The Lord is not slack concerning His promise, as some count slackness, but is longsuffering toward us, not willing that any should perish but that all should come to repentance. But the day of the Lord will come as a thief in the night, in which the heavens will pass away with a great noise, and the elements will melt with fervent heat; both the earth and the works that are in it will be burned up. Therefore, since all these things will be dissolved, what manner of persons ought you to be in holy conduct and godliness, looking for and hastening the coming of the day of God, because of which the heavens will be dissolved, being on fire, and the elements will melt with fervent heat? Nevertheless we, according to His promise, look for new heavens and a new earth in which righteousness dwells. Therefore, beloved, looking forward to these things, be diligent to be found by Him in peace, without spot and blameless.   2 PETER 3:8-14, NKJV

EVERYONE has experienced the disappointment of broken promises. Perhaps the most devastating of fractured pledges is that of a man who, having promised "to love and cherish as long as we both shall live," has an affair with someone new and divorces his lifelong partner.

As a pastor, I have suffered with some wonderful people who

had no clue that they were being betrayed by a false love. I remember a sixty-two-year-old man who abandoned his needy, sick wife for a younger woman. When questioned about the integrity of his wedding promise, he snapped his fingers indifferently and said, "Promises are like pie crusts, made to be broken."

Not so with God! There are no promises God has not kept. He promised through the ancient Hebrew prophets that Jesus would come. He kept that promise right on time. When Jesus came He also promised to come again. He said He would later return to the earth and set up His thousand-year kingdom. You may trust that this promise also will be kept on time.

Peter tried to explain this on a level that we humans could understand. God's promise to return was made two thousand years ago, but since God regards "a thousand years as one day" this pledge is but as a two-day-old promise. Human promises tarnish with age. Not God's! His Word is forever settled in heaven.

The term Peter uses is very reassuring to us: "The Lord is not slack concerning His promise, as some count slackness, but is longsuffering toward us"; that is, His Word endures "forever." And "the day of the Lord will come as a thief in the night." Peter used this metaphor to speak of His Glorious Appearing. In this passage those who are awaiting His coming will have already been raptured. Only the Tribulation believers who have not been martyred will be prepared for His coming by reading the signs of the times. Most of the post-Rapture world will continue on as people do now, ignorant of the promises of God. They will live unsuspecting lives. His coming for them will be "as a thief." They will not be prepared.

To be prepared for His coming is the point of all prophecy. But in this passage Peter tells us why Christ has so long delayed His coming. He is "not willing that any should perish but that all should come to repentance." Let every valiant pastor trumpet this from the housetops: God wants no one to be lost.

Somehow a false characterization of God has been spread by the deceiver. He has sponsored the stern notion that God is an angry taskmaster who delights in throwing people into hell. Nothing could be further from the truth! God loves humanity so much that He gave His Son to save us. He stands at the edge of hell weeping when anyone is lost. This compassion will extend beyond the Rapture. Many will be saved during the last half of the Tribulation. Surely this must prove how much God loves humankind.

Since God is "not slack concerning His promise," we know beyond a shadow of a doubt that Jesus is coming again. Our number-one need is to be ready when He comes. The only way we can be sure of our preparedness is to personally receive His Son, Jesus, as our Lord. Prepare yourself and draw near to the Savior.

TODAY'S PRAYER

Dear heavenly Father, thank You for Your love and interest in humankind. Thank You for saving me, and please use me to share Your Good News with others. I realize I need Your Holy Spirit to fill my life so I can become a channel of grace to others. So if there is anything in my life that would hinder me from being used of Your Spirit, please forgive me and cleanse me of the hindrance. In Jesus' name I pray, Amen.

78 ASHAMED AT HIS COMING

And now, little children, abide in Him, that when He appears, we may have confidence and not be ashamed before Him at His coming. If you know that He is righteous, you know that everyone who practices righteousness is born of Him. Behold what manner of love the Father has bestowed on

us, that we should be called children of God!
Therefore the world does not know us, because it
did not know Him. Beloved, now we are children of
God; and it has not yet been revealed what we
shall be, but we know that when He is revealed, we
shall be like Him, for we shall see Him as He is.
And everyone who has this hope in Him purifies
himself, just as He is pure. Whoever commits sin
also commits lawlessness, and sin is lawlessness.

1 JOHN 2:28–3:4, NKJV

LONG BEFORE believers in Christ were called "Christians," they were called "followers of the way." Society in first-century Israel was largely made up of Jews who observed a strict code of ethics, though sometimes it was highly legalistic. Along with these Jews there were Gentiles who, for the most part, did not believe in a God who had any claim on their personal conduct.

Christianity then was different than it is now. Jesus makes it clear that when we become His followers our lifestyles should change. A genuine conversion experience should change our appetites and our spirits, our whole set of values. Being born again is a supernatural occurrence!

A Vietnam veteran once told me he had come to Christ after the war. When I asked him in looking back what the first sign was that he had really become a Christian, he said, "After I went forward and received Christ, that very Sunday night as I was driving home, the thought suddenly hit me: I am going to have to get rid of that woman I have been living with!" No one had to tell him that. While no one at the church knew he was living that kind of lifestyle, the Holy Spirit spoke to him. He knew what he had to do. Eventually his live-in lover also accepted Christ and today has a Christian home of her own.

If I were to ask you what kind of life all Christians should live, how would you reply? I hope your answer would include the word "righteous." In our text for today, John teaches us that anyone who has a healthy expectation of Christ will purify himself just as He is pure. The healthy expectation of Christ's coming should have an effect on the way we live. It should produce holiness.

"The Lord helps those who help themselves," is a false proverb indeed. Salvation is the "gift of God, not of works, lest anyone should boast" (Ephesians 2:8-9, NKJV). But Christian living is a different matter. Those who call Christ Savior and yet live for themselves will be "ashamed before Him at His coming."

After church one Sunday, a certain lady in the church rebuked me at the church door. Her comment was, "I resent it when you put me on a guilt trip. When I go to church I don't want to feel guilty. I like to think I am doing a good thing." The woman only came to church once a week and never became involved in Bible study. She had no friends in the church and never witnessed to her faith. Her time was spent in civic affairs, garden clubs, and bridge parties. She had surrounded herself with women like her who had no concern for Christ and His kingdom.

Teaching on the Second Coming will give no hope to the carnal Christian who cares little for Christ. Such individuals have scant interest in what the Bible teaches about the future. Thus, they are rarely motivated to live wholly dedicated unto Him.

What kind of thoughts come up in your mind when you think of the Rapture, the judgment seat of Christ, or the marriage of the Lamb? These vital subjects are prophetic foretastes of all that God has prepared for those who love Him.

Are you ready for His coming?

TODAY'S PRAYER
Dear heavenly Father, thank You for not leaving us without a certain word on the second coming of Christ. We could be the

generation who will experience the Rapture. Is there some sin in my life? If so, make it clear to me. I want my heart to be unblemished as I await Your glory. In Jesus' name I pray, Amen.

79

THE PURIFYING HOPE

See how very much our heavenly Father loves us, for he allows us to be called his children, and we really are! But the people who belong to this world don't know God, so they don't understand that we are his children. Yes, dear friends, we are already God's children, and we can't even imagine what we will be like when Christ returns. But we do know that when he comes we will be like him, for we will see him as he really is. And all who believe this will keep themselves pure, just as Christ is pure. Those who sin are opposed to the law of God, for all sin opposes the law of God. And you know that Jesus came to take away our sins, for there is no sin in him. So if we continue to live in him, we won't sin either. But those who keep on sinning have never known him or understood who he is. Dear children, don't let anyone deceive you about this: When people do what is right, it is because they are righteous, even as Christ is righteous. But when people keep on sinning, it shows they belong to the Devil, who has been sinning since the beginning. But the Son of God came to destroy these works of the Devil. Those who have been born into God's family do not sin, because God's life is in them. So they can't keep on sinning, because they have been born of God.   1 JOHN 3:1-9

ONCE a person becomes a Christian he will live a different life. The Holy Spirit comes to live in our hearts as we call on the name of the Lord. But when this new spiritual nature comes to live in us, we should be different. What differences are we to expect? For one thing, we will come to love other Christians. The first verses of our passage make it clear that when we become children of God by faith, we must love one another.

John also says that "we do know that when he comes we will be like him," because we are His children. Just think of it! We shall be like Jesus in the resurrection! Most of us are dissatisfied that we sometimes live so little like Him. But one day we will!

In the meantime, we should take heart from the many evangelical young people who are wearing WWJD bracelets (What Would Jesus Do?). What a noble practice! We may never automatically respond in every situation as Jesus would because we are human. Still, when confronted by a temptation or decision it is wise to ask, "What would Jesus do about this?"

In a way, that is what John is challenging us to do in this text. "And all who believe this will keep themselves pure, just as Christ is pure." If these are indeed the last days, Jesus could actually come in our lifetime. Perhaps it is time for all Christians to purify their lifestyles.

We should not, however, get so paranoid about our lifestyles that we have no time to be evangelistic. Occasionally I meet Christians who brand almost anything done for fun as sinful. In verse 4, John makes clear what ought to be defined as sin. "Sin opposes the law of God." This definition recalls the first sin of Adam and Eve. They defied the will of God by eating of the tree of the knowledge of good and evil. It was not the fruit of the tree that killed them; it was the act of lawlessness. This disobedience eventually killed them.

For us the issue is the same. We have the Ten Commandments and know the basis of right and wrong. In the New Testament we have additional admonitions, commandments, and principles to help us determine righteous and unrighteous behavior. Further, the Holy Spirit within us serves as a spiritual umpire to call the shots in our struggle to live for God.

One day a man who owned a print shop came in to tell me he had an offer to go into business with another printer who had newer and bigger equipment. But I could tell that this young Christian didn't feel quite right about it. When I asked him if the man who would become his partner was a Christian, he answered, "No. Why do you ask?" I quoted Paul's advice, "Do not be unequally yoked together with unbelievers" (2 Corinthians 6:14, NKJV). He said, "I thought that only meant in marriage." When I responded with "not so" and explained that a business partnership, like a marriage, is a "yoke," his instant response was, "That settles it. If the Lord doesn't want me to do it, I won't." Less than a month later he discovered that his potential partner had mortgaged all the company equipment and fled to Mexico.

My friend won the battle the instant he confessed, "If the Lord doesn't want me to do it, I won't." That should be the attitude of every child of God, "especially now that the day of his coming back again is drawing near" (Hebrews 10:25). If there is anything in your life that you're not sure about, ask yourself this question: If Jesus came today, would I want Him to find me doing this or that? That question will invariably give you the best insight in every issue or decision.

Today's Prayer

Dear heavenly Father, forgive me for those times when I have defied Your will to serve my own. I want to walk in purity. Cleanse my heart. Wash me thoroughly so that I might be ready for the Rapture. In His name I pray, Amen.

80 THE HOPE OF THE CHRISTIAN

> And all who believe this will keep themselves pure,
> just as Christ is pure. 1 JOHN 3:3

THE SECOND COMING is the hope of the Christian. We have already seen how the Holy Spirit uses this hope to motivate Christians toward holiness. Only God can guarantee our future. And only He can predict it. Many have tried, but their prophecies never come to pass. Their followers twist and distort history in an attempt to make their predictions come true.

Our God is different. He has an unbroken chain of hundreds of accurately fulfilled prophecies. Remember Nebuchadnezzar's dream? Daniel interpreted it in such a way as to explain to the despot that four world empires would come and remain until the last days (Daniel 2:27-45). History has vindicated Daniel. All that he prophesied has been fulfilled. We have already seen the miracle of the Jews returning to Israel. The reason many other prophecies have not been fulfilled is that they are still in the future. That is what prophecy is: history written ahead of time! Anyone can make "iffy" predictions, but only God can write history in advance and have it come true.

Jerry and I are committed to writing prophetic novels of end-time events. We want Christians everywhere to become excited about Jesus' second coming. This isn't a matter of a guesstimate or supposition; it is a certified fact of the future. We can't guarantee Jesus will come in our lifetime, although we expect Him to. But we can guarantee He will come again, for He always does all He has promised.

When He does come, what will we be like? This is one of the most common questions we are asked at prophecy conferences. Jerry and I always answer confidently that we will be like Jesus, "for we will see him as he really is" (1 John 3:2).

I also use this verse whenever anyone asks how old he or she will be during the Millennium. Since Jesus was thirty-three when He rose from the dead and since, as John predicted, "we will be like Him" (1 John 3:2) in eternity, I'd like to assume we will all be thirty-three throughout the Millennium and into eternity.

Looking back, I can see now that thirty-three was a great time in life. It is the prime of life. At thirty-three we are old enough to be mature and young enough to enjoy great health. But better than being thirty-three will be being like Jesus! We will then have a resurrected body, like unto His own glorified body. That itself is enough to give us hope for the future.

Such hope is, as the apostle says, a confident expectation of life in the afterlife with our Lord (2 Corinthians 5:6). It is not a shaky hope like we admit to when we hope a friend will keep his word. It is God's hope we are considering. It is our eternal hope, as certain as His Word and as confident as His promise.

Not everyone shares this hope. Those who reject Christ have no hope. In the hour of death they may mouth our words, but their empty professions are hopeless. Christ alone can guarantee our rapture hope. Do you have this hope? Trust its author! You have nothing to lose and everything to gain. Someone has wisely said, "For a Christian, this present life is as bad as it will ever get. For the unbeliever, it's as good as it will ever get." The confident expectation of our resurrection at Christ's second coming makes the difference.

Today's Prayer

Dear heavenly Father, thank You for making Your plan of salvation so simple that a little child can understand it. Thank You for giving me a confident expectation that my future is guaranteed. Thank You for hope. In Your blessed name I pray, Amen.

81 WHEN HE IS REVEALED

Yes, dear friends, we are already God's children,
and we can't even imagine what we will be like
when Christ returns. But we do know that when he
comes we will be like him, for we will see him as he
really is. And all who believe this will keep themselves pure, just as Christ is pure. Those who sin
are opposed to the law of God, for all sin opposes
the law of God. And you know that Jesus came to
take away our sins, for there is no sin in him. So if
we continue to live in him, we won't sin either. But
those who keep on sinning have never known him
or understood who he is. Dear children, don't let
anyone deceive you about this: When people do
what is right, it is because they are righteous, even
as Christ is righteous. But when people keep on
sinning, it shows they belong to the Devil, who has
been sinning since the beginning. But the Son of
God came to destroy these works of the Devil.

1 JOHN 3:2-8

WHEN OUR Lord prayed in the Garden of Gethsemane (Luke 22),
He sweat drops of blood. On a recent trip to the Holy Land, I was
struck again with the importance of this dramatic event in the life of
our Lord. It was just before dusk when the ninety-eight people in our
touring group met in the Garden of Gethsemane outside the church
on the site. The crowd was so great we couldn't get into the church.
Our inability to get inside did not trouble me. There is little that is authentic inside this religious tourist site. The garden, on the other
hand, is most authentic. When you kneel in the garden, the twenty-
five-hundred-year-old olive trees give you an odd, yet real sensation
that you are truly kneeling where Jesus knelt to pray.

Somehow you feel like taking off your shoes, for you are indeed on holy ground. While our tour group stood silent in the awe of the twisted, eerie, beautiful grove, I read the Gethsemane account in Luke. Then someone quietly asked, "What would cause Jesus to sweat blood?" I had no answer. I have seen many people go through horrific times of suffering, but I have never seen anyone sweat blood. Still, something catastrophic must have happened for Christ to have such a physiological reaction.

I explained to our tour group that this kind of suffering is beyond our capacity to understand. Jesus had a divine nature and lived in complete holiness. Drinking the cup of our sin so that He could "taste death for everyone" (Hebrews 2:9, NKJV) was so repugnant to Him that He prayed, "Please take this cup of suffering away" (Luke 22:42). This statement does not mean that He was trying to dodge the Cross. He always knew that this would be His end. Indeed He said, "For this cause I have come into the world" (John 18:37, NKJV). The part Christ found horrifying was drinking humanity's sin into His holy nature. At His death, the act of becoming sin for us brought a strangling separation between Him and His Father.

In Gethsemane He prayed the prayer that saved our souls, "Father, if you are willing, please take this cup of suffering away from me. Yet I want your will, not mine" (Luke 22:42). That is the ultimate prayer for all Christians! We are never more authentic than when we pray "I want your will, not mine."

In this text, John shows us that sin is lawlessness. The root word here is "rebellion." All sin is rebellion—selfishness, anger, adultery, and murder. This makes it very hard to live without rebelling, doesn't it? But John gives us the recipe for holiness that lives above rebellion: "Everyone who has this hope in Him purifies himself, just as He is pure" (1 John 3:3, NKJV). Hope is the ticket! Hope purifies us with its focus. The constant expectation of the return of Christ is to be in our heart at all times. When it is, sin flees before our desire to submit to the will of God. When we lose sight of the imminent coming of Jesus, sin is magnified because our hope is gone. Then we tend to resist God and seek our own self-magnification.

John said, "We can't even imagine what we will be like when Christ returns. But we do know that when he comes we will be like him." Among other things, the true attitude of our hearts will be revealed when Jesus comes. Fix your mind therefore on Jesus' coming. Surrender every day to the will of God. Be sure of this: He will never ask you to do anything that is contrary to His Word. The same Holy Spirit whom you trust to direct your life also wrote the Word of God through His apostles and prophets. Live free of conflict and doubt, for God is never the author of confusion.

TODAY'S PRAYER

Dear heavenly Father, humbly I bow before You. Whatever You want me to do with my life, I will do. Lord, my spiritual vision is sometimes bad. I don't always see the need to do Your will. But I know by faith it is best for me in the long run. Help me to win in the struggle with willfulness and selfishness. Please forgive me and help me to remember each day that Jesus could come. Let that hope purify me and keep me from sin. In His name I pray, Amen.

82 KEEPING THE HOPE ALIVE

And everyone who has this hope in Him purifies himself, just as He is pure.   1 JOHN 3:3, NKJV

WE HAVE used this verse for several of our devotionals. Its riches are inexhaustible. This time let us focus on keeping hope alive. Most exciting things seem in time to become boring. Even the vital issues of life sometimes get bogged down in drab routine. Remember the first time you drove a car? It was exciting, maybe even a little frightening. My mother taught me to drive in an old car with a gearshift that rose from the floor like a stick of defiance. I had to operate it by the use of a clutch. Oh, the agony of coordination! How was I ever to keep the car going without looking down? I thought I would never learn to make my foot and my hand work together. Pushing the clutch down was no problem, but letting it back up without stalling the engine was a challenge. The first time I tried it, the car lurched out into the middle of the street and died. Traffic stalled around my poor coordination. Suddenly a big green-and-white city bus lurched upon me, screeching to a halt at my bumper. The bus driver honked his horn. I was so nervous I shifted too fast and stalled the car three more times! I'm glad my uncoordinated past is gone. Now I can shift without even thinking.

Most things are like that. Riding a bicycle, flying a plane, or negotiating the ins and outs of marriage. Things born in struggle eventually become commonplace and routine. Unfortunately, this can also be true of our expectation that Jesus might come at any moment. What was once thrilling to contemplate now for many seems ho-hum.

This must be why the Holy Spirit inspired John to challenge Christians everywhere to purify themselves by the hope of Christ's return. How do we keep this hope alive? This hope is bigger than just the Rapture. It includes meeting our Lord, appearing before the judgment seat of Christ, and receiving the rewards of faithfulness. After all of this, we shall then participate in the marriage of the Lamb. Then we shall "reign with him a thousand years" (Revelation 20:6).

Now these things are hope most glorious. But there is more. Whether we live until the Rapture or die in the Lord has nothing to do with the steadfastness of our Lord. If we should have to die, our deaths will not be a final parting. Death in Christ is but a temporary separation. Our Lord Himself has promised, "Because I live, you will live also" (John 14:19, NKJV). Further, He makes sure our confidence when He says, "We shall always be with the Lord" (1 Thessalonians

4:17, NKJV). Once raptured, we will be forever in the presence of Jesus. Satan, who troubles us often during life, will be bound and unable to tempt us ever again. We will have new and wonderful bodies like Jesus' resurrected body, a state of existence too glorious to describe.

Do you not feel your heart being warmed even as we rehearse these marvelous promises? It is this "promise rehearsal" that keeps hope alive. And how do we rehearse the promises? By reading, studying, hearing about, and thinking about our wonderful future.

Christians who never hear about the Second Coming rarely have this hope in the Savior's soon return. Their minds are cluttered up with "the cares of this life and the lure of wealth" (Matthew 13:22) and not focused upon Christ. Instead of promise rehearsal, their thoughts are occupied with stocks, bonds, sports, entertainment: things that cannot keep the hope alive.

The hope is better than anything this world has to offer. It gives our expectation confidence in His return. It purifies our morality. Knowing that Jesus could come today helps us to live clean and holy.

TODAY'S PRAYER

Dear heavenly Father, thank You for the great plan You have for my future. I know I don't deserve such a future, but I thank You that it is guaranteed by Your Word. Please keep this hope alive in my heart on a daily basis. Let me live every moment pleasing unto You and to Your Son who loved me and gave Himself for me. In Jesus' name I pray, Amen.

83 BE SURE TO EARN A FULL REWARD

Love means doing what God has commanded us,
and he has commanded us to love one another,
just as you heard from the beginning. Many

deceivers have gone out into the world. They do not believe that Jesus Christ came to earth in a real body. Such a person is a deceiver and an antichrist. Watch out, so that you do not lose the prize for which we have been working so hard. Be diligent so that you will receive your full reward. For if you wander beyond the teaching of Christ, you will not have fellowship with God. But if you continue in the teaching of Christ, you will have fellowship with both the Father and the Son.

2 JOHN 1:6-9

MOST CHRISTIANS have no idea that they can lose their earned rewards. Foolishly, they forget that they are supposed to "store [their] treasures in heaven, where they will never become moth-eaten or rusty and where they will be safe from thieves" (Matthew 6:20). Are our good works always secure in heaven? Yes, and only there!

It is impossible for us to lose our eternal rewards if we live for the Lord throughout life. The apostle Paul said of himself, "I have fought a good fight, I have finished the race, and I have remained faithful. And now the prize awaits me—the crown of righteousness that the Lord, the righteous Judge, will give me on that great day of his return. And the prize is not just for me but for all who eagerly look forward to his glorious return" (2 Timothy 4:7-8).

It is not enough that we start the race properly; we must also finish our race. We must complete the calling God has given us. The Bible challenges us to "remain faithful even when facing death" (Revelation 2:11, NKJV) and to "hold on to what you have, so that no one will take away your crown" (Revelation 3:11).

It would be an eternal tragedy for anyone to serve the Lord throughout life and then throw it all away just before the finish line. One of my college classmates served the Lord for many years. He was gifted and did a great job wherever he served. But at sixty-two years of age he walked into his home and announced to his wife of forty-two years that he had had it. "I'm out of here; please forward my mail to this address." With that he walked out of her life, resigned his ministry, and went off with a woman who had become the latest object of his ungodly affections. Of the forty-two or more years he served the Lord, I am confident he laid up many good works in his heavenly bank account. But this verse suggests that some of the rewards God intended for him will be lost.

David, the king of Israel, was known as "the man after [God's] own heart" (1 Samuel 13:14). He had a midlife crisis at about fifty years of age and played the fool. When he should have been leading his troops in battle, he stayed home and committed adultery. Then he murdered the husband of the woman he had claimed in an adulterous affair. He did all of this as a great man of God who had walked with God for many years.

Nathan the prophet confronted David with his sin. Convicted by the Holy Spirit, David confessed and made his heart right with God. He will not receive the reward he might have, but because of his repentance he will doubtless receive much. His right status with God was restored. However, sin takes its toll, and David's life was never again the same. Guilt followed him many years. He will not receive a full reward. Don't make David's mistake. Be faithful until Christ comes!

Today's Prayer

Dear heavenly Father, thank You for letting me see the truth that it is possible to lose my rewards through carnal living. As I know my heart today, I want to live the rest of my life fully committed to Your will. I pray with David, "Keep me from presumptuous sins" (Psalm 19:13, NKJV). Help me to keep my eyes on Jesus and His potential coming, living faithfully all the days of my life. In Jesus' name I pray, Amen.

84 ANTICHRIST IS A DECEIVER

Many deceivers have gone out into the world. They do not believe that Jesus Christ came to earth in a real body. Such a person is a deceiver and an antichrist. Watch out, so that you do not lose the prize for which we have been working so hard. Be diligent so that you will receive your full reward. For if you wander beyond the teaching of Christ, you will not have fellowship with God. But if you continue in the teaching of Christ, you will have fellowship with both the Father and the Son. If someone comes to your meeting and does not teach the truth about Christ, don't invite him into your house or encourage him in any way. Anyone who encourages him becomes a partner in his evil work.

2 JOHN 1:7-11

DANIEL THE prophet called the man of sin "the little horn" (Daniel 8:9, NKJV), and Paul called him "the lawless one" (2 Thessalonians 2:8, NKJV) or "the son of perdition" (2 Thessalonians 2:3, NKJV). The Antichrist is known by many names, even "the king of fierce countenance" (Daniel 8:23, NKJV). But one thing he is never called is "the anti-Christ." Yet that is the popular name or title of this all-powerful, self-willed leader of the followers of Satan during the Tribulation period.

Antichrist is best described as a spirit that is anti–Jesus Christ. The term "antichrist" is used by the apostle John near the end of his ministry. John outlived all the other disciples. At around eighty-five years of life, having been the pastor of the great church of Ephesus, he detected a spirit of deception that he considered dangerous. That deceptive spirit has plagued the church of Jesus Christ ever since. This spirit serves Satan and seeks to deceive people about Jesus' deity.

Satan knows that if he can get people to disbelieve the deity of Jesus or, as John said, not to believe that "Jesus has come in the flesh"

(1 John 4:2, NKJV), his deception has been complete. Christ's deity is the principal issue of the gospel. No one can be saved unless he or she believes this. Anyone who teaches otherwise is "an antichrist," deceived by the spirit of the Antichrist.

Recently a prominent minister announced to the world that Jesus was a good man, but not God. This American clergyman said that Jesus never claimed to be God and never performed any miracles. He went on to say that the Christian message was no better than any other religious teaching.

"Blasphemy!" I said in my heart. This man, masquerading as a minister, was grossly deceived by Satan and was confused about the most important subject in the world: the essential deity of Jesus.

Such a person not only is deceived about the deity of Jesus, he is trying to deceive others. Unfortunately, the secular press often endorses such heretics as though they were true representatives of the Christian faith. Even as I read of his blasphemy, I could not help but wonder if "Dr. Antichrist" had ever really read the fifth chapter of John where Jesus claims six times to be God.

Concerning Christ's miracles, Dr. Antichrist has two problems: First, the books of the Bible that were written by eyewitnesses of the life of Christ record thirty-nine supernatural miracles Jesus performed, from restoring blind eyes to healing ten incurable lepers at one time. Second, he must explain what brought such enormous crowds to hear Jesus unless it was His miracles.

We should expect such antichrists to appear more frequently as we approach the end of the age. Jesus warned thirteen times in the Olivet discourse that we should be careful not to be deceived by the false prophets or false teachers who would appear just before His coming. In these days, they appear in abundance. These deceivers fixate their deceptions on the nature of Jesus Christ. Some of them present Him as an impostor, others as less than God "come in the flesh" (1 John 4:2, NKJV). The incarnation of God in Christ is an event that is more than the fulfillment of prophecy; it was the miracle of creation so that God could sacrifice Himself and die for the human race.

That Christ was not God is the basic heresy that lies at the root of all cults. But more than this, it is the basic heresy that will characterize *the* Antichrist when he steps onto the world scene after Jesus raptures His church.

Today's Prayer

Dear heavenly Father, in an age of increasing deception I pray that I may avoid being deceived by Satan and his false teachers. Please give me a keen sensitivity to see and reject all attempts, no matter how clever, to distort the truth about Jesus' deity. And help me to think clearly in a fuzzy age. May I always be ready to "give a defense to everyone who asks [me] a reason for the hope that is in [me], with meekness and fear" (1 Peter 3:15, NKJV). In Jesus' name I pray, Amen.

85 ABIDING IN THE DOCTRINE OF CHRIST

For if you wander beyond the teaching of Christ, you will not have fellowship with God. But if you continue in the teaching of Christ, you will have fellowship with both the Father and the Son. If someone comes to your meeting and does not teach the truth about Christ, don't invite him into your house or encourage him in any way. Anyone who encourages him becomes a partner in his evil work.   2 John 1:9-11

JOHN is referred to in the Gospels as the beloved disciple because he laid his head on Jesus' chest during the Last Supper. He endeared himself to the church of Asia where he faithfully pastored for many years. He was the most venerated of church leaders at the end of the first century. Although he was well-known as the disciple of love, he felt only harshness toward those who deceive others concerning the doctrine of Christ.

Satanic deception will increase in the last days. John called this deception "the spirit of the Antichrist" (1 John 4:3). He said this spirit would deceive people about the deity of Jesus. John commanded Christians to "walk in [love]" (2 John 1:6). But then he turned and scathed those who allow themselves to be deceived by the spirit of antichrist. He warns that those who are so deceived will lose their rewards.

The antidote to such deception and false teaching, of course, is to "continue in the teaching of Christ," or, as the New King James Version translates it, "abide in the doctrine of Christ" (2 John 1:9). Abiding is a clear sign that we have "both the Father and the Son." John did not write about the virgin birth of Jesus; he just assumed it. In his Gospel, which was written long after both Matthew's and Luke's, he wrote to counteract the deceptive teachings of Satan, who was causing the faithful to question the doctrine of Christ. For that reason John did not try in his Gospel to present a chronological narration of the life of Christ. Instead, he presented seven of the most outstanding miracles in the life of our Lord to prove that Jesus was more than a man. He wanted the world to know Jesus was God in human flesh. For as Nicodemus said to Jesus, "Your miraculous signs are proof enough that God is with you" (John 3:2). John's conclusion, then, on how to avoid the end-time deception, is to saturate our mind (as he said, "abide in") with the doctrine of Christ. We can do that only through reading and studying the Word of God.

The Christian who reads and rereads the Word of God is not going to be deceived about Jesus! It is when we get away from reading the Bible regularly and from teaching it that we are open to the deceptions of the age. I once went to the home of a Christian who had renounced her faith and joined a cult. I doubted that she was truly a Christian. She had made an emotional decision to accept Christ, but she never seemed to have an understanding of Christ's deity. She had gotten into reading tracts and articles about New Age religions. Saturated by the occult, she had completely missed the Christ of love. This is why John commanded us to "abide in the doctrine of Christ."

Later, John adds: "If someone comes to your meeting and does not teach the truth about Christ, don't invite him into your house or encourage him in any way. Anyone who encourages him becomes a partner in his evil work." Today that sounds intolerant! But it shows just how dangerous it is to fellowship with those who do not hold to the deity of Christ. In the first century it was not even considered right to greet a heretic lest you give him a sense you approved of his heresies. Today, we are so tolerant of heretics that we politely refrain from publicly condemning their heretical views.

John tells us to "test the spirits" (1 John 4:1, NKJV). Jesus is the standard. We are to test all false teachings by standing them alongside His essential deity. Many minor doctrines separate Christians, which is why we have hundreds of different denominations today. One thing that will unite all Bible-believing Christians is the personal deity of Jesus. When we "contend earnestly for the faith" (Jude 1:3, NKJV), the main issue of our contending will always be the deity of our Lord. As it has been said, "If He is not Lord of all, He is not Lord at all."

Today's Prayer

Dear Lord, in this day of deception I want to thank You for those who have carefully steered me into truth. Thank You for all who had anything to do with my salvation, and please help me to be a tool in Your hand to teach others the truth they once taught me. In His blessed name I pray, Amen.

86 BOLDNESS IN THE DAY OF JUDGMENT

> Whoever confesses that Jesus is the Son of God,
> God abides in him, and he in God. And we have
> known and believed the love that God has for us.
> God is love, and he who abides in love abides in
> God, and God in him. Love has been perfected
> among us in this: that we may have boldness in
> the day of judgment; because as He is, so are we
> in this world. There is no fear in love; but perfect
> love casts out fear, because fear involves torment.
> But he who fears has not been made perfect in
> love. We love Him because He first loved us.
>
> 1 JOHN 4:15-19, NKJV

THE DAY of judgment plays a prominent role in end-time prophecies. For the Christian it is called the "judgment seat of Christ" and comes right after the rapture of the church. It is not a judgment of salvation, but of rewards (2 Corinthians 5:10).

The "Great White Throne Judgment" described in Revelation 20:11-15, on the other hand, comes at the end of the millennial kingdom and is the last thing to occur just before believers enter heaven for eternity. The reason the Great White Throne Judgment is reserved for this spot is so that everyone who has ever rejected God since the time of Adam can be included. Even the rebels at the very end of the Millennium will have their chance to decide whether or not they want Jesus to be their Lord. Their rejection shows that even God's material and spiritual utopia will not convince some people to surrender their lives to Jesus. Further, it shows just how deceptive Satan can be, deceiving even those who live during Christ's reign over the entire kingdom in the Millennium.

The fear of death and judgment is a nearly universal fear. Only the most blatant atheist would claim not to fear judgment. And many atheists are known to have changed their view just before death. But those who have received Jesus by faith have "the Holy Spirit to fill our hearts with his love" (Romans 5:5), and "perfect love casts out fear" (1 John 4:18, NKJV). John explains why the saved are fearless: "Love has been perfected among us in this: that we may have boldness in the day of judgment." Those who receive Jesus gain a boldness or faith that gives them a quiet confidence. Why? They no longer fear death and the judgment.

But John is saying that we should own something more than merely a lack of fear. We should "have boldness in the day of judgment." I came to Christ when I was only eight years old. Very honestly, it was not love of God or even of Jesus that led me to accept Christ. I was scared of going to hell! In fact, I had nightmares about getting in the wrong line on Judgment Day and ending up at the Great White Throne Judgment. At that time I didn't realize that Christians would never stand before God in final judgment. Being saved was wonderful. I had peace. I got my first good night of sleep the first night after I received Jesus. Years later, after I had become a preacher, I had a dream of confidence. I was standing at the Great White Throne Judgment, and the recording angel opened the book of my works. And what did he find? A bunch of blank pages! Christ had erased all entries. No single sin was recorded. The Bible teaches that "though our sins are like scarlet, they shall be as white as snow" (Isaiah 1:18, NKJV).

The confidence that our sins are forgiven is what gives us the boldness to contemplate Judgment Day and not be afraid. When we love God, "His love is shed abroad in our hearts" (Romans 5:5, KJV). And it is that love that gives us boldness when considering the Day of Christ.

TODAY'S PRAYER
Dear heavenly Father, thank You for the assurance that my sins are forgiven in Jesus' name and that they will never be

remembered against me. Thank You that I need not fear the Day of judgment, for Jesus took my judgment on Himself the day He died for me on the cross. I thank You that even if by some impossible mistake I were to get in the wrong line on Judgment Day, there would be nothing in the books to condemn me. In Jesus' name I thank and praise You! Amen.

87

THE MESSAGE OF THE FIRST PROPHET

> Now Enoch, who lived seven generations after Adam, prophesied about these people. He said, "Look, the Lord is coming with thousands of his holy ones. He will bring the people of the world to judgment. He will convict the ungodly of all the evil things they have done in rebellion and of all the insults that godless sinners have spoken against him."
>
> JUDE 1:14-15

ENOCH, the seventh in the lineage of Adam, was a prophet to his generation. We don't know much about him or the entire pre-Flood age, for that matter. The Bible spends little time on this era of history. But the flood of Genesis was real. The people who lived before the Flood had become corrupt. Their wickedness at last caused God to destroy them from the face of the earth. As you know, among this pre-Flood, decadent culture God found only eight people—the family of Noah—who were "perfect in all [their] generations" (Genesis 6:9, NKJV).

Enoch, who lived before Noah's family, of course, was a godly man. He "walked with God; and he was not, for God took him" (Genesis 5:24, NKJV). His walk of love caused him to be the first ever to be raptured. This man, "seven generations after Adam," was also a prophet. We have no other record of his prophecies, but we know of his prophetic life through the book of Jude.

How many times have we heard people say something like this: "I think that I will make it on Judgment Day. God will weigh my works on a scale, the good works on one side and the bad on another, and I am confident my good works will outweigh my bad." Usually such people break three to ten of the commandments just in making the statement. How foolish! It is but naïve pride that has come to see God as a big grandfather in the sky who is eager to disregard sin and congratulate sinners for being moderately good people.

There are many things wrong with this idea. The first is an attempt to provide salvation without Jesus. If being "kinda nice" would save us, then Jesus wasted His time coming to Earth. He certainly wasted His time dying on the cross. Yet the "kinda nice" theory of being saved has been wiped out by Peter, who said, "There is salvation in no one else! There is no other name in all of heaven for people to call on to save them" (Acts 4:12).

I don't know, of course, what prophetic truths Enoch preached, but I am confident they had something to do with the true nature of God. Studying prophecy has impressed upon me the correlation of holy men through time. The prophets were separated by centuries and yet they borrowed from each other in their prophecy. Jonah, for instance, says: "I knew that you were a gracious and compassionate God, slow to get angry and filled with unfailing love" (Jonah 4:2). Where did this rebellious prophet get that idea about God? From Joel, a Hebrew prophet who lived 120 years before him. Joel said of God, ". . . for he is gracious and merciful. He is not easily angered. He is filled with kindness and is eager not to punish you" (Joel 2:13). And where did Joel get that view of God? From Moses in Deuteronomy 4:31.

Enoch must have warned the people of his day to repent and return to their merciful God. Instead, the majority rebelled and went on living in their lust and sin. Someday, however, these rebels will stand before the righteous Judge of the universe who will convict them of their ungodly deeds. God's judgment won't be as easy as they envision it to be. It will not be a balancing of their good and bad works. Their small attempts at being good will run against the mighty standards of God.

Judgment Day! Who likes thinking of it? The powerful, towering Lord of all the earth must at last be answered. Perhaps that is why unsaved people prefer not to think of that coming day when, as Enoch said, the Lord will come "with thousands of his holy ones."

TODAY'S PRAYER
Dear heavenly Father, thank You for all the faithful prophets You have raised up to share Your truth and forgiveness. Thank You especially for those who patiently introduced me to Your love and mercy. Help me to help others find what they should in me. Let me be a point of hope in human despair. In the name of Jesus, our soon-coming Lord, I pray. Amen.

88 PAYDAY SOMEDAY

> Now Enoch, who lived seven generations after Adam, prophesied about these people. He said, "Look, the Lord is coming with thousands of his holy ones."
> JUDE 1:14

WHEN I WAS a college student, the late Dr. R. G. Lee came to Moody Bible Institute and preached his famous message, "Payday Someday," to a crowd of about four thousand. During his life he delivered that message over a thousand times. When he gave the invitation, three hundred people came forward to receive Christ. After about twenty minutes of extending the invitation, Dr. Lee turned to the president of Moody, Dr. Culbertson, said, "I never close a service while souls are still coming," and turned the invitation over to him. Dr. Culbertson urged the continued singing of the invitation hymn and another hundred or so came forward. Finally he turned the invitation over to Dr. Ironside, the pastor of Moody Church, and hundreds more responded. All in all, six hundred souls were gathered in following Dr. Lee's sermon.

"Payday Someday" is a message people need to hear today. Dr. Lee's message must have been much like the message of the prophet Enoch. Enoch said Christ was coming with His saints to "bring the people of the world to judgment. He will convict the ungodly of all the evil things they have done in rebellion and of all the insults that godless sinners have spoken against him" (Jude 1:15).

Millions of people in our day do not hesitate to use the matchless name of Christ in vain. There is something in the rebellious heart that has a need to blaspheme God. Many of these would say, "Oh yes, I take Christ's name in vain, but I don't mean anything by it. It's just idle talk." Not true! No one who really loves God would ever use His name in vain.

Railroad workers, like many other groups of heavy laborers, are sometimes known to use blasphemous profanity. I once read the testimony of a man named Charlie. He was a freight-train engineer who was famous for cursing loudly. Some said of him, "He could make the air blue with his blasphemy." But one weekend Charlie got saved. He had no sooner given his testimony than one of his friends said, "We will soon know if Charlie got the real thing by the way he talks." Needless to say, his fellow workers watched him carefully and were impressed that he was a changed man. That is, he seemed to be changed until just before quitting time on a particular Thursday. While trying to loosen a heavy bolt, his wrench slipped and he cracked his knuckles against a steel plate. Sure enough, Charlie lost it and swore in the Lord's name. His old friends quickly decided he had not really become a Christian.

Moments later, however, Charlie crossed to the other side of the engine room where the men who had overheard his profanity were standing. He knelt on the cinder track with tears running down his weather-beaten face and prayed, "Dear Lord, I am so sorry I blasphemed in your name again. Please forgive me and help me overcome this terrible habit. I really do love and worship You." Remorse is the state of the truly repentant believer.

Not so the ungodly! They are "grumblers and complainers, doing whatever evil they feel like. They are loudmouthed braggarts, and they flatter others to get favors in return" (Jude 1:16). While we have always had those who blasphemed God, they will evidently increase as we approach the end of the age. Jude tells his readers, "The apostles of our Lord Jesus Christ told you that in the last times there would be scoffers whose purpose in life is to enjoy themselves in every evil way imaginable" (Jude 1:17-18). May we suggest that they are already here?

It used to be that profanity was done secretly. This is not so today. Now it is heard on the radio, on television, and in movies. The blatant public use of our Lord's wonderful name is evidence that Jude spoke the truth. We are in the last time. Those who use profanity or speak blasphemy have no idea that their actions are but a fulfillment of ancient prophecies. Nor do they realize that when the Lord comes, it will be "payday today" for them.

Jude said, "Show mercy to those whose faith is wavering. Rescue others by snatching them from the flames of judgment. There are still others to whom you need to show mercy, but be careful that you aren't contaminated by their sins" (Jude 1:22-23). Don't become discouraged as the moral climate of our day continues to decline drastically. Blasphemy of our Lord's name will become even worse. I am sure old Charlie's friends were tempted not to invite him to their church evangelistic meetings, but they did anyway. And as a result, he was "[snatched] from the flames" and escaped "payday someday," gradually gaining the victory over the habits of his old nature.

TODAY'S PRAYER

Dear heavenly Father, I never cease to be amazed at the extent of Your mercy, patience, grace, and forgiveness. Thank You for "[saving] to the uttermost those who come to God through [Christ]" (Hebrews 7:25, NKJV)—even those who blaspheme against You. Please give me boldness to speak to those who use Your name in vain and live after their own lusts that they, too, may be forgiven of their ungodly deeds before Jesus comes again. In His name I pray, Amen.

89 ACCORDING TO HIS PROMISE

Since everything around us is going to melt away, what holy, godly lives you should be living! You should look forward to that day and hurry it along—the day when God will set the heavens on fire and the elements will melt away in the flames. But we are looking forward to the new heavens and new earth he has promised, a world where everyone is right with God. And so, dear friends, while you are waiting for these things to happen, make every effort to live a pure and blameless life. And be at peace with God.   2 PETER 3:11-14

OUR LORD and His apostles left us many promises that He would come again. Christianity rises and falls on the fulfillment of those promises. We have waited long and deeply desired that these promises be fulfilled. Many, like Paul, thought Jesus would come in their own lifetime. It is hard to wait on something so wonderful. So some wait patiently and some fitfully. Sadly, some lose sight of His coming altogether.

Let us not forget all those who once waited for His first coming. Isaiah wrote of it more than eight hundred years before it happened. Thousands before Christ read his prophecy and believed it. Many in those centuries died before Christ first came. But He did come, just as the prophets promised and right on schedule. Many saw Him, believed in Him, and were not disappointed.

As it was once with His first coming so it is now with His second. We wait! Sometimes patiently, sometimes not so patiently. But we are confident He will come. Our confidence is rooted in assurance. There are three times more second-coming prophecies than there are prophecies which relate to His first. Since His first coming is a certified fact of history, we can have three times the confidence for believing His second coming will also take place.

In this text, Peter offers his final challenge to the body of Christ. Tradition says Peter was crucified upside down shortly after he finished writing this epistle. He wanted Christians in all ages to consider what kind of people they should be and what kind of life they should live in light of the fact that on the Day of the Lord all things will be dissolved. We are only in this world for a short time. Jesus is coming soon, possibly in our own lifetime. So our primary interest should be in things eternal. The old spiritual song says it best:

> *This world is not my home, I'm just a-passin' through.*
> *My treasures are laid up somewhere beyond the blue.*
> *The angels beckon me to heaven's open door,*
> *And I can't feel at home in this world anymore.*

The Left Behind series has spawned hundreds of thrilling letters from readers exultant at how God is using these books to transform lives. Every day we receive hundreds of letters and E-mails, and around thirty thousand hits on our Web site. Each of these letters tells some heart-moving tale of God's work in people's lives. Our books have had a wonderful effect on their lives! Now they are fixed on things eternal.

During the rainy season, a Korean War platoon, headed by a young Marine lieutenant, slogged through mud and a bone-chilling drizzle to get to the battle zone. Finally, the lieutenant had the men make camp for the night. Just before he gave his final orders, he said in a loud voice, "Don't drive your tent stakes too deep because we are leaving early in the morning."

This is our Master's prophetic message for today. Don't drive your tent stakes too deep. We're leaving soon—be ready!

TODAY'S PRAYER

Dear Lord, it is so easy for me to take my eyes from the promises of Jesus' coming. Many times I spend too much of my time thinking of this world and all of its cares. Help me to maintain an eternal perspective and do what is necessary for my family. But never let me forget that heaven is my real home. Help me to so live that when I arrive there, I will have taken many with me. Use my life today. In Jesus' name, Amen.

90 HOW TO KEEP YOURSELF IN THE LOVE OF GOD

But you, dear friends, must continue to build your lives on the foundation of your holy faith. And continue to pray as you are directed by the Holy Spirit. Live in such a way that God's love can bless you as you wait for the eternal life that our Lord

Jesus Christ in his mercy is going to give you. Show mercy to those whose faith is wavering. Rescue others by snatching them from the flames of judgment. There are still others to whom you need to show mercy, but be careful that you aren't contaminated by their sins. And now, all glory to God, who is able to keep you from stumbling, and who will bring you into his glorious presence innocent of sin and with great joy. All glory to him, who alone is God our Savior, through Jesus Christ our Lord. Yes, glory, majesty, power, and authority belong to him, in the beginning, now, and forevermore. Amen.

JUDE 1:20-25

IN THESE brief thoughts on our Lord's return we have not touched on any of the prophetic events of the Revelation. This wonderful book is on reserve for the sequel, Lord willing, that we intend to do. The exciting future events of Revelation will require a book of their own. In addition, the Revelation is the only book of the Bible that reveals our Lord Jesus as He really is today.

However, we have saved the most significant challenge on how to live in readiness for our Lord's coming for this final devotional. It is no coincidence that the book of Jude was located right at the end of the library of God. It was written almost thirty years before the writing of the Revelation of Jesus Christ. The author of Jude was the half brother of Jesus and was inspired to write it between 65 and 67 A.D., just prior to the destruction of the city of Jerusalem by the Romans. It was not written to young Christians like many of Paul's books were. It was addressed to second-generation believers to urge them to "defend the truth of the Good News" (Jude 1:3). Many false teachers and heretics were trying to creep into the church and gain control of it for their own selfish ends.

The church has used Jude's masterful benediction (found in

verses 24-25) down through the centuries. It is one of the first, and certainly one of the finest, scriptural benedictions.

This short letter is a practical reminder to "live in such a way that God's love can bless you as you wait for the eternal life that our Lord Jesus Christ in his mercy is going to give you" (verse 21). This is the same challenge that Paul gave to Titus when he referred to "the blessed hope" of Christ's return (Titus 2:13, NKJV). It is, after all, at the rapture of the church when we will enter into eternal life. Keeping our eyes on this goal is one significant way we can remain in the love of God.

Jude teaches us that there are three things Christians can do to keep themselves in the love of God.

First, we can build ourselves up in our "holy faith." We hear a lot today about building ourselves up physically. Fitness centers and local gyms provide ample illustrations of men and women committed to bodybuilding. My physical-education instructor in the air force won the Mr. America title while I was stationed at the Las Vegas Army Air Base. We used to watch him work out in preparation for that contest. He was awesome! He took the excellent body that God had given him and made it a "Mr. America body" by sheer discipline.

If we are going to be strong Christians, we too must build ourselves up in the Word of God. This kind of disciplined Bible study produces spiritual "Mr. Americas." We can build a spiritual physique the world will much admire by hearing the Word taught, by reading it, by studying it, and by meditating on it. It has been said, "You are today what you have been becoming." As a Christian you will only be as strong as your spiritual workouts are requiring.

Second, we must make praying a vital part of our growth in Christ. God puts a vital premium on earnest, regular prayer.

Third, we must "live in such a way that God's love can bless [us] as [we] wait for the eternal life that our Lord Jesus Christ in his mercy is going to give [us]" (verse 21). We must fix our eyes on the permanent goal that Jesus is going to come and rapture all believers in Him (the dead and the living). Then, following the Tribulation, we will come to Earth with Him as He sets up His kingdom and join Him in His thousand-year reign.

In His rich mercy, God has saved us and given us an expectation for a glorious future. How can we do less than serve Him all the days of our lives? Nothing should matter more to us than the second coming of His Son. It is that glorious finality that brings to a conclusion all of God's plans for planet Earth. In exalting the promise of His coming, we keep eternity's values in view. In the last analysis, we are what our passions lead us to hope for. This, the grandest of human hopes, will at last fashion us into the image of Christ. This, the most noble of promises, creates a quality of life on earth that knows no parallel. Best of all, we will at last receive what our incessant desire fashions: an eternal companionship, a glorious heritage of thrones—life forever with the coming Christ.

TODAY'S PRAYER

Dear heavenly Father, thank You for the great mercy and love You have bestowed upon us. Thank You for the assurance of eternity, the certainty of heaven, and the hope of the coming of Jesus. Help me to live every day in the light of that mercy. The signs of our times seem to indicate that Christ's return cannot be far off. Please keep me in Your love as I watch for His return. In Jesus' name I pray, Amen.

ABOUT THE AUTHORS

JERRY B. JENKINS (www.jerryjenkins.com) is the writer of the Left Behind series. He is author of more than one hundred books, of which eleven have reached the *New York Times* best-seller list. Former vice president for publishing for the Moody Bible Institute of Chicago, he also served many years as editor of *Moody* magazine and is now Moody's writer-at-large.

His writing has appeared in publications as varied as *Reader's Digest*, *Parade*, in-flight magazines, and many Christian periodicals. He has written books in four genres: biography, marriage and family, fiction for children, and fiction for adults.

Jenkins's biographies include books with Hank Aaron, Bill Gaither, Luis Palau, Walter Payton, Orel Hershiser, Nolan Ryan, Brett Butler, and Billy Graham, among many others.

Eight of his apocalyptic novels—*Left Behind, Tribulation Force, Nicolae, Soul Harvest, Apollyon, Assassins, The Indwelling,* and *The Mark*—have appeared on the Christian Booksellers Association's best-selling fiction list and the *Publishers Weekly* religion best-seller list. *Left Behind* was nominated for Book of the Year by the Evangelical Christian Publishers Association in 1997, 1998, 1999, and 2000. *The Indwelling* was number one on the *New York Times* best-seller list for four consecutive weeks.

As a marriage and family author and speaker, Jenkins has been a frequent guest on Dr. James Dobson's *Focus on the Family* radio program.

Jerry is also the writer of the nationally syndicated sports story comic strip *Gil Thorp*, distributed to newspapers across the United States by Tribune Media Services.

Jerry and his wife, Dianna, live in Colorado.

DR. TIM LAHAYE (www.timlahaye.com), who conceived the idea of fictionalizing an account of the Rapture and the Tribulation, is a noted author, minister, and nationally recognized speaker on Bible prophecy. He is the founder of both Tim LaHaye Ministries and The Pre-Trib Research Center. Presently Dr. LaHaye speaks at many of the major Bible prophecy conferences in the U.S. and Canada, where his nine current prophecy books are very popular.

Dr. LaHaye holds a doctor of ministry degree from Western Theological Seminary and a doctor of literature degree from Liberty University. For twenty-five years he pastored one of the nation's outstanding churches in San Diego, which grew to three locations. It was during that time that he founded two accredited Christian high schools, a Christian school system of ten schools, and Christian Heritage College.

Dr. LaHaye has written over forty books, with over 30 million copies in print in thirty-three languages. He has written books on a wide variety of subjects, such as family life, temperaments, and Bible prophecy. His current fiction works, written with Jerry B. Jenkins—*Left Behind, Tribulation Force, Nicolae, Soul Harvest, Apollyon, Assassins, The Indwelling,* and *The Mark*—have all reached number one on the Christian best-seller charts. Other works by Dr. LaHaye are *Perhaps Today; Spirit-Controlled Temperament; How to Be Happy Though Married; Revelation Unveiled; Understanding the Last Days; Rapture under Attack; Are We Living in the End Times?;* and the youth fiction series Left Behind: The Kids.

He is the father of four grown children and grandfather of nine. Snow skiing, waterskiing, motorcycling, golfing, vacationing with family, and jogging are among his leisure activities.

THE FUTURE IS CLEAR

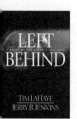

Left Behind®
A novel of the earth's last days . . .
In one cataclysmic moment, millions around the world disappear. In the midst of global chaos, airline captain Rayford Steele must search for his family, for answers, for truth. As devastating as the disappearances have been, the darkest days lie ahead.

0-8423-2911-0 Hardcover	0-8423-1675-2 Audio book—Cassette
0-8423-2912-9 Softcover	0-8423-4323-7 Audio book—CD

Tribulation Force
The continuing drama of those left behind . . .
Rayford Steele, Buck Williams, Bruce Barnes, and Chloe Steele band together to form the Tribulation Force. Their task is clear, and their goal nothing less than to stand and fight the enemies of God during the seven most chaotic years the planet will ever see.

0-8423-2913-7 Hardcover	0-8423-1787-2 Audio book—Cassette
0-8423-2921-8 Softcover	0-8423-4324-5 Audio book—CD

Nicolae
The rise of Antichrist . . .
The seven-year tribulation period is nearing the end of its first quarter, when prophecy says "the wrath of the Lamb" will be poured out upon the earth. Rayford Steele has become the ears of the tribulation saints in the Carpathia regime. A dramatic all-night rescue run from Israel through the Sinai will hold you breathless to the end.

0-8423-2914-5 Hardcover	0-8423-1788-0 Audio book—Cassette
0-8423-2924-2 Softcover	0-8423-4355-5 Audio book—CD

Soul Harvest
The world takes sides . . .
As the world hurtles toward the Trumpet Judgments and the great soul harvest prophesied in Scripture, Rayford Steele and Buck Williams begin searching for their loved ones from different corners of the world. *Soul Harvest* takes you from Iraq to America, from six miles in the air to underground shelters, from desert sand to the bottom of the Tigris River, from hope to devastation and back again—all in a quest for truth and life.

0-8423-2915-3 Hardcover	0-8423-5175-2 Audio book—Cassette
0-8423-2925-0 Softcover	0-8423-4333-4 Audio book—CD

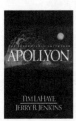

Apollyon
The Destroyer is unleashed . . .
In this acclaimed *New York Times* best-seller, Apollyon, the Destroyer, leads the plague of demon locusts as they torture the unsaved. Meanwhile, despite growing threats from Antichrist, the Tribulation Force gathers in Israel for the Conference of Witnesses.

0-8423-2916-1 Hardcover   0-8423-1933-6 Audio book—Cassette
0-8423-2926-9 Softcover   0-8423-4334-2 Audio book—CD

Assassins
Assignment: Jerusalem, Target: Antichrist
As a horde of 200 million demonic horsemen slays a third of the world's population, the Tribulation Force prepares for a future as fugitives. History and prophecy collide in Jerusalem for the most explosive episode yet of the continuing drama of those left behind.

0-8423-2920-X Hardcover   0-8423-1934-4 Audio book—Cassette
0-8423-2927-7 Softcover   0-8423-3682-6 Audio book—CD

The Indwelling
The Beast takes possession . . .
It's the midpoint of the seven-year Tribulation. As the world mourns the death of a renowned man, the Tribulation Force faces its most dangerous challenges yet. Time and eternity seem suspended, and the destiny of mankind hangs in the balance.

0-8423-2928-5 Hardcover   0-8423-1935-2 Audio book—Cassette
0-8423-2929-3 Softcover   0-8423-3966-3 Audio book—CD

The Mark
The Beast rules the world . . .
His Excellency Global Community Potentate Nicolae Carpathia, resurrected and indwelt by the devil himself, tightens his grip as ruler of the world. The battle is launched for the very souls of men and women around the globe as sites are set up to begin administering the mark.

0-8423-3225-1 Hardcover   0-8423-3231-6 Audio book—Cassette
0-8423-3228-6 Softcover   0-8423-3968-X Audio book—CD

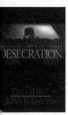

Desecration
Antichrist takes the throne

As His Excellency Global Community Potentate Nicolae Carpathia prepares to travel along the Via Dolorosa and then onward to the temple, his loyal crowds gather to see their potentate and take the mark in his presence. The lines are drawn between good and evil as God inflicts the first Bowl Judgment upon the flesh of those who have taken the mark, while his chosen ones flee to the wilderness, on the brink of Armageddon.

0-8423-3226-X Hardcover   0-8423-3232-4 Audio book—Cassette
0-8423-3229-4 Softcover   0-8423-3969-8 Audio book—CD
  (available fall 2002)

Watch for book 10 in this best-selling series to arrive summer 2002

Left Behind®: The Kids
Four teens are left behind after the Rapture and band together to fight Satan's forces in this series for ten- to fourteen-year-olds.

#1 *The Vanishings* 0-8423-2193-4
#2 *Second Chance* 0-8423-2194-2
#3 *Through the Flames* 0-8423-2195-0
#4 *Facing the Future* 0-8423-2196-9
#5 *Nicolae High* 0-8423-4325-3
#6 *The Underground* 0-8423-4326-1
#7 *Busted!* 0-8423-4327-X
#8 *Death Strike* 0-8423-4328-8
#9 *The Search* 0-8423-4329-6
#10 *On the Run* 0-8423-4330-X

#11 *Into the Storm* 0-8423-4331-8
#12 *Earthquake!* 0-8423-4332-6
#13 *The Showdown* 0-8423-4294-X
#14 *Judgment Day* 0-8423-4295-8
#15 *Battling the Commander*
    0-8423-4296-6
#16 *Fire from Heaven* 0-8423-4297-4
#17 *Terror in the Stadium*
    0-8423-4299-0
#18 *Darkening Skies* 0-8423-4312-1

Watch for the next Left Behind®: The Kids books, available spring 2002

Have You Been Left Behind®?
Based on the video that New Hope Village Church's pastor Vernon Billings created for those left behind after the Rapture. This video explains what happened and what the viewer can do now.

0-8423-5196-5 Video

An Experience in Sound and Drama

Dramatic broadcast performances of the first four books in the best-selling Left Behind series. Original music, sound effects, and professional actors make the action come alive. Experience the heart-stopping action and suspense of the end times for yourself. . . . Twelve half-hour episodes, on four CDs or three cassettes, for each title.

0-8423-5146-9 *Left Behind®: An Experience in Sound and Drama* CD
0-8423-5181-7 *Left Behind®: An Experience in Sound and Drama* cassette
0-8423-3584-6 *Tribulation Force: An Experience in Sound and Drama* CD
0-8423-3583-8 *Tribulation Force: An Experience in Sound and Drama*
                cassette
0-8423-3663-X *Nicolae: An Experience in Sound and Drama* CD
0-8423-3662-1 *Nicolae: An Experience in Sound and Drama* cassette
0-8423-3986-8 *Soul Harvest: An Experience in Sound and Drama* CD
0-8423-3985-X *Soul Harvest: An Experience in Sound and Drama* cassette
0-8423-4336-9 *Apollyon: An Experience in Sound and Drama* CD
0-8423-4335-0 *Apollyon: An Experience in Sound and Drama* cassette
0-8423-4338-5 *Assassins: An Experience in Sound and Drama* CD
0-8423-4337-7 *Assassins: An Experience in Sound and Drama* cassette
0-8423-4340-7 *The Indwelling: An Experience in Sound and Drama* CD
0-8423-4339-3 *The Indwelling: An Experience in Sound and Drama* cassette
0-8423-4341-5 *The Mark: An Experience in Sound and Drama* CD
                (available winter 2001)
0-8423-4342-3 *The Mark: An Experience in Sound and Drama* cassette
                (available winter 2001)

Discover the latest about the Left Behind series
and interact with other readers at **www.leftbehind.com**